A
SHORT HISTORY OF
ITALY

A SHORT HISTORY OF
ITALY

From Classical Times to the Present Day

H. HEARDER

*Professor of Modern History at
University College, Cardiff*

AND

D. P. WALEY

*Keeper of Manuscripts
at the British Museum*

CAMBRIDGE UNIVERSITY PRESS

CAMBRIDGE

LONDON   NEW YORK   NEW ROCHELLE

MELBOURNE   SYDNEY

Published by the Press Syndicate of the University of Cambridge
The Pitt Building, Trumpington Street, Cambridge CB2 1RP
32 East 57th Street, New York, NY 10022, USA
296 Beaconsfield Parade, Middle Park, Melbourne 3206, Australia

ISBN 0 521 09394 5

First published 1963
First paperback edition 1966
Reprinted 1974, 1977, 1979, 1980, 1983

Printed in Great Britain by
Hazell Watson & Viney Limited,
Member of the BPCC Group,
Aylesbury, Bucks

CONTENTS

CONTENTS

VII. MODERN ITALY

LIST OF MAPS

PUBLISHER'S NOTE

Most of the material and all the maps in this book were originally published by the Naval Intelligence Division of the Admiralty as part of a Handbook on Italy, in two volumes, for service use. By arrangement with the Controller of Her Majesty's Stationery Office, the original owner of the copyright, the historical sections are now reissued in this shorter form. The original contributors were the late Miss C. M. Ady and A. J. Whyte. Their work has been edited and brought up to date by Dr D. P. Waley and Dr H. Hearder, and Dr Hearder has added a section on the period since 1940. The first chapter was contributed by the late Professor Sir John Linton Myres and A. N. Sherrin-White.

Two companion volumes, *A Short History of Germany, 1815–1945,* by E. J. Passant, with contributions by C. J. Child, W. O. Henderson, and Donald Watt, and *A Short History of France,* by H. Butterfield, D. W. Brogan, H. C. Darby, and J. Hampden Jackson, with contributions by Sir Ernest Barker, A. Ewert, and I. L. Foster, were published in 1959.

CHAPTER I

CLASSICAL TIMES

1. ITALY BEFORE THE ROMAN CONQUEST

THE physical features of Italy have always divided the country into distinct and diverse regions and modified the characteristic life of each. The contribution of successive bodies of invaders tends to vary from region to region. In the earliest times the Central Apennines were almost impenetrable, and southern Italy had its own cultures and was in touch with lands beyond the Adriatic and the eastern Mediterranean long before it was affected by the cultures and migrations of the north. The ancient peoples and languages of Italy before the Roman conquests have left few traces; and though there is much archaeological evidence from sites and tombs, the identification of cultures with peoples and languages is often uncertain.

The peoples of ancient Italy are mainly distinguished by languages and by burial customs. Ethnographically the population always consisted of local breeds of 'Mediterranean' stock, progressively modified northward by immigrants of 'Alpine' descent. In the north there were also descendants of the 'Nordic' types representing invaders of Celtic and Teutonic speech.

LANGUAGES

All the ancient languages of the Peninsula, except Etruscan, were Indo-European. The oldest, the Venetic in the Alpine foothills and the Messapian in Apulia, were akin to some Balkan tongues. Less primitive, and very widespread, were the Italic languages, in two groups, of earlier and later arrival: Latin and kindred dialects were spoken in the western lowlands, Oscan and its cousin Sabellian, including Umbrian, spread from beyond the Northern Apennines throughout the Central Apennines and eventually reached the extreme south of Italy (Fig. 1).

North of the Apennines, in the Northern Plain and along the

Adriatic coast, Italic speech was wholly replaced about 600 B.C. by Celtic from central Europe; and Celtic (Gallic) raiders reached Rome in 390 B.C. Along the coasts of Sicily and southern

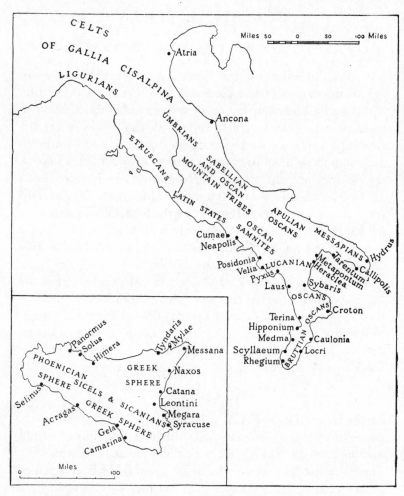

Fig. 1. Peoples, languages, and Greek and Phoenician settlements of Pre-Roman Italy

Italy south of Cumae, Greek settlements introduced their various dialects from the eighth century B.C. onwards. Etruscan in historical times was limited to the area of modern Tuscany. All these languages were gradually replaced by Latin, which was universally spoken in the Christian era, though Greek maintained itself as a second language in Sicily.

EARLY CULTURES

Civilizations, akin to those of other west Mediterranean lands, occupied all the principal regions of Italy, Sicily, and Sardinia, in the Bronze Age, and persisted in parts of south Italy and in Sicily almost into historic times. But in the more fertile and accessible regions these primary modes of life were twice modified by immigrant cultures in prehistoric times. In the late Bronze Age the 'Terramare' culture, notable for its hut-dwellings, spread from the north over the Po plain. In the Early Iron Age a civilization of Danubian origin, called 'Villanovan' in Italy after the 'Villanova' cemetery at Bologna, spread as far south as Latium and Campania. The characteristic of the 'Villanovan' way of life was the practice of cremation instead of inhumation of the dead which was the rule with other Italian peoples. The earliest culture of Rome was partly 'Villanovan', and in later Roman times both funeral rites were known. Meanwhile, in the highlands, along the Adriatic coast, and in southern Italy, survivals of the older cultures were transformed by intercourse across the Adriatic and by trade with Greek maritime colonies in Campania, Magna Graecia, and Sicily.

THE ETRUSCANS

In the west of the Peninsula between the Arno and the Tiber the Etruscans, Tuscans, or Tyrrhenians established, among a population of Italic speech and 'Villanovan' culture, a league of twelve principal cities, dominated by close-knit groups of related families (Fig. 2). Their language has no certain affinities and does not seem to be Indo-European. Ancient tradition that they came as refugees or colonists from western Asia Minor, during the disturbed centuries about 1200–1000 B.C., is supported by some elements in their life. Nevertheless much that is oriental about them is subsequent, superficial, and due to Phoenician and to Greek influence, of a date later than 800 B.C. But before these

3

later foreign influences appeared the Etruscans had adopted the 'Villanovan' culture of the natives. Later conquests spread their power through Latium, where Rome was an Etruscan strong-

Fig. 2. Central Italy in the fourth and fifth centuries B.C.

hold, southward into Campania; northward they reached through Umbria into the Northern Plain. The coming of the Gauls (about 600 B.C.) robbed the Etruscans of their holdings in the Northern Plain, and the revolt of the Romans about 510 B.C.

4

barred the Tiber crossing and the land route to the south. In 474 B.C. their sea-power was broken by the Sicilian Greeks at the battle of Cumae.

Veii, their chief southern fortress, was destroyed by the Romans in 397 B.C. After inveterate resistance they were crushed politically by 250 B.C., and gradually lost their language, religion, and distinctive culture. But the Romans believed that they owed much to Etruscan manners and beliefs; and both medieval and modern Tuscany retained features which may be Etruscan in origin.

GREEK COLONIES

The Ionian coast from Otranto to western Sicily was colonized intensively and permanently by the Greeks from about 730 B.C. onward. Greek colonies were quite different from Roman (p. 12). As their Greek name *apoikia* implies, they were 'a home away from home', and were used as a remedy for over-population and economic distress. Each usually duplicated and was organized by a 'mother-city' (*metropolis*) or group of such cities, and had a well-established political constitution for the mutual defence and maintenance of an agreed mode of life and conduct. But once founded, the new city-state retained only sentimental ties with the old; politically, and even economically, it was independent and sovereign in its own territory. Where the indigenous tribes were friendly, intercourse and Greek culture spread rapidly and far; where they were hostile, and especially when Etruscan or Phoenician rivals instigated resistance to Greek exploitation, there were long struggles, frequent territorial conquests, and a few failures. The principal regions of Greek settlement in Italy were as follows:

A very early settlement was made at Cumae in northern Campania. This founded a 'New Town' or Neapolis (Naples) and other cities farther south, like Paestum (Posidonia) in the lower Sele basin. Along the 'toe' of Italy and the Ionian coast a group of cities, of which Metapontum, Locri, Sybaris (Sibari), Croton (Crotone), and Rhegium (Reggio) were the chief, formed a 'Greater Greece' (Magna Graecia). The majority were estab-

5

lished by 700 B.C. and some had much older traditions. They formed a loose league with a federal sanctuary at Croton, and prospered on friendly terms with the natives till the Sabellian highlanders moved south about 400 B.C. and occupied their hinterland. Sybaris, one of the oldest and most prosperous, was destroyed by Croton in 510, but was refounded in 443 B.C. under the name Thurii.

Tarentum (Taranto) created a wide-reaching dependency in the 'heel' of Italy and bore the severest shocks of the Sabellian movement. Its great harbour, fisheries, and easy landward avenues gave it exceptional importance, and tempted it in later centuries to challenge the Roman protectorate over southern Italy. It became the supply base of Hannibal's expeditionary force, and suffered accordingly. Along the Adriatic coast Greek adventure and influence were slight. There were small early trading-posts at the mouth of the Po, and Ancona was founded in the fourth century B.C. as an outpost of Syracuse.

These numerous Greek settlements profoundly influenced the culture and economic history of southern Italy. Etruscan rivalry prevented Greek colonization north of Campania and broke its hold on Corsica. But Greek intercourse with Rome began early. After the revolt of Rome itself against the Etruscans in 510 B.C. the Romans supported the Greek cities against Etruscans, Phoenicians, and Sabellian highlanders alike, and consequently became involved, after the defeat of Carthage, in the politics of mainland Greece and Macedonia.

SICILY

Though geographically a continuation of the Italian peninsula, and populated for the most part by Italian stock, Sicily developed distinct social and political features in its later history, due mainly to foreign influences and to the circumstances of the Roman conquest. The aboriginal Mediterranean people survived, especially in the west, side by side with immigrants or 'Sicels' from Italy: Greek observers detected resemblances between the aboriginals and the 'Iberian' natives of Spain. Dense Greek colonization reduced most of the Sicel and aboriginal tribes to serfdom, from which they made determined but unsuccessful efforts to free themselves about 460–450 B.C.

There were minor Greek settlements on the north coast east of Phoenician Panormus (Palermo) to Messana (Messina), which latter controlled the Straits. The colonies of the east coast were more important: Naxos (near Taormina), Catana (Catania), Leontini (Lentini), and Syracuse (Siracusa), which later exploited the whole south-eastern upland. On the south coast were the great settlements of Gela and Acragas (Agrigento). Thence westward began the Phoenician sphere, in which was eventually planted the Greek colony of Selinus (Selinunte). The Phoenicians from Carthage who established their power in the west had much the same effect as the Etruscans in Italy, accentuating native differences, diverting produce and trade, forestalling Greek expansion, and eventually challenging the whole Greek occupation of Sicily from the end of the sixth to the middle of the third century B.C. It was in Sicily, rather than in south Italy, that Pyrrhus 'left so fair a battlefield to the Romans and the Carthaginians'. Principal Phoenician centres were Solus (Solunto) in the south-west, Motya and Lilybaeum (Trapani) at the western end, and Panormus (Palermo) with its great harbour on the north coast.

EARLY ROME AND LATIUM

The historical position of Rome results from its geographical situation in the centre of the Campagna and its command of the Tiber crossing between Etruria and Latium, at a point where the ancient 'salt-way' (Via Salaria) from the Tiber mouth (Ostia) struck north-east towards the Abruzzi. Within the Campagna Rome was one of thirty Latin 'peoples' which from the sixth to the fourth century B.C. combined in a League for mutual defence against the surrounding highlanders (Sabines, Volsci, and Aequi).

The original lowland Latin population of Rome, including many outlaws from neighbouring communities, had already been long dominated by Sabine clans from the hills when (c. 600–510 B.C.) three kings of Etruscan origin established a

7

powerful and splendid tyranny over Sabines and Latins alike, reorganizing the army, founding great buildings, and dominating the Latin League. After expelling this Etruscan dynasty in 510 B.C. the new Roman republic resumed the leadership of Latium, but ensuing quarrels with her allies led, in 348 B.C., to the dissolution of the League. Many communities were incorporated with citizen rights. The remainder were brought into separate dependence on Rome as allies (*socii*) with right of economic and social intercourse, and the duty of mutual defence under Roman control. By similar methods Rome proceeded in the following century to make herself mistress of the whole peninsula, which became a confederation of partly allied and partly incorporated peoples.

2. ROMAN CONQUEST OF ITALY

The principal stages in Roman domination of Italy (Fig. 3) were as follows:

1. The League of Latin cities was dissolved (348 B.C.).

2. The peoples of the Plain of Campania, liberated from Etruscan and Samnite rule (343–314 B.C.), were given partial citizen rights.

3. The Samnites and other members of the Southern Confederacy in Apulia and Lucania were conquered (327–290 B.C.). In accomplishing this Rome owed much to the loyalty of the Greek cities on the coast, but had thereafter to defeat Tarentum's claim to dominion in the south, supported by Carthage and by Pyrrhus, king of Epirus, who invaded Italy from beyond the Adriatic (280–275 B.C.).

4. The Etruscan cities resisted long, and were subdued gradually: Veii in 396 B.C. and the last in 295 B.C.; the Umbrians offered little resistance to Rome. These two peoples formed the Northern Confederates.

5. The Greek city-states of Campania and the south were recognized as specially privileged allies with equal rights. As most of them were ports and commanded the forests of their hinterland, they formed the nucleus of Rome's 'naval allies'.

Tarentum, the only recalcitrant, was conquered in 272 B.C., and Rome's new fleet was put to the test in the first Punic War.

Fig. 3. The expansion of Rome in Italy. Figures refer to dates (B.C.) of conquest

6. Common interests with Syracuse, which had created a dominion in Sicily over the other free cities and the more civilized natives, led to the first Punic War with Carthage (264–241 B.C.) and to the annexation of Sicily and Sardinia, which became the first oversea administrations or *provinciae*. Subject peoples were

9

on a different footing from the free allies of Italy. Yearly governors were sent out, but the principal Greek cities retained much
of their local autonomy.

7. In the second Punic War (218–201 B.C.) the Carthaginians
invaded Italy through Spain and Provence, and provided a
thorough test of the strength of the Roman Confederation. The
Samnites and also the Greeks of Campania, Tarentum, and
Syracuse seceded in vain, and after successful campaigns in Spain
and Africa Rome emerged as mistress not only of Italy but of the
western Mediterranean. The attempt to circumvent Roman sea-
power had failed.

8. The Northern Plain (Gallia Cisalpina) was dominated by
the Celtic-speaking Gauls. Those south of the Po and also the
Ligurian tribes of the Apennines were conquered between 225
and 160 B.C. The frontier of Italy, however, remained along the
Apennines and the Rubicon stream; in 49 B.C. Caesar did not
enter Italy until he crossed the Rubicon.

9. The Ligurian highlanders along the coast from Genua
(Genoa) into Provence were gradually conquered between 220
and 118 B.C. when the Provincia Narbonensis (Provence) was
organized as far as the north slope of the Pyrenees. The frontier
between Italy and Narbonensis was eventually fixed west of
Nicaea (Nice) along the Var.

10. After a civil war between the various members of the Confederation, the whole of Italy south of the Po was incorporated
into a single Roman State (90–89 B.C.).

11. The first Emperor Augustus (27 B.C.) incorporated the
rest of Gallia Cisalpina north of the Po and as far as the Alpine
foothills into Italy as part of the Roman State. The subjection of
the tribes of the Alpine foothills was completed by Augustus'
establishment of the provinces of Rhaetia and Noricum, which
included the non-Gallic peoples of the Alps, with their northern
frontiers on the Danube. These never became part of Italy.

The Roman conquest of Italy was greatly influenced by the
relief of the country. The first expansion of the Roman State
beyond the plain of Latium was south-east through the easy

Sacco-Liri valley into the Plain of Campania, but the second stage was north-east into the difficult country of Sabina and the Roman Apennines. This was necessary for defence against the hill-folk and to secure the flank of the great military route of the Flaminian Way through the Apennines to the Adriatic coast. Thus the Roman territory formed a block dividing the Peninsula into three sections and separating the Northern and Southern Confederates (Fig. 3). Among these the Oscan hillmen of the Central Apennines from the Abruzzi to the Ofanto river, and particularly the Samnites, were the most difficult to control. The greatest campaign was fought for the Benevento gap, where the capital of Samnium lay at Beneventum. The peoples of the open plateaux of Apulia and the scattered Etruscan and Umbrian communities of the Pre-Apennines gave less resistance, though the dense Ciminian forest then covering the North Latin hills at first limited the Roman advance into Etruria. Relatively few fortress-colonies were established in either Etruria or Apulia. By contrast, the inaccessible Ligurians of the Northern Apennines and Lucanian Oscans of the Southern Apennines were subdued only by long campaigns. In the Northern Plain conquest was relatively rapid despite the density of its population; the river Padus (Po) was in the late Republic a political frontier, and the river crossings at Placentia (Piacenza) and Cremona were of considerable strategic importance.

Throughout Roman history the Flaminian Way over the Apennines remained the key to the control of Italy. North of it no great Roman road crossed the Apennines until the Via Postumia from Genua. There is a notable similarity between the areas covered by the territory of the early Roman State and by the later medieval states of the Church. Both had the same basic strategic interest in the control of the Flaminian Way.

MILITARY CONTROL AND COLONIES

To protect allied and conquered territory, the only ancient alternatives were either to levy tribute and hire mercenaries, as some Greek cities did, or to enlarge the citizen-force itself. The Romans combined both methods, giving to the Latins and subsequently to other conquered peoples of Italy partial or complete citizenship with the obligation of military service, and exacting military levies from her allies. Tribute was also levied and all military forces were paid. Strategical points in conquered territories were garrisoned by settlements of Roman farmers (*coloni*), who remained full citizens of Rome, and by similar colonies with 'Latin rights', which, however, had a greater measure of local autonomy than the former. Citizen colonies were originally used to garrison the harbours and ports of Italy and acted as a substitute for a fleet; the havenless nature of the Italian coasts enabled Rome to dispense with a permanent fleet until the outbreak of universal piracy between 90 and 66 B.C. Many famous Italian cities originated as 'colonies'. The distribution of these 'Roman' and 'Latin' colonies is given on Fig. 4. Later, colonies were established far beyond the limits of Italy. Their influence in diffusing Roman ideas and modes of life was profound, replacing that of Sabellian hill-towns, Etruscan fortresses, and Greek city-states.

ROADS

Communications between Rome and the fortress-colonies were secured by a new device of warfare and policy, military roads, which had bridges, embankments, and even cuttings, and were the motorways of antiquity (Fig. 4). The most important (usually named from their builders) were, in approximate order of construction:

Via Latina from Rome into Campania, inland of the Alban hills.

Via Appia (312 B.C.) to Campania by the coast, then either
(*a*) to Tarentum (Taranto) and Brundisium (Brindisi) or
(*b*) to Rhegium (Reggio) by the Via Popilia (132 B.C.).

Via Salaria (361 B.C.) following the ancient 'salt-road' into the Central Apennines.

Via Flaminia (200 B.C.) to the Adriatic coast at Fanum (Fano); continued by the Via Aemilia (187 B.C.) to Placentia (Piacenza) on the Po.

Via Aurelia (123–108 B.C.) through Etruria to Pisa and Genoa; continued later (*a*) by the Via Postumia (148 B.C.)

to Placentia; (*b*) by the Via Julia Augusta through the Ligurian coastland into Provence.

Via Cassia (170 B.C.) also traversed Etruria.

Fig. 4. Strategic roads and colonies before A.D. 14

The main ancient routes across the Alps were those through the Julian Alps, the Brenner, the Splügen, the two St. Bernard passes, and the Mont Genèvre. These were mostly built by Augustus (29 B.C.–A.D. 14).

END OF THE REPUBLIC

The subsequent oversea conquests of Rome, though effected with the united resources of Italy, do not directly concern its territorial history. By 49 B.C. Italy ruled directly or indirectly the whole Mediterranean world, but the constant drain on fighting-men depleted Italian communities; foreign corn-supplies, especially from the provinces of northern Africa and from Egypt, did much to ruin Italian agriculture; the lure of city-life depleted rural communities; and immense wealth, easily won by Romans abroad, erected a barrier between the ruling class and the masses. Long discontent, exploited for party ends in Rome, led to a violent civil war between the more and the less privileged elements of the Confederation (90–89 B.C.) and to the eventual grant of full Roman citizenship to all Italians in Italy proper and Cisalpine Gaul as far north as the Alps. Economic and social grievances were, however, still neglected, and municipal government fell into disorder. These disaffections led to violent uprisings against the 'Republican' government (civil wars of 88–80 and 49–30 B.C.) which ended with the establishment by Julius Caesar (49–44 B.C.) and Augustus (27 B.C.–A.D. 14) of a thinly disguised monarchy.

Rome's conquest of Sicily (242 B.C.) and intervention in the politics of Greece, Macedon, and the new Greek kingdoms of Syria and Egypt (198–30 B.C.) had brought sudden and overwhelming contact with later Greek (Hellenistic) civilization, which stifled the development of indigenous Italian cultures. Yet Roman and Italian imitations of Greek architecture, sculpture, and other material arts have their distinctive qualities, and in Latin literature the influence of Greek conventions and technique is superficial. The Latin language matured under Greek scholarship, but remained a living and most eloquent tongue, the direct ancestor of medieval and modern Italian.

ITALY UNDER THE ROMAN EMPIRE

Julius Caesar (49–44 B.C.) planned the reorganization of Italy, but he did not live to put it into execution. After twenty years of civil war and anarchy, his legal heir Octavian, later called Augustus (27 B.C.–A.D. 14) came to the task of re-establishing public order in the empire, in Italy, and in Rome. In 27 B.C. he 'restored the republic to the Roman people', exchanging his dictatorial for equal but more constitutional authority, and continued as *princeps*, to watch over the working of the reformed Senate and republican magistrates, and of a growing civil service directly responsible to himself.

Italy was still administered by the Senate, in eleven 'regions' which included Cisalpine Gaul and extended from the Apennines to the new frontier provinces, Rhaetia, Noricum, and Pannonia, between the Alps and the Danube. New citizen colonies were founded, and the whole country divided up into self-governing communities, *coloniae* or *municipia*. Rome itself was much rebuilt and became a capital city worthy of the now vast Roman Empire, housing a population which grew greatly at least until the second century A.D., when it perhaps amounted to a million souls, 150,000 of whom were sustained by a dole of free corn. The rest were the personnel of the central administrative offices of the empire and the army, and also the retainers of the great princely families, which supplied the army with its officers and the administration with its governors (proconsuls and legates). A large percentage of the city population were of foreign and servile origin, and particularly included oriental elements which brought with them many mystical religions, such as Mithraism and Christianity.

Italy, like Rome, had shared in the decline of the republic. Together with political independence, exclusive privileges and responsibilities were vanishing. The overwhelming power of the emperor (*princeps*), and its abuse by individual rulers, bore most hardly on regions nearest the seat of government. This autocracy, expressed by the bestowal of divine honours on the emperor, was practised in many indirect forms, though technically forbidden in Italy. The municipal system was, however, consolidated, and extended into the provinces, especially in the west.

DECLINE OF THE EMPIRE, A.D. 180–476

From A.D. 180, when the first really worthless emperor, Commodus, was installed, to the accession of Diocletian (284), a few strong emperors—Septimius Severus (192–211), Aurelian (270–5), Probus (276–82)—postponed the dissolution of the empire by the barbarian invasions of the Goths (247–51), Franks (230–76), and Persians (260–70), in face of impoverishment by war, plague, and famine. The difficulties of the emperors were increased by the weakening discipline of the armies, which now consisted mainly of professionals and provincials with some recruits from the barbarian invaders, and also by the admission of barbarian settlers to lands within the empire. The separation of military and civil administration in the course of the third century, forecasting the Byzantine system, put an end to the old Roman conceptioı of citizenship and of the empire. Nevertheless, Diocletian's administrative and economic reforms probably saved the empire at a time when it appeared on the verge of collapse.

Diocletian's choice of Milan, of Trier on the Moselle, Sirmium on the Save, and Nicomedia on the Marmara (293) as administrative capitals of the empire, and Constantine's creation of a 'New Rome' (Constantinople) on the Bosphorus (325) gravely affected the prosperity and prestige of Rome, and thereby of the Italian homeland, whilst enhancing the importance of the Northern Plain over that of the Peninsula. The military position also was revolutionized when Aurelian (270–5) fortified Rome, and when Milan, Ravenna, and Aquileia became advanced bases for the defence of the Peninsula. The veiled autocracy of the early emperors had long become an open tyranny, sanctioned and swayed by the armies; Septimius Severus (192) abstained from seeking confirmation of his authority from the Senate, and himself exercised most of its functions; Diocletian finally freed the emperor from constitutional control, and assumed the title 'master' (*dominus*). In the elaborate administration which he created Rome and Italy were reduced to the level of the tribute-paying provinces, all alike now governed directly by imperial prefects and their subordinates.

The temporary division of the empire between Valentinian and Valens (364) and the permanent separation of East from West on the death of Theodosius (395) deprived Italy of the hitherto customary support from beyond the Adriatic. The sack of Rome by Alaric's Goths in 410 was reparable, but the temporary loss of Italy's granary and source of oil in Roman Africa

(Tunisia) to the Vandals (435) disorganized its artificial economy. The termination of the Western Empire in 476 by a barbarian chief, Odovacar, was accompanied by wide Teutonic settlements on the countryside, though the administration and the life of the cities do not seem to have been greatly disturbed.

3. ECONOMIC AND SOCIAL HISTORY

PRE-ROMAN ORIGINS

More important than political changes was the profound economic revolution which took place under Roman administration. The economic history of Italy has been greatly affected both by its geography and by its political developments. The distribution of the earliest rites and cultures indicates that the mountains of peninsular Italy long retarded settlement and that in the southern lowlands the primitive mode of life was pastoral rather than agricultural. The evidence also suggests that when cattle-breeding spread, it was at the expense of the forests, and consequently the surface soil was gradually transferred by the winter rains from the hill-sides to vast maritime fens like those of the Campagna, which in turn became cattle-ranches (*saltus*). Though nowhere nomadic, Italian herdsmen moved with the season between upland and lowland pastures; consequently the spread of agriculture was at the expense of winter grazing and a source of ill-will between cultivators (*coloni*) and herdsmen (*pastores*).

The fundamental economy of human settlement in Italy has not greatly changed since the introduction in prehistoric times of domestic animals, cereal crops, and the vine and olive. The essential means of subsistence, as in other Mediterranean lands, were, then as now, corn, wine, and oil, supplemented by other tree-fruits, by garden and dairy produce, and by meat and game. Geese and ducks were indigenous; fowls were introduced later from overseas. The nut-bearing forest trees, especially oak, beech, chestnut, and walnut, fed pigs and swineherds alike. Ox and ass supplied transport and drew the primitive plough, though there was much hoe-cultivation. The horse, though known in the later Bronze Age, was long used chiefly in war, and in small numbers.

Family life, and the larger clans and tribes, were strictly patriarchal; children were the father's property until he released them; women were the wards of parent or husband, but had their own dominion in the homestead and their own ceremonies. The primary settlements were village communities of associated clans under close patriarchal rule, crowded for defence on to defensible ridges and spurs which offered a safer refuge than the open farms. Much land was owned in common and farmed by individuals, but communal ownership—except on the pastures— early gave place to family freeholds. Society remained tribal, but was divided into local economic units (*pagi*). Government was shared among the landholders. Each community, large or small, had its council of ten or more elders (*decuriones*) and one, two, or four annual officers (*meddices, praetores*) for jurisdiction and to lead the tribal levy. Inter-tribal groups, however, only came into being for war, when a federal commander-in-chief (*dictator*) was appointed for each emergency. In such a community (*civitas*) 'civil' behaviour meant that of any ordinary decent citizen (*cives*): 'stranger' and 'enemy' were alike 'hostile' (*hostis*). Over-population was remedied by organized emigration of age-classes, to clear or to conquer new territory. The infertile and deforested highlands poured out their swarms (*populi*) into the plains: to 'populate' a territory (*populari*) meant to devastate it for resettlement. It was to check such raids that the original Latin League was formed and Rome's early wars were fought.

Early Italian houses were built facing inwards round a court with rain tank (*impluvium*) fed by the deep eaves of the house or a roofed colonnade; additional space and convenience were provided by a second court or (in towns) by an upper story. The settlements were close-built, with narrow alleys and a market-place. Temples were single chambers, with door and porch at one end; architectural styles, even the 'Tuscan', were borrowed from Greek traders and colonists, in the Po valley, Etruria, and Latium.

ROMAN SOCIAL AND ECONOMIC HISTORY

The economy of romanized Italy did not at first differ from that of the ancient Italic peoples. Conquered farms were distributed to Roman citizens in individual holdings, whilst conquered pastures were leased to Roman cattle-owners, that is, to the richer citizens. War captives and landless Italians were used to supplement the labour of the free tenant farmer and his family. Produce was still mainly consumed locally, though the growing population of the city of Rome called for all available surplus and was also looking overseas for its corn, to Sicily, and eventually to north Africa and to Egypt. But the wars with Carthage (264–204) and especially Hannibal's long occupation of parts of Italy (215–204) disorganized Italian economy. Grave losses of men, devastation of olive groves and vineyards, and prolonged absence of the farmers, both Roman and allied, on long war-service, were aggravated by the land-speculation of war profiteers. Few colonies were founded between 150 B.C. and the end of the republic, when the settlement of veterans on the land again became widespread. Aristocrats who had made fortunes in the wars overseas (200–49 B.C.) accumulated vast estates (*lati fundi*). Personal attention to farms gave place to bailiff management, hired men, and slave labour; and when foreign corn spoilt the Roman market, much land reverted to pasture, on which commercial profit was greater, and where slave herdsmen replaced peasant proprietors. There were slave risings in Etruria (196 B.C.), Apulia (185 B.C.), and Sicily (139 and 132–130 B.C.), and more widely in 73–71 B.C. As, however, the supply of slave labour diminished after the wars of conquest, there was increasing use of free tenant farmers.

The Civil Wars (89–80, 49–31 B.C.) renewed the disorganization first felt during Hannibal's invasion. Under the empire the peasant proprietor was at a disadvantage. Very large estates formed economic units in the hands of the imperial family and the aristocracy. Smaller estates were formed by lesser capitalists, but the smallholders still held out in remote uplands. The settlement of veterans in Italy was no longer successful—they preferred larger farms in the provinces. Such conditions characterized the Peninsula, but the broad lands of the Northern Plain were always more prosperous; and the 'restoration' of Italian agriculture was a constant aim and care throughout the early empire.

Trade and commerce played a large part in the economic life of Italy in the last years of the republic and the early years of the empire. Italy could, indeed, have been self-supporting, but the lure of high profits encouraged producers to concentrate on the export market and the production of luxury goods. In the towns of Tuscany and Campania there were many large enterprises for the production of raw materials and finished goods, including the manufacture of glass, pottery, metal, paper, and luxury goods. The main source of wealth, however, was the export of Italian wine and oil to the provinces on a large scale. The standing army overseas was also an important customer. Pliny the Elder said that two-thirds of the wine consumed in the empire came from Italy. This economic supremacy of Italy was not maintained. The vineyards and olive groves of Spain and Gaul stole the markets of the Italian producers even in Italy itself.

In this period also great public works—theatres, public baths and markets, harbours, roads, bridges and aqueducts—were built and waste lands reclaimed. Tax-farmers were gradually superseded by revenue officers, and financial administration was improved. Devastation by civil war was repaired partly by the settlement of veterans on derelict and confiscated properties, partly by systematic encouragement of agriculture, by a scientific review of resources, and by loans to farmers; and as agriculture recovered, municipal life revived.

SOCIAL SYSTEM OF THE EMPIRE

Wholesale introduction of war captives and slaves, mainly oriental, under the republic altered the composition of the people. Within the social and administrative hierarchy—the Senate, the capitalist, and mercantile class called the 'knights' (*equites*), and the agricultural, industrial, and urban populace (*plebs*)—ascent was easy, and the public service, which was entered from the army, attracted ever larger numbers, both from Italy and from the provinces. With Rome becoming an international city and with literature and the arts, as well as administration, passing into provincial hands, the political health of the country depended upon that of the self-governing municipal system. Local patriotism found its outlet in the embellishment of the towns, as at Pompeii, but the expenses of administration became burdensome, and—by the third century A.D.—local government was being neglected or was left to officials of the imperial administration.

The intrusion of barbarians after A.D. 300 did not check the agricultural decline. The population meanwhile became stationary or was reduced by pestilence, famine, and war; extension of state and municipal ownership testified both to anxiety over food-supply and to scarcity of private capital. Imperial ordinances for the people's welfare, however, failed to check the abuses of ancient customs.

Extension of Roman citizenship throughout the empire, and stabilization of frontiers, reduced the supply of slaves, the sale of whom by farmers was forbidden in A.D. 167 and 375. Aurelian compelled municipal councils to farm derelict lands, and Constantine (332) and Theodosius (433) forbade free tenants to leave their domicile. Out of such legislation there developed a system whereby the nominally free man was tied to the soil as a serf. These tenants were often grouped together in large agricultural 'colonates' owned by the emperor, by rich individuals, or by syndicates as an investment. These estates were operated by a large number of cultivators, called by the old name of *coloni*, nominally free men, but more and more restricted in their freedom to migrate, as the supply of slaves from abroad ceased. The larger of these 'colonates' came to have their own economic regime and salaried administration; they were managed by *procuratores* who were responsible to the emperor, but often not effectively controlled either by him or by the intermediate officials.

The building of Constantinople diverted the Egyptian supply of corn, and in 391 there was fear of famine, disorder in agriculture, and rioting in the country towns; tribute, levied now in

Italy as in the provinces, fell into arrears and had to be exacted by force. The barbarian invaders added to the demand for food, but were unable to produce it. The weaknesses of the Roman economy—shortage of manpower, technological backwardness, the existence of large unproductive classes of *rentiers* and bureaucrats, heavy taxation for a huge army—go far to account for the inability of the western provinces to resist barbarian settlement. Fundamentally the Italian social and agricultural systems remained much as they had been before the Roman unification, and many of their details have passed into medieval and even into modern times, outliving in Italy itself the higher grades of administration which barbarian conquest disorganized. The one permanent change in the Italian social system effected in Roman times was the substitution for peasant proprietorship of a system of wealthy landlords and impoverished tenants.

ROMAN MUNICIPAL INSTITUTIONS

The municipal institutions of the Roman Empire, on which depended its vitality, were developed from those of pre-Roman Italy.

The Roman custom was to confirm by treaty and charter the local self-governing institutions of the communities which they conquered (*civitates, municipia*) and to give similar constitutions to their own colonies (*coloniae*, p. 12). After the Social War (89 B.C.; p. 14) all 'colonies with Latin rights' and 'allied' states south of the Po on being incorporated into the Roman State became self-governing 'municipalities'. These *municipia* resembled a small English county rather than an urban borough. They retained their traditional magistrates, council, and massmeeting, and even their own local laws for the administration of their territories, which were sometimes considerable. The same procedure was followed in overseas provinces of the West. Within a large municipality the old subdivisions (*pagi*) were usually retained as administrative units. The inhabitants of municipal territories were everywhere Roman citizens, but outside Italy they were under the supervision of the provincial governors. The whole system was co-ordinated by Julius Caesar and Augustus. Throughout the empire Italy was a complex of several hundred municipalities, in whose hands the detailed administration of the country was placed.

4. *CHRISTIANITY AND THE ROMAN CHURCH*

Christianity, at once a new religion and a new society, was in part the creation of the empire, and blended Roman institutions and ideas with Greek culture and oriental mysticism. The new religion met a very real need, and is to be compared with 'mystery' cults such as Mithraism. Most ordinary people believed their lives to be controlled by chance or Fate's inexorable decree or by the stars, and sought deliverance from these usually malignant powers. The educated man might find solace in classical culture, which lived in the past, but for the majority the agnosticism of the Epicureans, and the impersonal deism of the Stoics, proved fatal to existing religions without putting anything in their place. Christianity appealed to the superstitious poor because it gave them salvation and the hope of a better world to come; and the Pauline presentation of the 'kingdom' to the 'Gentiles', and the high moral standards demanded in a degenerate age, satisfied the middle classes and the men of culture. The combination of appeals—to universal brotherhood, to the equality of all believers in the sight of God, and to a new social order—established Christianity as a proselytizing creed with a world-wide organization.

Rome was the centre of one of the earliest Italian Christian communities, which was probably founded by 'sojourners in Rome' during the Principate of Claudius (A.D. 41–54). The association of the two great apostles with the Church at Rome helped to make it one of the main Christian centres of the empire. This church was governed from apostolic times by a continuous succession of bishops or presbyters, the first of whom, Linus, had probably been appointed by St Peter.

Christian 'congregations', like Jewish synagogues, met for worship, teaching, and good works, and for the most part accommodated their mode of life to contemporary culture.

During the second half of the first and the early part of the second century the churches throughout the empire developed a form of organization which eventually produced episcopacy. Each church was governed by a number of presbyters (an elder; *presbyteros*), who together with the other members of the church elected one man as their leader. This man, who might be called *presbyteros* or *episcopos* (bishop; overseer), was not regarded during the first two centuries as being superior in kind to the other presbyters. But under the influence of the Roman notion of authority, and the Jewish conception of the priesthood, the bishop gradually rose above the presbyters and laity, over whom he gained considerable authority. The gap between the clergy and laity widened, when the Christian meetings, originally spontaneous and often led by illiterate men, gradually began to develop a set form of ritual which required educated men with specialized knowledge. Ordination soon became necessary before a man could speak publicly in church. This, without doubt, increased the power of the bishop, who claimed 'to preside in the place of God', and exercised political as well as ecclesiastical influence.

Each town had one church, and each church a bishop, who was, in theory, the equal of every other bishop. Christianity, which first took root in commercial cities visited by Jewish traders, gradually spread from the cities to the small towns around, and more slowly into the villages and the countryside. The smaller churches felt their dependence on the mother cities and this led to the development of something like the modern diocese. It is not surprising to find one of the largest Christian churches of the time in Rome, which was the capital of the empire. In such a church the chief presbyter was bound to assume great authority in the administration of so large a system, and he became vastly superior to the rest of the local presbyters or clergy. The bishops of Rome, therefore, had more local power than the bishops of most other cities, and tended to become the head of the church in the Italian peninsula. The first twelve bishops of Rome were Greek, the greatest being Clement. Victor, 189–98, was the first Latin-speaking bishop of Rome. The

Roman Church during the second century was noted for its zeal for order and good government, which were inherited from the bureaucratic traditions of imperial Rome.

The third century was marked by theological controversy resulting in the development of numerous doctrinal heresies, large-scale persecution of the Christians, and the gradual increase of the power of the Roman bishop. Controversy inevitably arose when the teaching of Christ and the apostles was formulated semi-philosophically by the apologists in order to appeal to the educated people of the day. The Church in Rome, however, was not so actively engaged in theological controversy, which was most rife in the philosophically-minded East, and its powerful episcopate helped to keep check on the growth of heresy. There were few theologians of note in Rome, where the bishops were more famed for their organizing ability.

Three severe persecutions greatly affected the Christian Church. The first of these took place in the West between 249 and 251, under the Emperor Decius, who considered the powerful Christian organization to be a source of danger to the State. Christians, who were estimated to comprise one-sixth of the population of the empire, were now found in every stratum of society. In Italy south of the Rubicon, Christians accounted for about half the population, whilst from the Alps to the Rubicon the number of Christians was smaller, though beginning to increase. Decius' attack was directed at the leaders of the Church, and aimed at breaking it up from within rather than a general massacre. Martyrs were, however, numerous, especially in Rome where two bishops were killed, and the great number of apostates caused much disturbance in the inner life of the Roman Church. The second persecution, under Valerian (257–61), was particularly severe in Rome, where many were martyred, church property was confiscated, and church services were forbidden. The Diocletianic persecution, at the beginning of the fourth century, attacked the clergy, the laity, and the Christian religion as a whole; though severe in Italy, it was of shorter duration there than in the East.

The fourth century saw the toleration of Christianity when, in

313, the edict of Milan proclaimed religious freedom for all. In the reign of Constantine (274–337) Christianity became the official religion of the empire, and many high officials and time-serving politicians became Christians, greatly to the detriment of the inner life of the Church. During the fourth and fifth centuries doctrinal problems became acute in the East, whilst the power of the bishop of Rome increased in the West. The heresy which most affected Italy was Arianism, because it was eventually adopted by the Christianized barbarians who over-ran northern Italy. The basic heretical element in Arianism was the reduction of 'God the Son' to the level of a *creature* and hence the denial of the full divinity of Christ.

The power of the Roman bishop increased during the third, fourth, and especially the fifth centuries, because there was no other church in the Italian peninsula which was so large, or that could claim apostolic foundation. In the third century the advice of the bishop of Rome was not regarded as sovereign by the other bishops of the empire; when Rome agreed with them they accepted her authority, but when Rome differed her bishop was a heretic, or at least in gross error. When in 381, at the second Council of Constantinople, the bishops of the four chief cities of the empire, Alexandria, Antioch, Constantinople, and Rome, were designated the 'patriarchs' of the Christian Church, the prelate of Rome refused the title and preferred to be called 'Papa' or Pope, which meant the same thing but sounded more archaic. He considered himself to be the head of the visible Church, and the equal of no other bishop. The increase of the power of the pope was largely the result of the establishment of the Eastern (Byzantine) Empire with its capital at Constantinople, and the transference of the seat of the western emperor to Milan and Ravenna. The pope was thus without rival in southern Italy and the islands of Sicily, Corsica, and Sardinia, and left to do what he could with the barbarian invasions. He made the best of his advantages and succeeded in converting the barbarians. In 443 the Emperor Valentinian recognized the supremacy of the bishops of Rome over the other bishops of the Western Church. The personal courage and forcefulness of the fifth-century pope,

Leo the Great, who amongst other things is reputed to have faced the barbarian Attila when the latter was at the gates of Rome, greatly increased the power and prestige of the popes. Leo claimed divine origin for the Papacy, but made no claim to temporal authority and was, when occasion arose, submissive to the emperors. After there ceased to be an emperor in the West (476) the pope tended still more to take the place of the emperor in all Italy. But Gregory the Great (c. 540–604) was the real founder of the present Papacy and of the Western Church (pp. 31-2). The split of East and West in the empire was also important in stressing the Latinity of the Western Church, though it was only gradually during the fourth and fifth centuries that Latin replaced Greek as the formal language of the Church. It was not, however, till the ninth century that the Eastern Orthodox and the Roman Catholic churches finally separated.

Christianity in the north of Italy, especially in the Northern Plain, developed considerably in the fourth and fifth centuries. The only bishoprics which have a date earlier than the fourth century are those of Ravenna (Classis, founded 200), Milan (240), Aquileia, Brescia, and Verona. Christianity came to the plains of Lombardy not from Rome, but from the Eastern Churches by way of the Po valley. Even in the fourth century the bishops of this region were Greek. For a short period during the fourth century it would appear that the Western Church recognized the dual hegemony of the pope and of the bishop of Milan, the metropolitan of northern Italy. This divided rule was especially felt during the life of St Ambrose of Milan (A.D. 340–97), who influenced the churches both of the Eastern Empire and of the West, particularly in Spain and Gaul, where the ecclesiastical authority of Milan was accepted as a natural and superior tribunal.

It was the existence of the Arian heresy in the Northern Plain, introduced by the barbarian conquerors, which led to the intervention of the Roman bishop in the fifth century and the final establishment of his ecclesiastical power in northern Italy.

CHAPTER II

EARLY MEDIEVAL ITALY

1. THE DARK AGES, 476–800

BARBARIAN INVASION AND GROWTH OF
PAPAL POWER

In 476 the last Emperor of the West was forced to abdicate, and Constantinople became the seat of the sole Roman emperor. From that time political unity ceased to exist in Italy. Not until 1870 was it again brought under the rule of one sovereign. Imperial authority was generally recognized, but the power of the Byzantine emperors could not be maintained in the face of barbarian invaders and the growing divergence between East and West. Centuries elapsed, however, before the last vestiges of imperial rule disappeared. Ravenna remained a seat of government, and a centre of Byzantine influence, until it fell to the Lombards in the eighth century. Sicily acknowledged the emperor until the Saracen conquest of the ninth century, and there were imperial officials in Calabria until the coming of the Normans. When the knowledge of Greek was all but lost to the western world, it was still spoken in southern Italy. Meanwhile, Goths, Lombards, and Franks in turn fought their way across the Alps. Although they conquered and settled in the Northern Plain, they failed to master the whole peninsula. Ravenna, under its exarch, maintained communications with Rome and barred the most convenient route to the south. The Italians, robbed of land and food by the barbarian armies, resisted them in the name of the Empire.

Into this struggle between ancient Rome and the new barbarian nations the temporal power of the Papacy entered as a third political factor. The adoption of Christianity as the official religion of the Roman Empire and the transference of the seat of empire from Rome to Constantinople gave new political significance to the Papacy. The popes were landowners on a large scale, and from the revenues of their estates, designated as the 'patrimony of the poor', they organized poor-relief. As the imperial government at Ravenna grew weaker, they were used more and more as agents of imperial administration. Such matters as the maintenance of public buildings in Rome and the payment of the army were dealt with by papal officials. It fell to the popes to defend Italy against the barbarian invaders and to negotiate with the conquerors. Realizing that little help could be expected from Constantinople they resented imperial interference in temporal and, still more, in spiritual affairs.

On the abdication of Romulus Augustulus, the ruler of Italy was the barbarian leader Odovacar, who claimed by his title of patrician to be the imperial representative. In 488 Theodoric, king of the Goths, invaded Italy with the support of the emperor, and Odovacar was overthrown after a five years' struggle. Theodoric had spent ten years as a hostage at the Byzantine court, and he knew the value of civilization. He strove to combine the functions of a military leader of the Goths with that of the wielder of imperial power. He ruled through Roman officials, and in association with the Roman Senate. He maintained even justice between Goth and Italian, Arian and Catholic. He carried out restorations in Rome and at Ravenna, where he built himself a palace. Yet he failed to establish a Gothic kingdom in Italy. His authority was undermined by the jealousy of the emperor, the suspicions entertained by Catholics of an Arian ruler, and the unrest caused among the Italians by the depredations of the soldiers. The last years of his reign were troubled, and his life-work did not survive him. The chief memorial of him in Italy is his unfinished mausoleum at Ravenna.

The years following Theodoric's death (526) were marked by the attempt of Justinian to revive imperial power in Italy. His aim was to be both conqueror and law-giver. He would drive out the Goths, champion the Catholic Church against Arianism, and 'give back to Rome, Rome's privileges'. Italy was conquered, after hard fighting, by the imperial generals Belisarius and Narses, but Gothic power was not brought to an end until the defeat of Totila in 552. The Pragmatic Sanction of 554 restored to the Roman proprietors their lands, revived Roman institutions, and reorganized the administration. These reforms imposed a heavy financial burden on a country ravaged by war, and increased its sense of subjection to Constantinople. Thus, when the emperor died in 565, Italy was in no condition to stand against her new invaders, the Lombards. Justinian left, however, a permanent mark upon Italian civilization. Byzantine art, which reaches its highest point in the splendid portraits of himself and the Empress Theodora in the church of San Vitale at Ravenna, was a great formative influence in Italian painting. The Roman Law, which he codified, continued to be administered in Italy and was identified with his name. Dante gives to Justinian a place in Paradise, saying that he, by the will of God, purged the law of the superfluous and the irrelevant. Raphael in his Vatican frescoes chooses Justinian's presentation of the Pandects, together with Pope Gregory IX's delivery of the Decretals, as the twin events in history which most appropriately illustrate justice.

LOMBARDS AND GREGORY THE GREAT

The Lombards, led by Alboin, appeared in the valley of the river Po in 568. Their power was more extensive and more enduring than that of earlier Teutonic invaders. For two hundred years Pavia was the capital of a kingdom which included modern Lombardy and the greater part of Venetia, Liguria, and Tuscany (Fig. 5). Independent warriors penetrated farther south and founded the duchies of Spoleto and Beneventum. Lombard custom was formulated in a written code, and the characteristic Germanic features of a loosely constructed society of free warriors, owing limited allegiance only to their king, were reproduced on Italian soil. The Lombards intermarried with the Roman population, adopted their language, and absorbed their culture. They aimed at conquering the whole country, but their numerical inferiority and their own lack of unity thwarted their designs. The effect of their period of power in Italy was to perpetuate its divisions. A significant development of the times was the growth of the temporal power of the Papacy. At the time when the Lombards were threatening Rome and the Byzantine government was showing itself increasingly incapable of defending its Italian dominions, a man of outstanding genius became pope (590). Gregory the Great was a scholar and a statesman,

Fig. 5. Italy about A.D. 600

who made his authority respected throughout the Church, and by his missionary zeal brought far-off England within the fold. He was also a Roman noble, nurtured in the tradition of his city's greatness, and determined to protect imperial Italy from the barbarians. He persuaded a Lombard duke to abandon the siege of Rome, and was instrumental in bringing about a general peace by which the exarch at Ravenna came to terms with the Lombards.

THE FRANKS IN ITALY

In the eighth century the dispute over the veneration of images known as the iconoclastic controversy widened beyond repair the breach between Rome and Constantinople. The Emperor Leo the Isaurian had already roused the hostility of the great land-owners by his new system of taxation when, in 726, he launched a decree forbidding the veneration of images of Christ and the saints, and ordering their destruction. On this, Italy revolted under the leadership of the Papacy. The immediate gainers by the revolt were the Lombard kings, who sided in turn with the emperor and the rebels until they felt strong enough to put an end to Byzantine power in Italy. In 751 Ravenna fell and the exarchate ceased to be. The popes had resisted the imperial decree against images in defence of their own spiritual sup-remacy. They now realized that this would be more directly threatened by a dominant Lombard than by an absent emperor, and so they sought a new protector from across the Alps. In 754 Pepin, king of the Franks, entered Italy at the invitation of Pope Stephen II, and, having driven the Lombards from Ravenna, he restored the lands of the exarchate, not to the emperor, but to the pope. Twenty years later Pepin's son, Charlemagne, com-pleted his father's work. He defeated and captured the Lombard King Desiderius, confirmed Pepin's grant to the Papacy, and himself assumed the Lombard crown. At about this time the document known as the Donation of Constantine first came to light. It purported to be a grant made by Constantine, on the removal of his capital to the East, to Pope Sylvester, handing over to him 'the city of Rome and all the provinces and cities of Italy' to be governed by him and his successors in perpetuity. Imperial sanction was thus given to papal rule in the former exarchate and also to the authority which the popes had long wielded in Rome and its territories. The nucleus was formed of the States of the Church. It only remained to complete the emancipation of Rome from Byzantine rule. This was achieved when the Empire of the West was revived in the person of the pope's Frankish champion.

2. THE HOLY ROMAN EMPIRE, 800–1015

CHARLEMAGNE

On Christmas Day in the year 800, Charlemagne knelt before the altar in St Peter's to receive the imperial crown from Leo III, and to be hailed as emperor by the Roman people. Few events in history have had more far-reaching effects. Rome was once more the seat of empire. The Frankish war leader was invested with the sovereignty of a Roman emperor. The ruler of the western world looked to Rome and the Papacy for guidance in matters of religion and culture. The Holy Roman Empire thus created lasted for a thousand years. It stood for the unity of Western Christendom under the joint auspices of pope and emperor, the one supreme in the spiritual, the other in the temporal sphere. As for Italy, the foundation of the Holy Roman Empire determined the main lines of her future history. By linking her fate with that of the northern nations it prevented her political development from taking its normal course.

Charlemagne's empire was held together by his own force of character. His arms extended the borders of Christendom, and kept heathen and Saracen at bay. His authority was exercised to promote religion, secure justice, and spread education among the peoples whom he conquered. On his death in 814 he was succeeded by his son, but the machinery of government which he created ceased to function when his controlling hand was removed. In the next generation his dominions fell asunder. By the Partition of Verdun (843) Neustria and the Teutonic lands east of the Rhine went to his younger grandsons, to become the kingdoms of France and Germany. Italy and the imperial title were held by the eldest brother Lothair, who ruled over a middle kingdom stretching from the North Sea, through the Netherlands, Burgundy, and Provence, to Rome.

SARACEN AND HUNGARIAN INVASIONS

The Arab conquest of Sicily marks the climax of Saracen expansion in Europe. It was begun in 827 by an expeditionary force from Tunisia, said to number seventy ships and 10,000 men, which landed on the south coast at Mazzara. By 843 the greater part of the island was overrun and for the next two and a half centuries Sicily was an Arab state. Palermo became the centre of a brilliant Moslem civilization, of which later Christian rulers of Sicily were the heirs.

Sicily also became a base for raids on the Italian mainland, and the task of dealing with the Saracen menace fell in the first instance to Lothair's son Louis II; for twenty-five years there was an emperor in Italy. Although the Frankish army co-operated with the Greek fleet against the Saracens, the Byzantine emperor viewed Louis with suspicion, as a usurper of his own authority. The Lombard Dukes of Benevento, whom Charlemagne himself had failed to subdue, encouraged the invaders for their own ends. Louis's achievements were eclipsed by Pope Leo IV's defence of Rome and the brilliant naval victory over the Saracens at Ostia (849), won by a league of southern republics with the pope at its head. In 875, when he was collecting a new army, Louis II died, and the hope of a united Italy was buried in his grave in Milan.

During the half-century which followed the final break-up of the Carolingian Empire in 888, power fell into the hands of local officers, who came to be regarded as magnates in their own right. Counts and marquesses competed for the crown of Italy, with which the supreme title of Emperor had come to be associated, and neighbouring kings joined in the struggle. The Magyars descended upon Lombardy, and the Saracens continued their raids upon Italy from Sicily, Africa, and their colony at Fraxinet on the Provençal coast. Owing to the preoccupation of the magnates with their own quarrels, the burden of defence against the invaders fell upon the cities and their representatives, the bishops. The cities grew, owing to the influx of refugees from the countryside; walls were built and ditches were dug. After Genoa had been sacked by the Saracens in 934, the bishop helped to organize a fleet which carried out reprisals against the raiders. Such were the humble origins of Genoese maritime power. The Magyars held the Lombard plain at their mercy, but when they attacked Venice they were defeated at sea by the Venetians under their Doge. In southern Italy the Byzantine Empire remained the greatest power, but it was hampered in its struggle with the Saracens by Lombard princes caring only for their own independence, and by the Italian maritime states of Naples, Gaeta, and Amalfi, which traded and allied themselves with the enemy. In Rome, the landowning aristocracy had triumphed over the clerical element in the Curia, and Roman nobles and their ladies controlled the Papacy. Marozia, the daughter of a Roman noble, was the mistress of one pope, the mother of another, and the grandmother of a third. Her son Alberic, as 'prince and senator of Rome', exercised secular authority in city and territory, and forced the Romans to elect his son as pope. When in 955 this young reprobate became Pope John XII the Papacy was little more than a hereditary city despotism.

THE SAXON EMPERORS

From this state of disintegration and degradation Italy was rescued by the revival of the Western Empire under Otto I. The chief motive which inspired Otto I's Italian exploits was the need for establishing his authority in Germany. As ruler of Saxony he was only the strongest of the great dukes, having precedence over the others with the title of king. His principal support, outside his own duchy, came from the Church, and as emperor and protector of the Papacy his control over the Church would be greatly increased. Opportunity to intervene in Italian affairs came through Adelaide, the widow of the late King Lothair II, who appealed for help against her husband's rival and successor, Berengar, marquess of Ivrea. Otto crossed the Brenner pass in 951, defeated Berengar, married Adelaide, and assumed the Italian kingship. His victory over the Magyars at Lechfeld in 955 freed northern Italy from their molestations. So long as Alberic ruled in Rome, Otto's southward path was barred, but in 962

John XII appealed for his aid, and crowned him emperor. When John attempted to shake off the imperial yoke, his misconduct gave ample grounds for proceedings against him. Otto presided over a synod held in Rome which declared John XII deposed, and elected a fresh pope in his stead. Imperial control over the Papacy was further secured by making the Romans swear not to proceed to an election until the emperor had named a candidate. Otto's third Italian expedition had as its object the extension of his authority over the turbulent south. This involved a clash with the Byzantine Empire which ended in the marriage of Otto's namesake and heir to the Greek princess Theophano. Otto II took his Italian responsibilities seriously, and devoted as much of his brief reign as he could spare from Germany to warring against the Saracens. The career of his son, Otto III, shows the effect of the magic of the name of Rome upon a romantic boy brought up under ecclesiastical influences and in the traditions of Byzantine imperialism, imbibed from his mother. He built himself a palace on the Aventine, and dreamed of a world-wide Christian empire having Rome as its centre. His cousin, Gregory V, the first German to ascend the papal throne, shared his ideals. Gregory's successor, Sylvester II, was Gerbert of Aurillac, a Frenchman, and the most learned man of his age, who saw himself as a new Sylvester working with a new Constantine for the triumph of civilization over barbarism. Neither Sylvester II's intellect nor Otto III's energy and resourcefulness sufficed to overcome the opposition which their schemes aroused. When the emperor died in 1002, the Romans had expelled him from his capital, and Germany was on the brink of revolt.

The revival of imperial power by the Ottos brought to Italy increased security, the renewal of commerce, and the expansion of civic life. They created a new political system uniting Germany and Italy under a single ruler, who could claim only a vague supremacy over the rest of Europe. During the coming centuries the king elected by the German magnates became, as of right, king of Italy, and a candidate for coronation as emperor. A German monarch alone possessed a legitimate title to rule over a united Italy.

3. EMPIRE AND PAPACY, 1015–1250

NORMANS IN SOUTHERN ITALY AND SICILY

Among the outstanding developments in Italy during the eleventh century was the establishment of Norman rule in the south. About the year 1015 certain Norman knights, who had visited southern Italy as pilgrims, settled there to seek their fortunes. A century had elapsed since Norse pirates had settled in the Seine valley and there became Normans. They had embraced Christianity with the ardour of converts, and had adopted Frankish institutions, but they were still pirates at heart, eager for adventure, whether by sea or land, and greedy for gain. In southern Italy, where Greeks, Lombards, and Saracens warred with one another without respite, the Normans found a field upon which their mastery of the technique of fighting earned swift reward. At first they played the part of mercenaries, aiding Lombard against Greek and Greek against Saracen. Soon they asked, in payment for their services, not merely gold and horses but land. After the grant of Aversa to a band of Normans by the duke of Naples in 1030, a stream of landless men came from Normandy to conquer and to settle. Among them were the twelve sons of Tancred of Hauteville, who succeeded in asserting their supremacy over their fellow adventurers and in welding the territories wrested from their former employers into a single state. The subjection of southern Italy to Norman rule was the work of Robert Guiscard, the sixth of the Hauteville brothers, 'a man of great counsel, talent and daring'. In his conquest of Calabria he led the life of a robber chief, supporting himself by cattle-lifting and other forms of plunder. So great were the sufferings caused by the Normans that the Papacy was stirred to take arms against them. At the battle of Civitate in 1053, Leo IX was defeated and taken prisoner. The pious Normans knelt to receive their captive's blessing, released him, and continued their aggressions. The advantage which alliance with this powerful body of churchmen might bring to the Papacy was quickly perceived. In 1059 Pope Nicholas II

37

invested Robert with the lands he had conquered as a papal fief, and the cattle-thief could now style himself 'By the grace of God and St Peter, Duke of Apulia and Calabria, and hereafter of Sicily'. This action at once legitimized Norman rule, and formed the basis of the papal claim to suzerainty over south Italy and Sicily, which was to be a useful weapon in the papal armoury in the centuries to come.

The conquest of the island of Sicily from the Saracens was accomplished by Robert's youngest brother Roger. When Robert died in 1085 both the mainland and the island portion of the future kingdom of Sicily were held by the house of Haute-ville. Roger's son and namesake united the territories won by his father and uncle; in 1130, with the consent of an antipope, Roger II was crowned in the cathedral of Palermo as king of Sicily.

The organization of the Sicilian kingdom in the twelfth century gave proof that the Normans possessed a genius for administration at least equal to their skill in fighting. Compared with the population of the kingdom as a whole, the Normans were few in numbers, and they were called upon to rule over Greeks, Saracens, Italians, and Frenchmen, each with their distinctive customs and language. Each separate race was allowed to retain, as far as possible, its own way of life. At the same time, use was made in the central government of every institution, every tradition, of both conquerors and conquered, which would serve to strengthen the power of the Crown. According to the feudal arrangements imported from Nor-mandy, princes, dukes, and counts holding their fiefs by military tenure from the king became typical figures in Sicilian society. Thus Sicily was separated in its political structure from the rest of Italy. Roger II's kingly power, however, was not the limited authority of a feudal monarch but the absolute sovereignty of a Byzantine emperor. His financial system was borrowed from the Arabs; his fleet was officered by Greeks. This adroit mingling of diverse elements made Norman Sicily a model of efficient administration. Its only possible rival in twelfth-century Europe was Norman England. The presence of Thomas Brown, once chaplain and fiscal officer to Roger II, among Henry II's exchequer clerks is but one of many instances of the intercourse between the two kingdoms. In the churches founded by the Norman kings, as for example the great cathedral of Monreale, Roman, Norman, Greek, and Arabic elements are combined in a new harmony of form and colour. The Norman court became the meeting-place of Jewish, Greek, and Arabic scholars, and the channel by which their learning passed to western Europe.

Norman rule in Sicily was challenged by both eastern and western emperors; it was hampered by rebellion at home and the intermittent hostility of the popes. The Norman kings not only met these dangers, but attempted to extend their dominions beyond the borders of Sicily. Shortly before his death Robert Guiscard crossed the Adriatić and took Durazzo, as a preliminary to his designs upon the imperial throne of Constantinople. Roger II went far towards making himself master of the Mediterranean by taking possession of Malta, and establishing a Norman dominion in Libyan Tripoli. In so doing he anticipated the policy and ambitions of modern Italy. Roger's son and grandson succeeded him on the throne and worthily maintained his traditions, but William II, dying in 1189, left no legitimate male heir. The passing of the succession to a woman marked the end of Norman rule which has left a permanent mark upon the Sicilian kingdom.

REFORM OF THE CHURCH

While the Normans were forging southern Italy into shape, a change was coming over the character of the Papacy. The popes of the eleventh century emancipated themselves from the control of the Roman nobility and placed themselves at the head of a reform movement in the Church. The aims of the reformers were to raise the moral and intellectual standards of the clergy, and to emphasize the distinction, which had become largely obliterated, between the ecclesiastical and the lay members of feudal society. They opposed simony, clerical marriage, and the control of the secular powers over ecclesiastical appointments, practices which alike tended to approximate the outlook and way of life of the higher clergy to those of the lay nobility. They strove to organize the Church on the model of the Roman Empire, and to secure that throughout Europe bishops were answerable to the pope, and priests to bishops, all being bound together by one law and one administrative system. The lay rulers at once took up this challenge to their right to determine the personnel and command the obedience of the ecclesiastical estate, which, as a land-owning body, contributed largely to their armed forces, and, through its monopoly of education, provided their chief ministers of state.

While all Europe was involved in the controversy, Italy and Germany became the battlefields on which the struggle between pope and emperor was fought out. Among the emperors of the period were those who tried to do their duty, as protectors of the Papacy, by cleansing it from scandals, and restoring to it the moral leadership of the Church. But thus they raised up rivals to themselves. In 1046 the Emperor Henry III came to Italy and, having secured the deposition or resignation of three unworthy popes, helped to place Leo IX on the throne. Leo was a German and related to a former emperor. Devout, learned, and states-manlike, he became the leader of the reform movement, and the first of a succession of popes whose conception of the nature and scope of their authority brought them into inevitable conflict with the empire. The new papal claims also worsened relations with the Greek Church and this severance of Orthodox from Catholic combined with the Norman conquest to destroy the last vestiges of Greek imperial authority in south Italy.

HILDEBRAND AND HENRY IV

A decree of a council held at the Lateran (1059), placing the business of papal elections in the hands of the cardinal-bishops, formed an important landmark in the progress of the reform movement. It put an end to the usurpations of Roman nobles, and to the practice of imperial nomination, while it emphasized the independence of the Papacy and the spiritual character of its authority. In the same year Hildebrand, the protégé of Leo IX, was made archdeacon of Rome, to become from that time the

moving spirit in the campaign for reform. The aim of Hildebrand's life was to make the righteousness of God prevail upon
earth; the means to that end, as he conceived it, was obedience
to the Church's law and to the pope, upon whom, as the successor
of St Peter, must fall the awful responsibility of judging between
right and wrong. From being the power behind the papal throne,
he was in 1073 himself elected pope, by the unanimous vote of
the cardinals, and amid the acclamations of the Roman people.

As Gregory VII Hildebrand set himself to impose upon the
Emperor Henry IV, first by persuasion and then by force, his own
ideal of righteousness. The struggle which had for some time past
been raging in Milan between the champions and opponents of
reform provided the occasion for open conflict between pope and
emperor. The peculiar customs of the church of St Ambrose, and
the tradition of government attached to the capital of the Lombard
kingdom, made the ruling classes in Milan resentful of outside
interference. They objected to the calling of a synod by papal
legates on their city, and rejected their demands for obedience to
Rome on such matters as simony and clerical marriage. On the
other hand, the more democratic elements in Milan were ardent
reformers, and the ecclesiastical controversy became a civic
feud. In 1072 the anti-reform candidate for the archbishopric,
whom the pope refused to recognize, received investiture with the
ring and staff of his office from the emperor. This started the chain
of events which led to the decree of 1075, forbidding lay investiture, to the excommunication of Henry IV, and to his dramatic
humiliation before Gregory VII. For three days in the winter of
1077 the emperor stood a suppliant for absolution in the courtyard of the castle of Canossa, where Gregory was staying as the
guest of the Countess Matilda of Tuscany. When, after promises
of submission, he was forgiven, the triumph of the Papacy seemed
complete, though Gregory had no way of ensuring that Henry's
apparent acceptance of his claims was genuine.

Canossa was only the first round of the duel. The quarrel broke
out again with greater violence. Gregory excommunicated and
deposed Henry, recognizing Rudolph of Swabia, the choice of
Henry's German enemies, as king. A council of German bishops

decreed Gregory's deposition and elected as anti-pope Arch-bishop Guibert of Ravenna, the leader of the Lombard bishops in their revolt against papal authority. Henry prepared to invade Italy to enforce the council's decrees. In a conflict waged with temporal weapons, Gregory was no match for the emperor. He had a warm supporter in Countess Matilda, who, at about this time, made over her lands to the Church, receiving them back as a fief of the Papacy. But, for the most part, northern Italy was his enemy, and Robert Guiscard, for whose aid he appealed, was engaged on his expedition against the Eastern Empire. Thus in 1084 Henry entered Rome in triumph and was crowned emperor by the anti-pope. Succour came at last from the Normans, but at the price of a three days' sack of Rome, in which the atrocities committed by the champions of the Papacy exceeded those of earlier barbarians. When it was over, Gregory could not be left to the mercy of the angry populace; he was carried off by the Normans to Salerno, where he died in 1085.

SETTLEMENT OF THE INVESTITURE QUESTION

'I have loved righteousness and hated iniquity, therefore I die in exile', were Gregory VII's dying words. Although they marked a personal failure, the years which followed witnessed the triumph of his cause. His successors in the Papacy were men who shared his ideals. Urban II was a monk of Cluny, the centre of the mon-astic revival which played so large a part in the reform movement. To him it fell to rouse Europe to a Holy War against Islam by preaching the First Crusade. The marshalling of a great army under the crusading banner was an impressive demonstration of the reality of papal leadership. By the Concordat of Worms, made between Calixtus II and the Emperor Henry V in 1122, a com-promise was reached on the investiture question which constituted a real gain for the Papacy. While a large measure of control over episcopal elections, especially in Germany, remained with the emperor, he surrendered for ever the right of investiture with ring and staff. This recognition that bishops were something more than imperial vassals vindicated the independence of the Church. It gave expression to the belief that there were aspects of human life which belonged to the realm of the spirit and could not be made subject to temporal rule. The effect of the investiture controversy upon Italy was to weaken the authority of the emperor and to strengthen all those forces making for separatism. Vassals of the empire took occasion to throw off the yoke of their suzerain; the Normans welcomed the opportunity of attacking a power which threatened their own. Some of the cities, increasing in size and wealth, found in the ecclesiastical quarrel a means to secure new powers of self-government. The eleventh and twelfth centuries saw the rise of the Italian commune.

DEVELOPMENT OF CITY-STATES

The rebirth of Mediterranean commerce, after the interruptions caused by the Saracens, and the beginnings of trade and industry in a society hitherto almost entirely agricultural, led to the development of town life throughout western Europe. Italy, owing to her geographical advantages, and to the peculiarities of her political system, was in the van of the urban movement, and the growth of her cities was at once more rapid and more complete than that of other nations. She was the half-way house between East and West, the channel through which the amenities of the older civilizations flowed to the western peoples who were becoming eager to acquire them. She was besides the heiress of ancient Rome. Although the continuous existence of the institutions of the Roman municipal system cannot be proved, the traditions of civic life survived. Italian city-dwellers, by the close of the eleventh century, had enough of classical learning and legal training to conceive of themselves as the Roman people in miniature, to call their chosen officers consuls, and to claim rights of self-government as their lawful heritage. In many cities the bishop rather than a count had become the representative of imperial authority. The investiture controversy provided opportunities for the citizens to win autonomy at the expense of the bishops. Sometimes the emperor himself purchased the support of a city by granting it a charter. Sometimes the bishop, thinking more of his own position than of imperial interests, entered into an agreement with the citizens which recognized their rights to co-operate with him in the government. Sometimes a city rose in revolt against a bishop whose attitude on the questions of ecclesiastical reform did not meet with popular support. Thus throughout northern and central Italy there came into being city-states, which had not only made good their rights to rule within their own city walls, but which forced the nobles of the surrounding countryside to acknowledge their supremacy.

Foremost among the Italian cities were the maritime republics of Venice, Genoa, and Pisa. All three had formed fleets, originally for their own protection, and had found them a passport to the favour of popes and emperors. The origins of Venice lay in the flight of the people of the mainland to the lagoons before barbarian raids. As early as the sixth century Belisarius was glad to avail himself of the boats and harbours of these struggling groups of refugees during his siege of Ravenna. In 697 the separate communities were brought together under their first Doge, and Venice emerged as a republic, which Charlemagne recognized as a part of the Eastern Empire. An expedition against Dalmatian pirates in 1100 established Venetian supremacy over the Adriatic. Meanwhile Pisa and Genoa waged war against the Saracens in the western Mediterranean. In 1016 a joint Pisan and Genoese expedition drove the Saracens from Sardinia, which became henceforth the scene of bitter commercial and political rivalry between the two cities. Urban II wrote personally to Genoa, urging her participation in the First Crusade, and for all three maritime republics the Crusades marked the opening of improved opportunities for commerce and colonization in the Levant. Inland cities owed their prosperity to their situation. Milan and Verona lay at the foot of Alpine passes; Piacenza guarded a crossing of the river Po; Bologna was the most important of a line of cities which sprang up along the Via Emilia; Florence had a route to the sea on the river Arno and controlled two roads to Rome. Many others, and especially those of the fertile Lombard plain, were the market towns of busy agricultural districts. Varied in their history and character, they were alike in their fierce local patriotism, which showed itself in their struggle for autonomy and in their ceaseless rivalry with their neighbours.

BARBAROSSA AND THE CITIES

In 1154 the recently elected emperor, Frederick I of Hohenstaufen, crossed the Alps for the first time. Barbarossa, as the Italians called the red-haired stranger, was determined to assert the imperial rights and to reduce Italy to order and unity under his rule. Circumstances seemed favourable to his enterprise. All Italy, save Venice and the Sicilian kingdom, acknowledged imperial suzerainty. The pope sought his aid in order to crush the republican movement in Rome, led by Arnold of Brescia. The lesser Lombard communes hailed him as their champion against the aggressions of Milan. The barons of the south urged him to attack the Sicilian kingdom. Only gradually was it realized that Frederick's conception of his rights and duties ran counter to Italian development during the last hundred years. Frederick's refusal, when he was in Rome for his coronation, to lead the pope's palfrey or hold his stirrup challenged the Hildebrandine idea of papal supremacy and marked the beginning of a new duel between Papacy and Empire. At the Diet of Roncaglia (1158) the Roman Civil Law as interpreted by the imperial lawyers appeared as the enemy of civic autonomy. The destruction of Milan (1162), far from crushing the spirit of rebellion, led to the formation of the Lombard League, in which the greater number of the communes sank their differences and united in defence of their liberties. They received active support from Pope Alexander III, William of Sicily, and the Venetians. The building of a new city, named Alessandria after the pope, marked the drawing together of the most vigorous elements in Italian political life in resistance to a common danger. In 1176, at Legnano, Frederick's German knights were defeated by the forces of the League. The emperor determined to admit the papal claims, and a year later he knelt in the church of St Mark at Venice to receive the pope's kiss of peace. Peace with the Lombard cities was finally made at Constance in 1183. The suzerain rights of the emperor were recognized, but these communes (but not those of Tuscany) were left free to manage their own affairs both within and outside their city walls. In 1186 Barbarossa made his sixth and last appearance in Italy for the marriage of his son Henry to the Norman Constance, aunt of the Sicilian ruler and heiress presumptive of the kingdom. Sicily was a prize which would go far to compensate for the humiliation which Frederick had undergone from pope and communes. He probably saw in its possession a means by which his successor could make himself master of Italy. In fact, this increase of imperial power only served to strengthen the opposition to Hohenstaufen domination.

INNOCENT III AND THE STATES OF THE CHURCH

After a great emperor came a great pope. The reign of Innocent III (1198–1216) marked the zenith of papal power in matters both temporal and spiritual. If his fame in English eyes rests chiefly on John's submission to him as the temporal suzerain of his kingdom, if his sanction of the Order of St Francis of Assisi is perhaps his greatest service to the Church, in Italy he may claim to be the real founder of the States of the Church. His accession coincided with the death of the Emperor Henry VI. Henry had succeeded in conquering Sicily, crushing Norman resistance to German rule with relentless cruelty. The widowed Constance now sought papal protection for her infant son, Frederick, and Innocent assumed direct rule over the Sicilian kingdom. He also constituted himself the arbiter between the rival candidates for the empire, Philip of Hohenstaufen and Otto of the Welf house of Brunswick. Otto, in return for papal support, confirmed Innocent in the possession of all territories contained in earlier imperial privileges. He thus proclaimed the undisputed right of the Papacy to lands stretching from Radicofani on the Tuscan border to the Sicilian Kingdom at Ceprano, also to the Duchy of Spoleto, the March of Ancona, the Exarchate of Ravenna, and the Matildine inheritance, embracing territories as far north as Ferrara and the river Po. Henceforth the twofold aim of papal policy was to perpetuate the separation between Sicily and the empire, and to make papal rule a reality throughout the territories recognized as belonging to the Church. The Senate of Rome was brought under papal control and papal rectors replaced German governors in central Italy. When Otto, now secure on his throne, refused to take seriously the pope's claims to temporal dominion, Innocent secured the election of his ward, Frederick, as king of the Romans, and extracted from him promises to respect the States of the Church and not to hold the Sicilian kingdom in union with the empire. Thus, on the death of Innocent III the stage was set for the final round of the duel between the popes and the Hohenstaufen emperors. In the course of a thirty years' struggle Frederick II (1194—1250), the most remarkable figure of his age, was checked by the Papacy and by defiant towns.

FREDERICK II, GUELFS AND GHIBELLINES

Frederick II concerned himself little with Germany. Himself half a Norman, and born and bred in the south, his first aim was to strengthen and develop his Sicilian kingdom, and thence to extend his authority over the rest of Italy. Northern and central Italy were to be divided into five imperial vicariates. The communes which commended themselves to him retained their rights of self-government but became members of a federation of which the emperor was the head. Among his supporters were local magnates such as Oberto Pelavicini and Ezzelino da Romano, who with the aid of his German troops made themselves masters of a group of cities. The popes rallied round themselves every element of opposition to the imperial power. As Frederick's rival for the empire had been the Welf Otto, the popes and their allies in Italy began to call themselves Guelfs. The imperialists, italianizing the Hohenstaufen battle-cry 'Hie Weibling', became known as Ghibellines. Into this great struggle were caught up all the rivalries, whether between cities or factions, which divided Italy, and the names Guelf and Ghibelline were used to distinguish opposing factions long after their original significance had been lost.

The course of the trial of strength between Frederick II and three successive popes was briefly as follows: In 1220 Frederick was crowned in Rome by Honorius III (1216–27), thus gaining papal sanction for the union (against his previous promise) in his person of the crowns of Sicily and the empire. He took an oath to go on a crusade and was excommunicated for postponing his departure. Having embarked for Palestine under papal censure, he made a treaty with the Sultan which gave Christian pilgrims access to the Holy Places. Then, in the Church of the Holy Sepulchre, excommunicate and alone, he crowned himself king of Jerusalem. He defeated the revived Lombard League at Cortenuova (1237), and Gregory IX (1227–41) as the champion of the cities excommunicated him afresh. At the Council of Lyons (1245) he was deposed by Innocent IV. From that time he encountered a number of setbacks. He was defeated at Parma. His son Enzo was taken prisoner at Fossalta, to spend the rest of his life in captivity at Bologna. Disaffection showed itself in Sicily. During 1250 the fortunes of war still swayed either way, but Frederick's death in that year marked the decline of imperial power in Italy.

Frederick's strongly centralized state was built on Norman feudalism and on the bureaucracy of his Byzantine and Saracen predecessors. The code of law which he promulgated was inspired by the principles of Roman jurisprudence. Jews, Mohammedans, and Christians enjoyed equal religious liberties within his dominions. His court was the centre of a rich and varied civilization, the home of Arab medical science and philosophy no less than of Italian vernacular poetry. Frederick himself was the friend and correspondent of philosophers; he was at once his own chief counsellor in matters of government, warrior, diplomat, scientist, and poet. The multiplicity of his talents and interests, and his sceptical spirit, excited the admiration and amazement of his contemporaries. They condemned him as a heretic and called him *Stupor Mundi*, the Wonder of the World.

CHAPTER III

THE LATER MIDDLE AGES AND EARLY RENAISSANCE, 1250–1402

1. THE AGE OF DANTE, 1250–1313

END OF IMPERIAL POWER

The problem before the Papacy during the latter half of the thirteenth century was how to reap the fruits of its victory over the Empire. The first question calling for solution was the disposal of the Sicilian kingdom in such a way as to secure for the popes a temporal lieutenant who would assist in the establishment and maintenance of their supremacy throughout Italy. On the death of Frederick II, Innocent IV proceeded to hawk the crown of Sicily round the courts of Europe, promising investiture with the kingdom to anyone prepared to come and conquer it. A prince on whose behalf the offer was accepted who did not come was Edmund, younger son of Henry III of England. Frederick II had left Sicily to his only surviving legitimate son, Conrad, but Conrad's centre of interest was Germany, and he survived his father only by four years. The heir of Frederick's Italian policy, and also of his talents and interests, was his illegitimate son Manfred. This brilliant prince, first as regent and then as king of Sicily, dominates Italian history during the years 1250–66. At one stage Innocent IV himself was prepared to recognize his possession of Sicily. Yet he was a Hohenstaufen, and an alliance between the Papacy and the son of Frederick II was too unnatural to last.

Papal opposition grew until it became the immediate cause of Manfred's fall. Besides this, the nature of the supremacy which he was able to establish in Italy had in it weaknesses which in the end proved fatal. Except in Sicily his ascendency was merely that of a party leader. Both in Lombardy and Tuscany his period of power ensured the triumph of the Ghibellines and the downfall of the Guelfs. He was made senator of Rome as the champion of Roman republicanism against papal autocracy. Siena with his aid won her solitary victory over Florence at the battle of Montaperto (1260). The cities which placed themselves under his protection did so with the object, frankly expressed by a leading citizen of Siena, 'to gain advantage' for themselves. In 1261 a Frenchman became pope as Urban IV, and he determined to secure for the Papacy a French champion. The objections hitherto raised by St Louis of France to the acceptance by his brother of the Sicilian crown were overcome, and Charles, count of Anjou and Provence, came to Italy to win his kingdom. In 1264 he became senator of Rome, at the invitation of the Guelf faction, and in 1266 he defeated and killed Manfred at the battle of Benevento. Two years later the house of Hohenstaufen made its last forlorn attempt to regain possession of its Sicilian dominion. Conradin, the sixteen-year-old son of Conrad, led an army across the Alps, but it went down before Charles of Anjou's superior generalship at Tagliacozzo (1268). After a mock trial, Conradin was beheaded in Naples; Charles was undisputed king of Sicily, and the Guelf cause was triumphant throughout Italy.

INTERVENTION OF THE FRENCH

The coming of Charles of Anjou marked a turning point in Italian history. The French became the predominant foreign power in Italy. The death of Conradin brought about the extinction of the Hohenstaufen dynasty. In 1273 the interregnum in the empire which had followed the death of Frederick II ended with the election of Rudolf of Habsburg. Rudolf's life-work was the re-establishment of monarchical power in Germany, and in this he gained invaluable support from the Papacy by a policy of non-intervention in Italy. In return for papal recognition as king of the Romans, he recognized the papal rights over the States of the Church (to which he added Romagna) and Charles of Anjou's possession of Sicily. Imperial rights over northern Italy remained as before, but Rudolf made no attempt to press them, and he did not even come to Italy to be crowned. Henceforth, save during one or two transient episodes, the German emperors ceased to be a decisive factor in Italian politics. On the other hand, Charles of Anjou was the first of a succession of

French princes who in the course of the next three centuries crossed the Alps in search of territory and influence. His career in Italy formed the basis of claims which were to make French intervention a constant menace to Italian independence.

Far-reaching as were its results, Charles of Anjou's expedition proved a disappointment both to himself and to the popes. Heavy taxation and the insolence of foreign troops and officials goaded his new subjects to revolt. On Easter Monday, 1282, the mishandling of a Sicilian woman on her way to church by French soldiers in Palermo, raised the cry of 'Death to the French'. The Sicilian Vespers were the prelude to a wholesale massacre of the foreigner throughout the island. The leaders of the revolt were already in alliance with Peter, king of Aragon, the husband of Manfred's daughter Constance, and with the Byzantine ruler, Charles's enemy Michael Palaeologus. Aragonese forces, supported by their excellent fleet, swept all before them, and by September the island portion of the Sicilian kingdom was lost to the Angevin for ever. The kingdom created by the Normans was now divided between Angevin and Aragonese monarchs, each contesting the claim of the other, and each aspiring to unite the whole dominion under their rule. In the focusing of Spanish interests and ambitions on Sicily from 1282 onwards may be seen the prelude to Spanish domination in Italy.

EMERGENCE OF THE MIDDLE CLASSES

Manfred's fall meant little more than a change of the party in power. The Guelfs returned to their respective cities, and the Ghibellines took their places in exile. Faction continued with unabated violence, and the support which the Guelfs gave to the head of their party was determined less by devotion to the papal cause than by their own local interests. Thus the popes were forced to depend more and more on the foreigner whom they had brought into Italy; they were in danger of allowing Charles of Anjou to become their master, rather than their temporal lieutenant. In the cities a new middle class was rising into prominence which found its trade hampered by warfare, and its civic life disturbed by street-fighting. The people passed laws to curb the nobles, whether Guelf or Ghibelline, and strove to be rid of faction in order that each city-state might pursue its own path in security and peace. The unrest of the age showed itself in matters of religion, no less than in politics. There was widespread criticism of the wealth and worldliness of the Church, and demands for its return to the simplicity of the Gospel standard. There was much questioning of fundamental articles of the Christian faith. A cardinal of the Church, Ottaviano Ubaldini, was credited with the saying: 'If I have a soul, I have lost it for the Ghibellines.' The pontificate of Boniface VIII (1294–1303) showed the height of power to which a great pope could attain, yet his career ended in a tragedy, and with him fell the medieval Papacy.

BONIFACE VIII AND THE TEMPORAL POWER

'It is necessary for salvation that every human being should be subject to the Roman Pontiff.' These words from the bull *Unam Sanctam*, with which Boniface VIII challenged the autonomy of the realm of France, indicate the nature of his claims as the spiritual head of Christendom. He, like Gregory VII, insisted that the pope was the sole interpreter and judge of the moral law, but whereas Hildebrand was concerned only with the maintenance of his spiritual supremacy, Boniface used the authority which he claimed as pope to establish a temporal dominion in central Italy. The treatment of his political opponents as sinners goes far to explain the bitterness aroused in the minds of his enemies. Italian opposition to Boniface emanated from four principal quarters. Nearest home were the members of the great Ghibelline house of Colonna, who, like their rivals the Orsini, held estates and fortresses in the Campagna, and competed with them for the control of the city of Rome and of the College of Cardinals. Boniface himself was a Roman noble, of the house of Gaetani. Assured at least of the acquiescence of the Orsini, he set himself to destroy the power of the Colonna, and to enrich his own relatives at their expense. The devastation of their fortress of Palestrina made every Colonna his implacable foe.

At the beginning of his reign Boniface had cause to hope that he had achieved a final solution of the Sicilian problem. James, the second son of Peter of Aragon, had succeeded him in Sicily, but when the death of his elder brother gave him the throne of Aragon, Sicily was no longer his first interest. In 1295 the pope brought about a settlement by which James yielded the island of Sicily to Charles II of Anjou, in return for the renunciation of French claims over Aragon, and a promise of papal investiture with Sardinia and Corsica if he succeeded in expelling from them the Pisans and Genoese. The treaty was rendered ineffective by the rebellion of the Sicilians under Peter of Aragon's third son Frederick, and this prince and his subjects were added to the list of Boniface's enemies.

FLORENCE

Thirdly there were the Florentines. Since the expulsion of the Ghibellines which followed the battle of Benevento, Florence had been a purely Guelf city, and from 1282 her chief magistracy was drawn exclusively from members of the trade-guilds. Yet this did not put an end to civic strife. The magnates, whether land-owning nobility or members of the greater guilds, would not submit their interests or their quarrels to the direction of the commune, and they continued to wreck the peace of Florence by their crimes of violence. A split in the Guelf party provided a new source of disturbance. As usual in Italian faction, personal and family rivalries played a large part in the feud which broke out in the last decade of the thirteenth century between Blacks and Whites. The Cerchi, leaders of the party which later became the Whites (the names were derived from those of rival factions at Pistoia), were wealthy bankers, magnates, yet willing to compromise with the rising merchants and craftsmen of the Popolo. Corso Donati, head of the rival interest, stood for an older, feudal, tradition among the nobility: he was unbending in his opposition to the Popolo and its legislation. Florence's internal disunity made it possible for Boniface VIII to seek a foothold in Tuscany by allying himself with the Blacks and posing as the restorer of peace. When a member of the Florentine banking house of Spini and his associates in Rome were condemned by their government as conspirators against the State, Boniface demanded a reversal of the sentence. The city magistrates replied that the pope had no right to interfere with 'the processes and sentences of the Florentine commune'. Thus spake the free spirit of the Italian city-state, determined to be master in its own house, and to resist the demands of the pope, that it should be 'obedient to his will'.

FALL OF BONIFACE VIII

To these three groups of political enemies there was added the religious opposition of the Fraticelli or Spiritual Franciscans, who were urging their own rule of poverty as a standard of life for the Church as a whole. Boniface VIII's predecessor in St Peter's chair had been Celestine V, a saintly hermit, whose lack of knowledge of the world had reduced the administration of the Church to chaos. He had, however, shown favour to the Fraticelli, and when he resigned the Papacy after a reign of five months they held Boniface to be directly responsible for his resignation and for his subsequent death. By antagonizing one of the most vigorous religious movements of the day, Boniface had placed a powerful weapon in the hands of his enemies. The accusations of heresy and immorality made against him originated in the Fraticelli. 'O Pope Boniface,' sang the Franciscan poet, Jacopone da Todi, 'the world is not a horse that you can bridle and ride at your will.'

In the face of his many enemies, Boniface sought military aid from France. Charles of Valois, the brother of King Philip IV, came to Italy at the pope's invitation. As 'pacificator' in Tuscany he made possible the exile of the Whites and the establishment of a Black regime in Florence. Then, with forces augmented by contingents from Tuscany, he marched into Sicily in order to crush the rebel Frederick. His enterprise ended in failure, and by the Treaty of Caltabellotta (1302) Boniface VIII had to recognize Frederick's possession of the island of Sicily with the title of 'King of Trinacria', that of 'King of Sicily' being retained by the Angevin rulers on the mainland. Charles of Valois's intervention taught Philip IV that he had the pope at his mercy, and his reply to an attack made by Boniface on the royal authority in France was to demand the summons of a general council which should bring the pope to account for the crimes of which he was accused. A French official, Nogaret, was sent to Italy to secure Boniface's presence at the Council. Here he joined hands with Sciarra Colonna, and other enemies of the pope, and together they took Boniface prisoner in his summer residence at Anagni. Boniface was released after three days, owing to popular pressure, but he returned to Rome only to die (October, 1303). In 1305 a Gascon was chosen pope; Clement V took up his residence at Avignon, and more than seventy years elapsed before Rome became again the seat of the Papacy.

DANTE

Among the members of the White party exiled from Florence in 1302 was Dante Alighieri. The most famous citizen of Florence had acquired no great name for himself hitherto. As a member of one of the greater guilds he had taken his share in public life, serving on various councils, and holding office for two months as one of the chief magistrates or Priors. Yet the same could be said of any other Florentine citizen of the dominant class. If the late thirteenth and early fourteenth centuries in Italy is called the Age of Dante, it is not because of Dante's achievements as a statesman, but because the *Divina Commedia*, the work of his exile, is an indispensable guide to the history of the times. Here Dante takes upon himself to pronounce judgment on his age, on its leading figures and on its manners and ideals. Our view of Manfred, Boniface VIII, the Emperor Henry VII, and of many lesser men, is largely affected by the place which he assigns to them in Hell, Purgatory, or Paradise. The bitter hatred shown in the *Commedia* for Boniface VIII is due in part to his personal responsibility for Dante's exile. A deeper cause is Dante's veneration for the Papacy as the supreme spiritual power, and his conviction that it was degraded and turned from its true purpose by its assumption of temporal prerogatives. The Papacy under Boniface had usurped the function of the empire. 'Rome . . . used to have two suns, which lighted the roads of the world and of God. Now one has extinguished the other, the sword is joined with the pastoral staff, and the two together must perforce go ill' (*Purg.* XVI, 106–111). Because it was by nature unfitted for the exercise of temporal authority it had fallen victim to the alien power of France; at Anagni 'Christ was made captive in the person of his Vicar' (*Purg.* XX, 87). Yet Dante believed that Italy's imperative need was for some form of political unity. As he wandered from city to city, a homeless exile, he saw everywhere life, energy, genius, political, literary, and artistic. Everywhere, this immense capacity for good was thwarted by senseless civil war. Every city had its band of exiles plotting with external enemies to overthrow the government. Those within the city lived in constant fear of attack, those without lived in poverty or on the charity of strangers. Dante's hope for Italy was for a reign of peace which would allow her creative power to develop. It was his conviction that this could only be brought about by a revival of the Roman Empire. An emperor, representative of the sovereign people of Rome, and able to put into effect the Roman law, was the sole legitimate temporal ruler of Italy. The fact that the emperor at this stage of history was chosen, not by the Roman people, but by seven German Electors, was brushed aside in the relentless logic of Dante's political philosophy as set forth in his treatise *De Monarchia*.

HENRY VII IN ITALY

When in 1308 Henry, count of Luxemburg, was elected king of the Romans, an opportunity arose for testing the value of Dante's scheme for the salvation of Italy. Henry had few dominions of his own, and as lord of a French-speaking province of the Empire he was bound by no close national ties. He made it the purpose of his life to revive imperial power in Italy, and to establish a reign of law which would know neither Guelf nor Ghibelline. Circumstances seemed at first to favour his enterprise. Clement V saw in it an opportunity for detaching himself from French leading strings; he confirmed Henry's election and agreed to send cardinals to crown him as emperor in Rome. When Henry crossed the Alps in the autumn of 1310, Italian nobles of both factions flocked to meet him. A letter which Dante addressed to the rulers and people of Italy at this time reflects the hope of better days which the coming of the *Rex Pacificus* aroused among all classes. Henry's success was expected to bring to Italy not only peace but power. She would become once more the seat of Empire, and Italians, as members of the imperial household, would rule the world. Less than three years later these high hopes were buried in Henry VII's grave at Pisa.

The causes of Henry VII's failure do not differ in essentials from those which led to Boniface VIII's downfall. Both owed something of their misfortunes to their own personality. Henry was not a fighter as was Boniface, nor had he a biting tongue to goad his enemies into fury. He was rather an obstinate idealist who believed rashly in the good intentions of his opponents, and when he found that he had been deceived, took over-severe measures against those who had betrayed his confidence. His plan of obliging the cities of Lombardy to restore their exiles, of whatever faction, was conceived in a spirit of justice, but it caused general unrest. When rebellion followed it was ruthlessly suppressed, and the punishment meted out to cities which submitted stiffened the resistance of others. Thus, most of the summer of 1311 was wasted over the siege of Brescia, and it was not until 1312 that Henry reached Rome for his coronation. He persuaded himself that it was possible to arrive at a good understanding with Robert of Anjou, king of Sicily, although it was quite obvious that Robert had everything to lose from a revival of imperial power in Italy. His error was brought home to him when he found that the Vatican quarter in Rome was in possession of hostile Angevin forces, and that the imperial coronation must take place, not in St Peter's, but in the Church of St John Lateran. Among Henry's first acts after his coronation were the promulgation of a sentence against Robert, as a rebel vassal, and a treaty with his rival, Frederick of Aragon. His quarrel with Anjou cost Henry the support of the Papacy, for Robert was the representative of France in Italy, and Clement V was not a free agent where the French king was concerned. Threatened by the fate of Boniface at Anagni if he continued to favour the imperial cause, Clement extended his protection to its opponents. Thus, the power of France, established in Italy by papal policy, contributed to Henry VII's failure. A still more formidable obstacle in his path was the tradition of liberty in the city-states, and their refusal to tolerate interference from any external authority. In a letter to the Florentines, reproaching them for their opposition to Henry VII, Dante accuses them of seeking 'to establish new kingdoms, making the civic life of Florence one, and that of Rome another'. Such indeed was the ideal which inspired the Italian communes, and which made Florence the centre of resistance to the imperial plans. She kept alive the spirit of revolt in Lombardy by sending letters and money to the cities which held out against Henry's armies. She infused energy and courage into Robert of Anjou's somewhat half-hearted opposition. She strengthened her own fortifications to resist imperial attack, and Henry was still in Tuscany, having been forced to raise the siege of Florence, when he died of fever in August 1313. 'He who came to reform Italy before she was ready for it' (*Par.* xxx, 137–8) is Dante's description of Henry VII. It is a just sentence on the events of the age. Neither the head of a world-wide Church nor a German monarch was best suited to bring about Italian unity, yet their disabilities as national leaders were not the chief cause of their failure. The Italians of the early fourteenth century had no desire to be united.

2. DESPOTS AND REPUBLICS OF THE FOURTEENTH CENTURY

After the dramatic events and outstanding figures of the preceding period the history of Italy from 1313 to the great days of the Renaissance is apt to appear confused and uninteresting. Its importance lies in the development, both constitutional and territorial, of the separate city-states. There is a general tendency towards the rise of despotism, while the larger cities draw the smaller into their orbit and mark out for themselves spheres of influence. At the same time one power after another strives to establish a hegemony over the rest. As each in turn fails of its purpose, there emerge five principal states—Naples, the Papal States, Venice, Florence, and Milan—varying greatly in character but more or less equal in importance, which, during the fifteenth century, control between them the national destinies (Fig. 6).

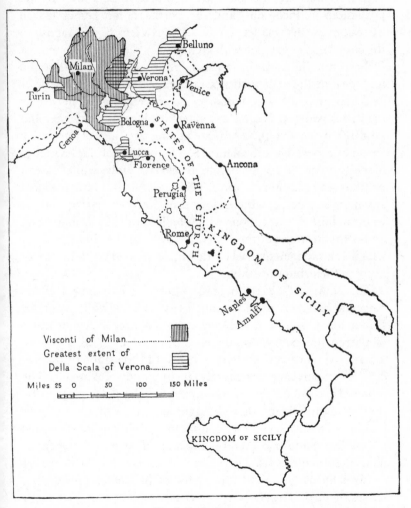

Fig. 6. Italy about 1340

THE KINGDOM OF NAPLES

In 1313 the central figure in Italian politics was Robert of Anjou, who four years earlier had succeeded his father as count of Anjou and Provence, and king of (mainland) Sicily. As count of Provence, with the popes resident in his dominions at Avignon, he was the connecting link between the Papacy and Italy. He had possessions in Piedmont, and the north Italian Guelfs looked upon him as their leader. He was Papal Vicar in Romagna; in the course of the struggle with Henry VII, Clement V appointed Robert Imperial Vicar in Tuscany, while the Florentines granted him the lordship of their city for five years. As his title 'Robert the Wise' suggests, he was a man of considerable gifts. Boccaccio found his court at Naples a congenial place of residence, and Petrarch writes of him as 'unique among the kings of our day, a friend of knowledge and virtue'. The University of Naples, under his rule, attracted students from all parts of Italy, while Tuscan painters and sculptors worked in his capital. Robert's personal advantages, together with the long tradition of monarchy and the well-established institutions which he had inherited, made him by far the strongest of the Italian powers. In the Guelf reaction which followed Henry VII's death, it seemed as if he might become the arbiter of Italy.

The course of his reign made plain the weaknesses of the Angevin kingdom of mainland Sicily as a rallying point for Italian unity. Southern Italy was a poor country with wide tracts of barren soil and a population weakened by class divisions. There was no organized middle class, and the trade of the few cities of importance was largely in the hands of Tuscans. The monarchy retained the essentially feudal character given it by the Normans. During their struggle to win and maintain their dominion, the Angevins had bought the nobility by lavish grants of privileges, and had thereby increased their own dependence upon their feudatories. There was a sharp contrast between the civilized life of the capital and the rest of the kingdom, where the nobles reigned like petty sovereigns over their estates, hampered only by the turbulence of a backward and poverty-stricken peasantry. Apart from the difficulties which he had to encounter at home, Robert lived under constant menace of attack from insular Sicily. His reluctance to pursue a forward policy in northern and central Italy can be explained by his fear that any failure there would provide an occasion for Frederick of Aragon (p. 54) to attack his rear. After an abortive Italian expedition made by the Bavarian Emperor Louis (1327–9), the Guelfs had less need of Robert, and his dream of uniting Italy faded.

When Robert died in 1343, he was succeeded by his grand-daughter Joanna I, and the Angevin kingdom entered upon a period of decline. Joanna's four husbands involved her in many quarrels but gave her no heirs. Before her death her kingdom was seized by her cousin, Charles of Durazzo, and she died a prisoner in his hands. As Charles III he reigned for four years (1382–6), to be succeeded on the throne of Naples (as the mainland portion of the Sicilian kingdom was coming to be called) in turn by his son and daughter. Theirs was a purely Italian dominion, as Provence fell to a Frenchman, Louis, duke of Anjou. Ladislas of Naples was a man of adventurous spirit, and during his reign (1386–1414) the union of Italy under an Angevin supremacy became again a possibility. He took advantage of the papal schism to make him-self master of the territory round Rome and the fortress of St Angelo within the city, conquests which were regarded as stepping-stones to the fulfilment of wider ambitions. His death, wrote a contemporary Florentine, 'brought release from fear and suspicion to Florence, and all other free cities of Italy'. The acces-sion of Joanna II, the last Angevin ruler of Naples, reopened the succession question. The rival candidates were Louis III of Anjou and Alfonso, king of Aragon and Sicily, who were in turn adopted by Joanna as her heirs. During her reign (1414–35) Naples was the scene of almost incessant warfare. The adminis-tration suffered at the hands of the queen's favourites, and the *condottiere* captains who came thither in search of employment turned to their own advantage the misfortunes of the kingdom. Not until seven years after Joanna's death was Alfonso of Aragon able to secure victory over his rival and enjoy his conquest in peace. During his reign the two portions of the old kingdom of Sicily, the island and the mainland, were united.

THE STATES OF THE CHURCH

During the absence of the popes from Italy (1305–76) the cities belonging to the States of the Church set up despots, who, while paying nominal allegiance to their suzerain, ruled as independent princes. This process had begun before the fourteenth century, the Este holding power at Ferrara alternately with Salinguerra from the early thirteenth century. In 1308 the death of Azzo VIII without legitimate heirs enabled Clement V to bring Ferrara under his direct rule, and for nine years it was governed by Robert of Anjou as Vicar of the Church. Then, in 1317, the citizens rose and recalled the Este family. Excommunication and interdict from Avignon were powerless against a *fait accompli*, and in 1332 John XXII was obliged to recognize three Este brothers as his vicars in Ferrara. From that time the Este lords went from strength to strength, despite the greedy eyes which both the Papacy and Venice cast upon their city. By skilful diplomacy they played off one great power against the other, preserved the independence of Ferrara, and won for it a world-wide reputation as a centre of civilization.

As the seat of a university, dating at latest from the twelfth century, famous throughout Europe for its law school, the city of Bologna had an importance beyond its size, and more than its share of civic pride. Resentful of outside interference, that of its suzerain the pope not excepted, the violence of its factions stood in the way of ordered communal life. In the first half of the fourteenth century it enjoyed an interlude of peace under the lordship of the local house of Pepoli. The pope, as in the case of Ferrara, recognized a rule which he could not prevent by making Taddeo Pepoli his vicar. In the lesser cities of Romagna the movement towards despotism was also visible. The Ordelaffi of Forli, the Manfredi of Faenza, and the Malatesta of Rimini are among the native families who were recognized by their fellow-citizens as lords, and by the popes as their vicars.

When no longer the residence of the popes, Rome itself became only one of the cities in the Papal States, in which Orsini, Colonna, and other powerful families struggled for supremacy, and the Roman people, while claiming the right to rule the world, gave proof of their incapacity to rule themselves. It was the urgent need for some form of settled government in Rome that made possible the career of Rienzi. This fantastic being, half hero, half charlatan, so captured the imagination of the Romans that they proclaimed him Tribune of the People in 1347. The titles which he assumed—Liberator of Rome, Champion of Italy, Friend of the World—indicate the magnitude of his notions. Not content with establishing a reign of peace, order, and prosperity in Rome, he invited the cities of Italy to send representatives to a parliament, and proposed to the despots that he should confirm their titles to lordship. He even called upon England and France to make peace, and summoned the rival emperors, Louis the Bavarian and Charles of Luxemburg, to appear before him as arbiter. As at other times in her history, the association of the Roman Republic with world-wide authority hampered the establishment of stable government in Rome. Pope and emperor were alarmed by Rienzi's pretensions, the more powerful despots ignored him, and the cities which attended his parliament were chiefly intent on safe-guarding their own independence. Florence might style herself 'Rome's most glorious daughter', but she would not yield an iota of her autonomy to her mother. Thus Rienzi's attempt to unite Italy under the aegis of the Roman Republic was doomed to failure, and it was followed by the overthrow of his authority in Rome. Faced by a formidable attack from the nobility, he fled from the city within a year of his rise to power. His career ended in a violent death when, in 1354, he returned to Rome with the title of senator given him by the pope, who hoped to use him for his own ends.

The sequel to Rienzi's adventures was a determined effort on the part of the Avignon popes to revive their power in Italy. Cardinal Egidio Albornoz was appointed Legate, and entrusted with the task of bringing the States of the Church under the direct rule of their suzerain. In the course of his mission (1354–67) he succeeded for a time, despite hesitant papal backing, in estab-

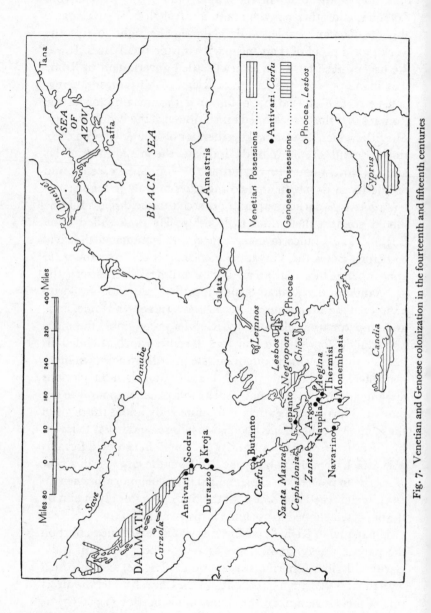

Fig. 7. Venetian and Genoese colonization in the fourteenth and fifteenth centuries

lishing a considerable degree of order and unity. Bologna was recovered from the Visconti, to whom it had been sold by one of the Pepoli. The despots of Romagna and the Patrimony were brought to heel, and the cities gave up their keys in token of submission to the representative of the Papacy. Albornoz crowned his work by the issue of the Egidian Constitutions for the organization and administration of the March of Ancona. Urban V ventured to come to Italy in 1367, but returned to Avignon in 1370. Much of Albornoz's work perished with him, yet his Constitutions remained to form the basis of government in the States of the Church until the nineteenth century.

Gregory XI returned to Rome in January 1377, and the end of the 'Babylonish Captivity' of the Papacy was hailed with general rejoicing. When he died a year later, the Italian Urban VI was elected to succeed him in Rome, but within six months many of the cardinals regretted this choice and elected at Fondi Clement VII, a Genevan who settled with his court at Avignon. Europe was plunged into the scandals of the Great Schism, and until the election of Martin V by the Council of Constance in 1417 there were at first two, and then three rival candidates for the allegiance of Christendom. The existence of rival popes seriously weakened the hold of the Roman pontiff over his Italian dominions. Every lordling of the Romagna had an excuse for repudiating papal suzerainty; every adventurer in search of territory looked on the States of the Church as his prey. As an example of the expedients to which the Papacy resorted to preserve even the semblance of its authority may be cited the grant of the office of Papal Vicar made by Boniface IX to the city magistrates of Bologna. When Martin V returned to Rome in 1421 there was hardly a city that acknowledged his right to rule. With him began a process of recovery which was to place the temporal power of the Papacy upon a firm basis and make of Rome a splendid Renaissance capital.

VENICE AND GENOA (FIGS. 7, 8)

For the cities of northern and central Italy the fourteenth century was a period of great commercial activity. Geographical ad-

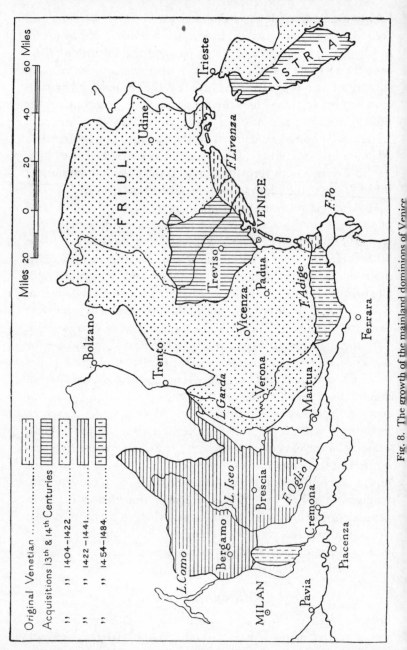

Miles 20   0   20   40   60 Miles

Original Venetian ....
Acquisitions 13th & 14th Centuries
    ,,   ,,   1404–1422...........
    ,,   ,,   1422–1441...........
    ,,   ,,   1454–1484...........

Fig. 8. The growth of the mainland dominions of Venice

66

vantages and the energies of her citizens had combined to make Venice the focal point of medieval commerce. Her carrying trade was developed during the first three Crusades; the Fourth Crusade, diverted in conformity with her interests from an attack on the infidel to the conquest of Constantinople (1204), laid the foundation of her dominion in the Levant. At the height of her power she held Crete, Corfu, and many islands in the Aegean, a strip of coast in the Morea, and the Dalmatian coast from Trieste to Albania. Treaty rights at Constantinople, Trebizond, Alexandria, and other ports made the Black Sea and the eastern Mediterranean free to her vessels. Thus trade with the East was in Venetian hands. Twice a year, from the beginning of the fourteenth century, the 'Flanders galleys' set sail from Venice taking with them spices, sugar, pepper, and other eastern products, by way of Gibraltar and Southampton to Bruges. Thence they returned laden with wood and furs from Scandinavia, English wool, Flemish cloth, and French wines. Other goods from the East were conveyed on pack-horses across the Alps to supply the needs of the cities of Germany. In 1299 Venice made a treaty with the Turk which ensured protection for pilgrimages to Palestine made under her auspices. This gave her a monopoly of the tourist traffic, and the masters of Venetian galleys earned substantial profit from the pilgrims from all parts of Europe who sailed with them to visit the Holy Places of Christendom.

The sole maritime rival to Venice among the Italian cities in the fourteenth century was Genoa. At the naval battle of Meloria (1282) Genoa inflicted a defeat on her neighbour and rival Pisa from which she never recovered. From that time began the decline of Pisan power and prosperity which ended in the conquest of the city by Florence (1406). The control over Corsica and Sardinia which Genoa now hoped to exercise unhindered was, however, disputed by the Aragonese kings of Naples. In Corsica, Genoa maintained her supremacy and the administration of the island passed into the hands of her great trading corporation, the Bank of St George. In Sardinia, Genoese intrigues kept alive the spirit of revolt, postponing its final conquest by the Aragonese until the fifteenth century. A special sphere of Genoese commercial activity was the coast of north Africa, where Genoese merchants established trading colonies, penetrating into the interior in search of gold, and setting up depots as far afield as the Atlantic ports of Sala and Safi.

In the Levant, the rivalry between Venice and Genoa was unceasing. Venice had been the mainstay of the Latin Empire set up in Constantinople during the Fourth Crusade, but when the Greek Empire was restored under the house of Palaeologus in 1261 the advantage passed to Genoa. Whereas the Venetians could expect nothing but hostility from the Greeks, the Genoese, who had aided their restoration, were given a quarter in Constantinople, and such trading rights as the emperor had to bestow. Genoa gained more than one conspicuous naval victory at the expense of Venice during the course of their struggle. The superior seamanship of the Genoese commanders won the battles of Curzola (1298) and Sapienza (1354), and brought the enemy to the gateway of Venice in the War of Chioggia (1379–80). Nevertheless, the close of the fourteenth century saw the decline of Genoa as a naval power and left Venice undisputed mistress of the seas.

The triumph of Venice was due to the unity of her citizens and the efficiency of her government. The city was free from the bane of faction, taxation was light, justice strong and impartial. Every class, from the nobles, who since the closing of the Grand Council in 1297 had the monopoly of political power, to the workers in the state arsenal and the rowers in the state galleys, had a direct interest in the security of the republic and the success of her commercial enterprises. Danger and defeat were incentives to patriotism, moving patrician and plebeian alike to offer their possessions and their lives to the common cause. The fortitude with which the Venetians met and overcame adversity contrasted with the exhibition of weakness and party rivalry which accompanied a crisis in Genoa. Here commercial activity was directed not by state organization but by the particular interest of a few powerful families. The plebeian classes regarded with distrust and jealousy the wealthy patricians whom they excluded from political power, but they proved incapable of managing the affairs of the republic single-handed. The acceptance of French suzerainty in 1396 marked the end of the independent republic and the beginning of Genoa's decline as a commercial and colonial Power.

FLORENCE (FIG. 9)

In the course of the later Middle Ages the merchant families of Florence succeeded in making their city the leading commercial and financial centre of Europe. The wool trade was at its zenith in the early fourteenth century. English wool and dyes from the East, together with the secrets of the Florentine *Arte della Lana* (Wool Guild), produced the heavy red cloth which was marketed throughout the civilized world. Despite Flemish competition, Florentine cloth maintained its supremacy, and the *Arte della Lana* employed some five to six thousand workmen. Writing of the great banking houses of the period, Villani, who was himself a member of one of them, says that they 'supported by their dealings a great part of the commerce and traffic of Christendom'. Their loans were the mainstay of many a hard-pressed government, but the failure of the Bardi and Peruzzi banks in 1342, owing to the rashness of their lending to Edward III of England, involved other firms in their fall, and shook confidence for the time being in Florentine credit.

With increase of wealth went great achievement in the arts. The second half of the thirteenth century was a period of great building activity. Among its products were the first palace of the commune, now known as the Bargello, the Franciscan church of Sta. Croce, the Dominican church of Sta. Maria Novella, and many private palaces. The last decade of the century saw the foundation both of the cathedral and of the Palazzo Vecchio, their architect being Arnolfo di Cambio. The building and decoration of the cathedral were throughout the fourteenth century the special charge of the *Arte della Lana*. Under its auspices Giotto planned the Campanile which bears his name, sculptors from Andrea Pisano to Ghiberti executed bas-reliefs, and finally in 1434 Brunelleschi finished his great dome. Another merchant guild, the *Arte di Calimala*, concerned with the dressing and dyeing of

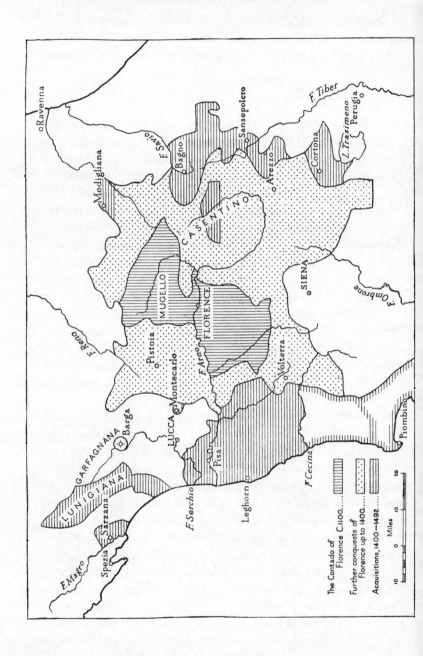

foreign cloth, made itself responsible for care and enrichment of the ancient Baptistry of S. Giovanni. Fourteenth-century artists covered the walls of Sta. Croce, Sta. Maria Novella, and other churches with frescoes. Thus the wealth of the Florentine merchant families was lavished on the adornment of their city. Their patriotism gave an impetus to artistic development which enabled a sixteenth-century historian to claim with truth that 'the three most noble arts of painting, sculpture, and architecture have reached that degree of supreme excellence in which we find them now chiefly by the toil and by the skill of the Florentines'.

Because of the power of the merchant guilds, Florence was able to resist the prevailing political tendency of the day, and preserve her republican government from subjection to a despot. During the revival of Ghibellinism which marked Louis the Bavarian's appearance in Italy (1327–9), the lordship of Florence was conferred for a term of years on the son of Robert of Anjou. In an effort to restore Florentine credit and allay internal unrest, after the financial crisis of 1342, Walter de Brienne, titular duke of Athens, was made lord of the city for life. Both these experiments in despotism proved transitory. The death of their Angevin protector was hailed with as much enthusiasm by the Florentines as that of their chief enemy, the Ghibelline lord of Pisa. Walter de Brienne was hounded from the city after a year of office by the very people who had proclaimed him lord.

Internally, the patricians remained in control, but they met with considerable difficulty in maintaining their authority. Amid competing commercial interests, and the aspirations of the plebeian classes after the political power to which they were entitled constitutionally, the patricians were able to secure their own predominance by means of the Parte Guelfa, a political club to which considerable indirect share in the government was entrusted. The captains of the Parte Guelfa, drawn chiefly from the nobles and the greater merchants, had the right to search out and punish citizens tainted with Ghibellinism, and were also entrusted with the administration of the estates of exiled Ghibillines. This enabled them to manipulate finance and justice in the interests of their friends, and to become the virtual rulers of

Florence. The struggle between oligarchs and democrats reached a climax in the rising of the Ciompi (1378), when the lesser guilds combined with the unenfranchized artisans to wrest political power from the dominant faction. For a time the chief magistrate of the republic was a wool-comber and the democrats were able to impose their will on the commune. But the oligarchs, as the chief employers of labour, held the master card, and in four years' time they were once more supreme in the republic. Henceforth they ruled Florence, not through the Parte Guelfa, whose power was finally overthrown, but under the leadership of one of their own number. Maso d'Albizzi, a member of a powerful family of cloth merchants, directed the affairs of the city, and won for it both territory and prestige. The failure of his son Rinaldo to retain the confidence of his fellow-citizens paved the way for the rise of Cosimo dei Medici to the first place in Florence.

VERONA AND CAN GRANDE

Perhaps the most far-reaching effect of Henry VII's Italian expedition was the recognition which he accorded to Can Grande della Scala of Verona, Matteo Visconti of Milan, and other north Italian despots. Each was made Imperial Vicar of the city which already acknowledged him as lord, and the right to rule conferred on him by the people was given the added prestige of a title emanating from the emperor. The chief characteristic of the Italian city despotism is its popular character. It originated, in almost all cases, through the delegation of authority by the republic to a single man, who was, more often than not, himself a citizen. The benefits expected from his rule were the suppression of faction within the city and its increased wealth and prestige. In early phases of the *signoria* the lord might be elected to a special position receiving *arbitrium*, or full legislative, administrative and judicial powers. At this stage he might also take an oath to protect the interests of the city. The first object of the despot was to win and maintain popular favour, his second was to find means of making himself, as far as possible, independent of popular support. The title of Imperial Vicar conveyed few clearly defined powers, but as a representative of the emperor, its holder became the leader of the Ghibellines and had opportunities for extending his authority over other cities in the district. The position held by Can Grande della Scala at his death in 1329 shows how authority derived from the people, together with imperial recognition, could be adroitly used to build up a despotism.

Can Grande's grandfather was a Veronese citizen, according to tradition a maker of ladders; his father was chosen as lord of Verona for life, and succeeded in handing on his authority to his sons. After Henry VII's death, Can, the only survivor of three brothers, became the champion of the Ghibelline cause in eastern Lombardy, and created for himself a dominion which included Vicenza, Padua, and Treviso. He was the first of the native despots to establish a brilliant court as a means to the increase of his power, Verona under his lordship offered hospitality not only to exiled Ghibellines but to men of talent of every kind. The most famous guest of the court was Dante, who dedicated the *Paradiso* to his host and possibly looked to him to restore peace and unity to Italy in the imperial name. With the death of Can Grande the great days of the della Scala were ended, but their rule in Verona continued until 1387, when the last lord fell before the advancing power of the Visconti.

MILAN AND THE VISCONTI DOMINION (FIG. 10)

The grant of an imperial vicariate to Matteo Visconti marked the final victory of his family over the rival house of della Torre, who for the past sixty years had vied with the Visconti for the lordship of Milan. After Henry VII's death (1313) Matteo gave protection to neighbouring cities, such as Pavia and Cremona, which were threatened by Robert of Naples, receiving in return an acknowledgement of his own supremacy. This was the beginning of an expansion of the Visconti dominion, both east and west of Milan, which continued throughout the century. During the career of Gian Galeazzo Visconti (1379–1402) the Visconti lordship rose head and shoulders above other despotisms of the Lombard plain. Both as conqueror and organizer, Gian set his mark upon the future history of Italy. His first task was to weld the cities, in which the Visconti were recognized as lords, into a centralized monarchical state. When in 1379 he became lord of Pavia, in succession to his father, his uncle Bernabò was lord of Milan; by seizing and murdering Bernabò, Gian transformed a family supremacy into the rule of an individual. His officials collected taxes and executed justice throughout the dominion, vast schemes·

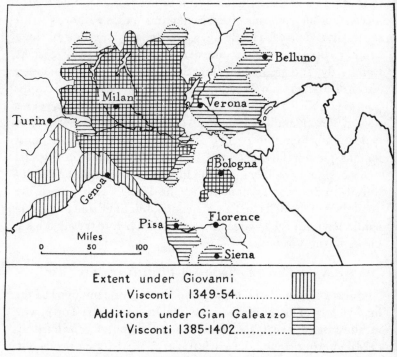

Fig. 10. The Visconti territories, 1349–1402

for material improvement were initiated, and his subjects experienced the unwonted blessings of peace. Persons from all parts of the dominion were drawn to Milan, as to the capital and seat of the government, while the more vigorous life of the city was marked by the building of the cathedral. At the same time Gian founded and built the Certosa, outside Pavia, making this splendid Carthusian monastery a propitiatory offering to Pavian pride, wounded by subordination to a Milanese government. In

1395 the investiture of Gian Galeazzo as duke of Milan by the Emperor Wenzel crowned his work of centralization.

The way had already been prepared for the acceptance of the Visconti by the princely families of Europe as one of themselves through a series of brilliant marriage alliances. Gian's first wife was Isabella of France, his father having, as Froissart states, 'bought the daughter of King John for 600,000 francs'. His sister married Lionel, duke of Clarence and his nieces, the daughters of Bernabò, married into the ruling houses of Austria and Bavaria. Finally his daughter Valentina became the bride of Louis, duke of Orleans, it being stipulated in the marriage contract that she should inherit her father's dominions in default of male heirs. This famous clause is the origin of the French claims to Milan which brought the armies of Louis XII across the Alps a century later.

From his duchy of Milan, Gian's conquering armies pressed forward until they seemed about to bring all Italy within his grasp. In the north his power extended from the frontiers of Piedmont to Padua and the March of Treviso. South of the river Po he controlled the Via Emilia from Piacenza to Bologna and established a protectorate over Romagna. His possession of Lucca, Pisa, and Piombino cut off Florence from the sea, while his occupation of Siena and Perugia blocked the two main roads to Rome. Venice kept, as far as possible, aloof from the struggle. The smaller states, trembling for their safety, hastened to make terms with Visconti. Florence alone offered stubborn resistance to his advance. In August 1402, when all hope seemed lost, Gian Galeazzo died of fever, and Florence was saved as by a miracle. Visconti's methods were those of an able and ruthless tyrant, who by a cunning mixture of force and fraud made himself the arbiter of Italy. In order to achieve his purpose he strained his resources to breaking-point, leaving behind him an exhausted dominion which broke in pieces when his strong hand was removed. If he had succeeded in establishing an enduring supremacy and extinguishing the *libertas* which Florence's propagandists declared her to be upholding, Italy in the fifteenth century would probably have been better governed and more peaceful, and possibly more prosperous.

CHAPTER IV

THE AGE OF THE RENAISSANCE,
1402–1515

WITH the death of Gian Galeazzo Visconti the union of Italy under one ruler passed out of the realm of practical politics for many years to come. The history of Italy during the age of the Renaissance is that of her five chief states. Up to 1454 each was engaged in enlarging its borders or consolidating its power (Fig. 11). There were many petty wars which created a golden age for a peculiar product of Italian civilization—the *condottiere*, or soldier of fortune. After 1454 there followed a period of comparative peace, in which the chief states strove to further their individual interests, without having recourse to war, by an elaborate system of alliances. These were years of immense artistic and intellectual activity, when the Italian states both great and small became centres of a rich and varied culture. With Charles VIII's descent upon Italy in 1494 began the period of foreign invasions, but between 1494 and 1527 the fruits of the earlier period of peace came to maturity in the midst of political turmoil. The Renaissance was at its height, and its light was reflected throughout Europe.

The history of the duchy of Milan during the miserable reign of Giovanni Maria Visconti (1402–12) was one of territorial loss and internal anarchy. On his death his younger brother, Filippo Maria, set himself to reconstruct the dominion which had once been his father's. He found the chief cities of the duchy in the hands of local despots or of soldiers of fortune. Beginning with Pavia and Milan he brought them one by one under his control, until his dominions stretched from the river Sesia on the west to the river Mincio on the east. With the ejection of the Swiss from the Val d'Ossola and the Val Levantina, the keys of the Simplon and St Gotthard passes were again in Milanese hands. The recovery of Parma and Piacenza brought Visconti power south of the river Po, while the conquest of Genoa was the crowning triumph of a decade of achievement. Filippo Maria Visconti was no soldier, but he was an excellent financier. The resources at his disposal enabled him to buy the services of the chief military

Marquisate of Saluzzo................1
Montferrat................................2
Marquisate of Mantua 3
Ferrara 4
Modena 5
Republic of Lucca 6
Venetian Territory ....
Small Independent States

Fig. 11. Italy in 1454

leaders of the day, and his diplomatic skill was employed to make the most of their victories. Under his rule the whole duchy, and in particular the city of Milan, increased in wealth, population, and industry.

The rapid recovery of Visconti power aroused the apprehensions of the two neighbouring republics. Florence, who had been mistress of Pisa since 1406, found her newly acquired maritime interests threatened by the Visconti regime in Genoa. Venice had embarked upon a policy of mainland conquest which had already brought her western frontiers to the river Mincio, and was determined that Milan should not recover undisputed control of the Lombard plain. In 1423 Florence declared war on Milan, and two years later Venice entered into an offensive alliance with her sister republic. From that time until the Treaty of Lodi in 1454 fighting was almost incessant.

THE 'CONDOTTIERI'

Until the end of the fourteenth century the professional soldiers engaged in Italian warfare were for the most part foreigners. Sir John Hawkwood, who with his White Company of Englishmen came to Italy after the Peace of Brétigny (1360) and fought there for over thirty years, is typical of the crowd of adventurers—Spanish, German, French, and English—who sought to make their fortunes at Italy's expense. In the fifteenth century the profession of arms had become italianized. Braccio and Sforza both received their military training under Alberico da Barbiano, the founder of the first purely Italian mercenary company. As leaders of the two principal Italian schools of soldiery they attracted to their ranks men of all classes and from all parts of Italy. The *condottiere* looked on war as a fine art, and he brought to his profession both technical skill and enthusiasm. From the standpoint of the ruler, however, the system was far from satisfactory. The interests of employer and employed were divergent. The *condottiere* sought wealth, fame, and a territory of his own. He was bound by no patriotic ties to the cause for which he fought, and changed his employer as his own interests demanded. Rulers could not afford to leave important captains to be bought up by their enemies, and were thus obliged to multiply their forces beyond their needs or their ability to pay for them. In the long struggle between Milan and her enemies, the characteristics of *condottiere* warfare were fully displayed. The conflict produced stirring episodes in which feats of much endurance, skill, and daring were performed. It saw the tragedy of Carmagnola, who, having transferred his services from Milan to Venice, was convicted of treachery, and decapitated by the Venetians in their place of public execution.

The outcome of over thirty years of fighting was that Venice extended her western frontiers to include Brescia, Bergamo, and other places between the river Mincio and the river Adda, and that Francesco Sforza rose from the position of a landless adventurer to become duke of Milan.

MILAN AND THE SFORZA

The first Sforza was a native of an obscure townlet in Romagna, who won his reputation as a soldier in the Neapolitan succession wars. On his death in 1424 his son Francesco succeeded to the command of his forces and transferred himself to the fresh scene of warfare now staged in north Italy. He fought first for Milan and then for Venice, until Filippo Maria Visconti sought to attach him permanently to his side by marrying him to his illegitimate daughter Bianca. On the death of Visconti in 1447 Milan declared itself a republic, and Francesco Sforza who had hoped to rule the city as duke was forced to serve the republican government as its captain. Three years later, having turned his forces against his some-time employers, he was able to starve Milan into surrender. The chief assembly of the republic invited him to enter the city, where he was acclaimed as the successor of the Visconti (1450).

Francesco Sforza owed his success firstly to his own military genius and secondly to the support given him by Cosimo dei Medici. Florence and Venice had combined to limit the power of Visconti, but it now appeared to Cosimo that the greater danger to Florence lay in the domination of Venice. He had formed a personal friendship with Francesco Sforza when the latter was in charge of the Florentine-Venetian armies, and he saw in his acquisition of Milan a means to the peace and security of Italy. So Florentine resources and diplomacy assisted Sforza's rise to power and then helped to secure his acceptance by the Italian states as duke of Milan. Four years of fighting followed Sforza's entry into his capital until, by the Treaty of Lodi (1454), he secured peace with Venice at the price of a small cession of territory.

THE ITALIAN LEAGUE

There followed a defensive league between Milan, Florence, and Venice, to which Alfonso of Naples gave his adherence and which Pope Nicholas V ratified with his blessing. The Italian League of 1455, in which the lesser powers were included as allies of the five chief powers, represents the nearest approach to Italian unity achieved in the fifteenth century. It was designed in the first place to prevent any one of the greater powers from increasing at the expense of its weaker neighbours, but it also stood for a common national front against external attack. The fall of Constantinople (1453) emphasized afresh the Turkish menace, which, for different reasons, was a matter of vital concern to both Venice and the Papacy. Francesco Sforza and the king of Naples, Alfonso of Aragon, alike had cause to fear a French invasion. This was seen to be a real and immediate danger when Charles VII of France, on the death of the last Visconti duke, at once put forward the claims of the duke of Orleans to Milan, and continued to support the cause of his Angevin cousins in Naples. As for Florence, her interests as a trading community, having close commercial ties with France, were bound up with the preservation of peace.

While the Italian states were not without appreciation of their common ideals and common dangers, they had yet to learn to prefer these to their particularist interests. When opportunities for individual gain presented themselves, loyalty to the principles of the League was forgotten, and the peace which it came into existence to preserve was frequently broken. Nevertheless, the League remained a factor in Italian diplomacy for at least forty years. Friendship between Milan, Florence, and Naples continued with only occasional intermission, and more than once the intervention of these three powers was employed to check a war of aggression. Peace being again secured, it was usually followed by a renewal of the League. The appreciation shown by the smaller states of the benefits which they derived from the system is expressed by Giovanni Bentivoglio, the leading citizen of Bologna. 'This most holy League', he writes, 'upon which depends the welfare of all Italy, and in particular, the welfare of our city.' A respite from serious warfare was secured, which enabled the members of each city-state to concentrate their energies upon the arts of peace. The outcome was a contribution to civilization which cannot easily be over-estimated.

POPES OF THE RENAISSANCE

Among the characteristic developments of the fifteenth century was the emergence of the Papacy as an Italianized temporal power. When the Council of Constance ended the Great Schism by electing Martin V as pope, the task which confronted the Papacy was the recovery of its lost prestige. The means to this end adopted by Martin and his successors was the creation of an Italian state which could hold its own against its neighbours, and the identification of the Papacy with the literary and artistic movements of the age. Martin V was a Colonna; it was a great advantage to him that he could rely on the support of members of his own family in the College of Cardinals, the city of Rome, and the Campagna. With the help of his relations and by his own firmness and moderation, he gained some measure of recognition for his authority throughout the States of the Church. To the Romans his reign brought some return of order and prosperity and the restoration of the city's half-ruined buildings.

Eugenius IV's difficulties with the Council of Basel reacted on his position in Italy. His enemies fomented a revolution in Rome which set up a republican government and forced the pope to fly for his life. He spent the years of his exile in Florence, where in 1439 he presided over the Council of Reunion attended by representatives of the Greek Church. Thus he was brought into contact with Greek scholars, and with the artistic and literary interests of the Florentines. When he was able to return to Rome he was accompanied by a learned Greek, Bessarion, now a Cardinal of the Roman Church. Florentine humanists were given posts as papal secretaries, and Florentine painters and sculptors were employed at the Vatican. The Renaissance had come to Rome.

Nicholas V (1447-55) was himself a professional humanist. Having studied at the University of Bologna, and acted as tutor in two Florentine families, he won the notice of a cardinal who made him his secretary, and set his feet on the ladder which led to the papal throne. In his early days Nicholas V had said that if he were ever rich he would spend his money on books and buildings. As pope, he realized his ambition to the full. He set scholars to translate Greek authors, and papal agents to search Europe for manuscripts, so that the Vatican Library became a centre for classical studies. A memorial of his services to art survives to-day in the exquisite little Chapel of Nicholas V in the Vatican, decorated with frescoes by Fra Angelico, and complete in its furnishings as when it was originally designed. Among those who enjoyed his patronage was Leon Battista Alberti, poet, scholar, architect, and sculptor, a man who went far towards realizing the Renaissance ideal of universal genius. Alberti made plans for the complete rebuilding of Rome, and under his care the dismantling of the old St Peter's prepared the way for the new and splendid basilica which was later to be erected.

Among the popes of the fifteenth century, Pius II (Aeneas Sylvius Piccolomini, 1458-64) most fully expresses the spirit of the times. Like Nicholas V he was a humanist who owed his advancement to his talents; he was perhaps the best man of letters and the best speaker who ever wore the papal tiara. The story of his life is told by Pinturicchio in the series of frescoes which adorn the Piccolomini Library at Siena, and also in his own *Commentaries*. These last show him as a keen classical scholar and an even more enthusiastic student of his own age. An experienced diplomat, an indefatigable sightseer, he was interested in everything and most of all himself. He strove to set his mark on the Papacy by recovering for it its world-wide supremacy, and he found his opportunity in the promotion of a crusade. Presiding over a Congress at Mantua, he devoted his eloquence to rousing the Powers of Europe to the task of driving the Turk from Constantinople. Disappointed in the response to his appeal, he determined to shame others into activity by becoming himself a crusader. He died at Ancona, where he was awaiting the Venetian galleys which were to convey him to the East.

The pontificate of Sixtus IV (Francesco della Rovere, 1471–84) is noteworthy for his determined effort to turn the States of the Church into a strong, well-armed dominion, and his employment of his numerous nephews as agents to this end. Hitherto the popes had been content with securing the recognition of their suzerainty over Romagna, leaving the rule of the cities in the hands of local despots. Their policy had accorded with the principles of the Italian League, and they had, for the most part, refrained from acts of aggression. Sixtus IV set up his nephew Girolamo Riario as lord of Imola and Forli, and married him to Caterina Sforza. Finding Lorenzo dei Medici an obstacle to his designs in Romagna, he tried, and failed, to bring about his murder, and then made war on Florence in alliance with Naples. Later he joined with Venice in an attack on Ferrara, which was parried by the intervention of Florence, Milan, and Naples in defence of the house of Este. Other Riario and della Rovere nephews made diplomatic marriages, or were raised to the rank of cardinal, and under their leadership Rome enjoyed the gaiety and luxury of a secular Renaissance Court. Under Innocent VIII (1484–92) the secularization of the Papacy continued, rendered only less harmful to the peace of Italy by the pope's submission to the diplomatic guidance of Lorenzo dei Medici. With the accession of Rodrigo Borgia as Alexander VI (1492–1503) the tendencies which had been visible throughout the fifteenth century reached their full development. Cesare Borgia, the illegitimate son of the pope, brought all Romagna under his direct rule. The position and standpoint of the Papacy was that of a temporal, Italian power. Rome was distinguished from other centres of the Renaissance chiefly by its greater extravagance and its more open vice.

THE ARAGONESE KINGDOM OF NAPLES

In 1442 Alfonso, king of Aragon and Sicily, was recognized by the Neapolitans as their king, and the succession promised to his illegitimate son Ferrante. For the next fifty years each successive monarch strove, through the development of a system of monarchical absolutism, to overcome the hindrances to his authority presented by the suzerain rights of the Papacy over Naples, the rivalry of Angevin claimants to the throne, and the unruly Neapolitan baronage. Alfonso was an Aragonese in speech and outlook, but after his state entry into Naples he never returned to Aragon. He established friendly relations with the Papacy, and before his death had entered into a close alliance with Milan. His passion for learning and love of splendour attracted scholars and artists from all parts of Italy to Naples, and even drew his own feudatories to the court. On his death in 1458 Aragon and Sicily passed to his brother John, while his son Ferrante was hailed in Naples as an Italian king. Nevertheless, the Angevin party again raised its head, and René of Anjou came from France to contest Ferrante's rights. The success of the Aragonese cause, after a four years' war, was due in large measure to the active support given to Ferrante by the chief Italian powers. 'It will not conduce to the freedom of Italy if the French obtain the kingdom', said Pius II ; 'in protecting Ferrante, Italy is protecting herself.' Ferrante ruled Naples with a heavy hand. The limitation of their privileges and the arrest of some of their leaders stirred the nobility to revolt, and Innocent VIII, who had Angevin sympathies, supported their cause by demanding the renewal of the annual tribute formerly paid by the king of Naples to the Papacy. The Barons' War (1486–7) ended in victory for the king, but the treacherous cruelty with which Ferrante avenged himself on his enemies caused fresh grievance among the malcontents. Prominent members of the nobility fled to France to tell of disaffection at home, and to promise swift success for an expedition to Italy in support of the Angevin claims. When Ferrante died in January 1494, preparations for Charles VIII's invasion were already well advanced.

FLORENCE AND THE MEDICI

The sixty years which lie between Cosimo dei Medici's rise to power in 1434 and the fall of his great-grandson in 1494 constitute the golden age of Florence. The historian Guicciardini, writing amid the troubles of the sixteenth century, thus describes the Florence of Lorenzo dei Medici in which his childhood was spent: 'The city was in perfect peace, the leading citizens were united, and their authority was so great that none dared to oppose them. The people were entertained daily with pageants and festivals; the food supply was abundant and all trades flourished. Talented and able men were assisted in their career by the recognition given to art and letters. While tranquillity reigned within her walls, externally the city enjoyed high honours and renown.' All the features upon which Guicciardini dwells—the internal peace and prosperity of Florence, her artistic and literary pre-eminence, and the prestige which she enjoyed throughout Italy—were due in large measure to the direction of her affairs by the Medici. Cosimo dei Medici's rise, and the fall of his rival Rinaldo d'Albizzi, represented a change of persons rather than of system. Albizzi and Medici alike belonged to the class of merchant oligarchs who had long controlled the destinies of Florence. Giovanni dei Medici, the father of Cosimo, was a banker, and one of the richest men in Florence. Although he took little part in politics during the Albizzi supremacy, his co-operation was consistently sought by the ruling faction. When rivalry arose between Cosimo and Rinaldo, the association of the name of Medici with the popular cause at the time of the Ciompi rising, together with Cosimo's great wealth and superior ability, assured his success. In 1434, after a year spent in exile, he returned to Florence amid the acclamations of his fellow-citizens, while Rinaldo and his friends were driven from the city.

The peculiarity of the Medici regime in Florence consisted in the rule of an individual under the forms of a republic. Throughout the fifteenth century supreme constitutional authority lay with the Gonfalonier of Justice and the eight Priors, known as the Signoria. Cosimo held the office of Gonfalonier for three periods of two months only, in the course of his whole political career. Lorenzo died before he was old enough to be eligible for election as the chief magistrate of Florence. While they remained nothing more than private citizens each in turn dominated Florence as completely as any formally constituted despot. They maintained their ascendancy partly by so manipulating the elections as to secure a Signoria made up of their supporters, but the real basis of their power lay in the recognition by the leading citizens that their rule served the interests of Florence. The swift expulsion of Lorenzo's son Piero, when in 1494 he forfeited the confidence of the great merchant families who had hitherto supported him, shows the extent to which the Medici rule rested upon public opinion.

The popularity of the Medici was due in large measure to their identification with all that was best in Florentine life. On the death of the humanist, Niccolò Niccoli, Cosimo acquired his collection of books and built a place to house them attached to the convent of San Marco, thus creating the first public library in Florence. Through his initiative Marsilio Ficino was trained to become the head of the new Platonic Academy, which was to make Florence the centre of Platonic studies. He supplied Donatello with models from the antique which inspired his sculpture. Michelozzo was employed to build the Medici palace, and Benozzo Gozzoli (by Cosimo's son Giovanni) to decorate its chapel with frescoes which depict the colour and gaiety of a Florentine spring in the form of the Procession of the Magi. Lorenzo grew up in the atmosphere which his grandfather had helped to create; he was the pupil of the scholars and philosophers whom Cosimo delighted to honour. To the men of genius of his own day he was less a patron than one of themselves, an artist among artists. The poetry of Lorenzo dei Medici reflects the spirit of Renaissance Florence no less faithfully than do the paintings of Botticelli. Beyond the walls of Florence the Medici had their villas and their share in the life of the Tuscan countryside. Here the young men of the family had their hawks and horses, the ladies saw to the oil and the cheeses and Cosimo talked of farming, as if he never did anything else but farm.

The banking connexions which they maintained all over Europe gave the Medici special advantages in the sphere of foreign policy, and this was the department of government which they kept more exclusively in their own hands. Lorenzo's services to the cause of peace and his great social gifts made him an honoured guest at the princely courts of Italy. Class distinctions in Italy had never been rigid, least of all in the age of the Renaissance when talent was the key to all doors. Private citizens such as the Medici or the Bentivoglio of Bologna made marriage alliances with ruling families or with the old aristocracy, and there was constant intercourse between one court circle and another.

Each city had its gala day, usually the festival of its patron saint, when the leaders of Italian society gathered from all parts to celebrate the event by banquets, tournaments, and pageants. The smaller courts vied with the larger in the magnificence of their entertainments, and all had their special contribution to make to civilization. New ideals in education were practised in Vittorino da Feltre's school for princes at Mantua. Ferrara was the home of poets, and the scene of a revival of dramatic art initiated by duke Ercole d'Este. The palace at Urbino, built by the soldier-scholar duke Federico da Montefeltro, was perhaps the finest specimen of domestic architecture of the age, and a treasure house of books and works of art. Artists and men of letters passed from one city to another, bearing with them recommendations from their old to their new patrons. Absorbed in their own ambitions and rivalries, these rulers fell an easy prey to the powerful national states which were rising on their frontiers.

FRENCH INTERVENTION

Charles VIII's victorious march on Italy was made smooth for him by a quarrel between Milan and Naples. Lodovico Sforza, a younger son of Francesco, had seized supreme power at the expense of his nephew, the rightful duke, whose wife was Isabella, the grand-daughter of king Ferrante of Naples. After the death of Lorenzo dei Medici (1492) had removed the one influence which might have preserved peace, Lodovico began to encourage French intervention as a counter to Neapolitan attack on his own state. Thus Charles VIII crossed the Alps as the ally of Milan, while Florence, Naples, and the Papacy combined to resist his coming, and Venice stood aloof from the contest.

Before this period the Medici policy of mutual friendship and support among the Italian Powers had caused no break in the traditional Guelf alliance of Florence with France. Now Florence was at open war with France in defence of Naples, and opposition to the country with which Florence's economic ties were strongest was unpopular with all classes in the city. When Piero dei Medici's pursuit of this policy ended disastrously and obliged him to yield four Florentine fortresses to Charles VIII, he was driven from the city. For the next four years the dominant influence in Florence was that of the Dominican Friar—Girolamo Savonarola. Savonarola's aim for Florence was first of all the revival of religion; closely associated with it in his mind were the establishment of effective republican government and the identification of the republic with the French cause. At first he and the republican reformers carried all before them. The constitution was reformed after the Venetian model; even after the chief Italian Powers united to drive Charles VIII from Naples, Florence remained true to the French alliance. The Florentines gave themselves to prayer and good works; religious processions and the burning of 'vanities' took the place of horse-racing and carnivals. When his political programme failed to achieve the results expected from it, and the wave of religious enthusiasm subsided, the Florentines turned against their prophet. In May 1498 Savonarola was burned as a heretic on the Piazza della Signoria in Florence. The republic associated with his name lasted until 1512, when, on the collapse of the power of Louis XII in Italy, the Medici were recalled to their position as unofficial rulers of Florence.

Charles VIII made himself master of Naples almost unhindered. His soldiers, said Alexander VI, had no need of swords, but only of chalk with which to mark up their lodgings. Yet he was back in France little more than a year after he first crossed the Alps, and before the end of 1496 all his Italian conquests had melted away. Lodovico Sforza turned against him once his immediate object was served, and Spanish troops were sent by Ferdinand the Catholic to re-establish his cousins of the illegitimate line of Aragon in Naples. During the years which followed the power of Lodovico Sforza was at its height and the court of Milan outshone all others in brilliance. On the death or murder of his nephew, Lodovico became duke of Milan, receiving investiture with his duchy from his friend, the emperor Maximilian. His young wife, Beatrice d'Este, was the centre of gaiety, and Leonardo da Vinci the presiding genius of the court.

The apparently fruitless expedition of Charles VIII had, however, disastrous consequences for Italy. Spain and the empire had been taught by France to turn their thoughts towards Italian conquests. The Italian Powers, demoralized by the ease with which Charles VIII had been expelled, saw in foreign intervention a convenient method for furthering their own political ends. In 1498 Louis, duke of Orleans, succeeded to the French throne and at once prepared to enforce his claim to Milan. Alexander VI and Venice accepted his proffered alliance, the one in order to gain support for Cesare Borgia in his conquest of Romagna, the other in order to win fresh territory at the expense of Milan. Lodovico Sforza was left without a friend in Italy, while heavy taxation and high-handed methods of government had aroused formidable opposition to him in his own dominions. The presence of a prominent Milanese—Gian Giacomo Trivulzio—among Louis XII's generals contributed not a little to his rapid conquest of the duchy. Sforza fell into his enemy's hands, and ended his days in a French prison. The French occupation of Milan was followed by a treaty between Louis XII and Ferdinand the Catholic (1500) for the partition of Naples between France and Spain. Thus, according to Machiavelli, Louis made the fatal error of introducing into Italy a powerful stranger capable of rivalling his own authority. The illegitimate line of Aragon was easily dispossessed and the kingdom of Naples was divided, but, in a few years, the French were ejected from their portion and the whole of the ancient Sicilian kingdom was once more united under the rule of Spain. From this time shrewd observers began to perceive that the real threat to Italian independence came from Spain rather than from France.

VENICE AND THE LEAGUE OF CAMBRAI

During the years which followed the first French invasion, when Florence, Milan, and Naples had in turn suffered at the hands of the foreigner, Venice alone had gained rather than lost by the disturbance of the times. She had won ports in Apulia on the plea of helping to overthrow French rule in Naples; she had gained fresh territory from Milan as the price of the assistance which she gave to Louis XII; she had taken advantage of the fall of Cesare Borgia to add to her possessions in Romagna. Not only was her mainland territory at its widest extent, but her commercial supremacy had not yet felt the effects of the mortal injury done to it by the Portuguese discovery of the ocean-route to India and the consequent breaking of the Venetian monopoly of the spice trade. In the first decade of the sixteenth century Venice stood at the apex of her prosperity and power, and it was, moreover, the period of her greatest contribution to the art of the Renaissance. Giovanni Bellini was still painting, Carpaccio was at the height of his reputation, and Giorgione and Titian were coming to maturity. The oriental splendour of Venetian life, the serenity of the Venetian temperament and its sensuous delight in beauty found expression in their work.

Venice was probably no more selfish than her neighbours, but she was considerably more efficient. The successful policy of aggression which she had pursued throughout the fifteenth century raised up for her a band of enemies. In the League of Cambrai (1508) all those Powers which had suffered loss of territory from Venetian expansion combined to strip her of her mainland possessions. The members of the League included France, Spain, the Papacy, the Empire, Mantua, and Ferrara. Venice was defeated at the battle of Agnadello (May 1509) and suffered temporary loss of her entire mainland dominion. Yet quarrels among its members soon broke up the League and Venetian power rallied. The cities of the mainland, mindful of a century of good government under the auspices of Venice, gladly returned to her rule. Recent acquisitions and cities stolen from the Papacy and Naples were finally lost, but a dominion bounded roughly by the Alps, the Adriatic, the river Adige, and the river Adda was recovered. This territory remained Venetian so long as the republic lasted, and enjoyed greater prosperity and greater freedom than any other part of Italy.

POPE JULIUS II AND THE TEMPORAL POWER

Alexander VI was succeeded, after the brief pontificate of Pius III, by Cardinal Giuliano della Rovere, who took the name of Julius II (1503). One of his earliest bulls declared that he was determined, as his bounden duty, to recover full possession of the States of the Church. This product of Sixtus IV's nepotism set his face against using the papal power for the advancement of his own family, and made the strengthening of the Church his consistent aim. Perugia submitted to him without a struggle, and Bologna, which had successfully resisted Cesare Borgia, opened her gates to him. As a member of the League of Cambrai he recovered possession of the towns in Romagna which had been seized by Venice. The Este in Ferrara alone succeeded in parrying his attacks. With this exception the day of small states under papal suzerainty was ended, and before his death Julius II was master throughout his dominions.

The years of Julius II's pontificate saw the culmination of the artistic and literary revival in Rome. Artists and men of letters, thrown out of employment through the fall of so many princely patrons, came to Rome in search of fresh opportunities, and found them in the pope's grandiose schemes for the enrichment of his capital. With Bramante as architect-in-chief, the foundation stone of the new St Peter's was laid and the Vatican galleries were built. Raphael began to work on his series of frescoes in the pope's private apartments; Michelangelo decorated the ceiling of the Sistine chapel, and prepared sculptures for the great tomb which Julius II ordered in his lifetime to serve as a memorial of his pontificate. In place of the medieval city with its narrow and filthy streets, and its fortress-like palaces, a new and spacious Rome of the Renaissance came into being. Meanwhile the humanists laid stress on the harmony between the classical and the Christian tradition, and extolled Julius II as the lord of both worlds.

Julius II's ambitions looked beyond Rome and the Papal States; his aim was to unite all Italy under his leadership, and to free her from the foreigner. Having reduced Venice to submission, he broke up the League of Cambrai and formed the Holy League (1511) in which Venice, Spain, and the Papacy combined to drive out the French. The major engagement of the war, the battle of Ravenna (1512), was a French victory, but the death of the French leader—Gaston de Foix—and the descent of the Swiss on Milan in support of the League brought disaster on the victors. Louis XII's conquest of Milan had been achieved with the help of the Swiss, but he had failed to retain their friendship. Now at the instigation of Julius II they succeeded in conquering Milan for themselves, setting up Massimiliano Sforza, the son of Lodovico, as their puppet duke. When Julius II died in February 1513 the French were once more driven from Italy, a Sforza was back in Milan, the Medici were back in Florence, and it seemed as if the happy days before 1494 might return again. A papal federation was, however, no solution of the Italian problem in the sixteenth century. The ruling families had not rallied to the side of Julius; the Este on the contrary had found in the French alliance the means of preserving their hold on Ferrara against papal attack. Thus the Pope's successes had been won chiefly by means of foreign aid; Italy had been freed from the French only at the price of increasing the power of the Swiss and of Spain.

MACHIAVELLI

In the year 1513 Giovanni dei Medici, a son of the great Lorenzo, became Pope Leo X, and the *Prince* of Machiavelli, perhaps the most famous of all political pamphlets, was written. As secretary to the Ten (the executive body concerned with foreign affairs) and as an emissary in France, southern Germany and Italy itself, Machiavelli had studied politics at first hand during the years 1498–1512. His purpose in the *Prince* was to give advice to the Medici, who controlled the Papal State and Florence and had, he believed, the possibility of gaining power over much of Italy and of freeing the peninsula from the French and Spaniards. His lessons he claimed to have learned from Cesare Borgia, son of an earlier pope, whom he had known personally. Machiavelli's intention of persuading the Medici to take him into their employment is clear; he disliked inactivity and could not afford to be without a post. The *Prince,* which concludes with a peroration urging the Italians to drive out the foreigner, is a handbook for despots. This does not, however, mean that Machiavelli, who had served the Florentine republic, had abandoned republican ideals. In his *Discourses on Livy,* written in the following few years (*c.* 1514–7), Machiavelli produced a wider and more analytical book in which he attempted to found a science of politics on the lessons of Roman history. In the *Discourses* Machiavelli shows a preference for republicanism as a better form of government in an 'uncorrupt' society. The despotism of the *Prince,* then, is an unavoidable evil in a time of crisis. Neither of these brilliantly written works influenced the conduct of rulers of the time—or indeed of later times. It would have been difficult for them to do so, since their advice is generic and their justification of 'Machiavellian' conduct superfluous.

ITALY THE TEACHER OF EUROPE

In 1515 Francis I, newly succeeded to the French Crown, defeated the Swiss at Marignano and established himself as duke of Milan. Four years later Charles of Austria, ruler of Spain and the Netherlands, was elected emperor, and Italy became the battlefield on which the struggle for supremacy between Habsburg and Valois was fought out. All that the native Italian rulers could do was to play off one foreign Power against the other, in the hope of retaining some measure of their independence. Italy fell before the foreigner, but at the same time her civilization conquered Europe. The French kings took the Renaissance back with them to France; Tudor England made Italy its model in letters and manners; an Italian tour came to be regarded as part of a liberal education. Thus, in the midst of her political degradation Italy became the standard of appeal for all Europe in matters intellectual and artistic. As the home of the Renaissance she established an enduring supremacy over the mind of man.

CHAPTER V

THE CENTURIES OF FOREIGN DESPOTISM

1. SPANISH DOMINATION, 1521–1713

THE struggle between Charles V and Francis I in Italy began in 1521, when imperial troops drove the French from Milan and set up Francesco Sforza, the younger son of Lodovico, as duke. Although his first act was an assertion of imperial suzerainty, Charles's real stake in Italy was as ruler of Spain. Sicily, Naples, and Sardinia were part of the heritage which he had received from his grandfather, Ferdinand the Catholic, and which he was resolved to hand on undiminished to his successors. French power in Italy challenged the Spanish hold on Naples, hampered the communications between Spain and the Empire, and, in alliance with the Turk, imperilled the position of Spain in the Mediterranean. Thus Charles V's Italian policy was throughout directed towards the exclusion of French influence from Italy. He had no desire to acquire further territory, and was content to preserve the native Italian rulers in their states, provided that Spain was recognized as the dominant Power. His non-aggressive policy, the long tradition of Aragonese rule in Naples and Sicily, and his own steady perseverance in the face of difficulties are perhaps the chief factors which led to the defeat of France and the establishment of Spanish domination in Italy.

THE SACK OF ROME

Francis did not readily abandon his claims to Milan and Naples, and the struggle in Italy continued with little intermission until 1529. At the battle of Pavia (1525) Charles, contrary to expectation, won a sweeping victory over his rival, who was left a prisoner in his hands. The emperor's success alarmed the Italian Powers, and Pope Clement VII (Giulio dei Medici), who had hitherto supported Charles, now turned against him. He was the prime mover in the formation of the League of Cognac in which the chief Italian states united under the leadership of France to overthrow the power of the emperor. Charles sent an army under the duke of Bourbon to march on Rome. Bourbon was killed outside the walls, and in May 1527 some 20,000 German and Spanish troops, leaderless and mutinous, poured into the Holy City, to sack and plunder without mercy or discrimination. The Sack of Rome has been said to mark the end of the Renaissance. Over and above the irreparable destruction of works of art which took place, the event is symbolic of the disappearance of the old life of Rome—free, gay, and pagan—under the stifling influence of Spain and the Counter Reformation. During the next hundred years Rome was to become even more magnificent with the completion of St Peter's and the building of its great Baroque churches. But, with the exception of Michelangelo, the leading artists who had worked there were dead, and the spontaneity and variety of its culture had vanished.

CHARLES V'S SETTLEMENT OF ITALY

After the Sack of Rome Charles for a time lost ground in Italy to France and her allies. In the spring of 1528 the two fortresses of Milan and Naples alone remained in Spanish hands. A turning-point came about through a quarrel between Francis I and Andrea Doria, who transferred his allegiance and that of his city of Genoa to the emperor. With the passing of sea-power from France to himself, Charles V began to recover lost ground, and in 1529 he was able to dictate a settlement of Italian affairs. By the treaties of Cambrai and Barcelona, Francis I renounced his claim on Italy and Clement VII consented to invest Charles with Naples. In return, he was promised imperial forces with which to overthrow the last Florentine Republic, and reinstate the Medici. Florentine republicanism had raised its head in the confusion which followed the Sack of Rome. Now the republic fell in a blaze of glory, holding out courageously for a year against the imperial armies with Michelangelo acting for a time as director of fortifications. The outcome of this gallant struggle was that Florence, at long last, had to submit to the rule of an official despot. Alessandro dei Medici, the son of the younger Lorenzo, was given the title of duke and married to the emperor's illegitimate daughter, Margaret. On 24 February 1530, in the

Fig. 12. Italy in 1559

church of San Petronio at Bologna, Clement VII crowned Charles as emperor. Francesco Sforza, who had taken arms against his imperial suzerain, was forgiven and married to Charles's niece. Federico Gonzaga was rewarded for the steady devotion of his house to the imperial cause by the erection of his marquisate of Mantua into a duchy. The pope was persuaded to recognize the rule of the Este in Ferrara and Modena. Thus, surrounded by a circle of Italian families bound to him by ties of kinship and interest, Charles V was the arbiter of Italy.

Further wars between Charles and France followed, the disposal of Milan, after Francesco Sforza died without heirs in 1535, being a recurring cause of dispute. Tuscan republicans, and supporters of the Angevin cause in Naples, found a refuge in France and were persistent in urging the king to undertake fresh enterprises in Italy. Not until the Treaty of Câteau-Cambrésis (1559) was a definite settlement reached. The terms of the treaty mark the tightening of the Spanish grip on Italy and the triumph of monarchy over republicanism. In 1540 Charles had invested his son Philip with the duchy of Milan, and transferred all imperial rights over Italy to the Spanish monarchy; Henry II of France now recognized the accomplished fact by a further renunciation of his claims (Fig. 12).

In 1537 Cosimo dei Medici, of the younger branch of the family, succeeded to the dukedom of Florence. He was to prove one of the ablest rulers of the sixteenth century. When Siena rose against the imperial representative in the name of 'France and Liberty', Cosimo aided in the overthrow of the republic and was rewarded by the grant of Siena as a fief of Spain. To guard against any too great independence on his part, certain Tuscan ports, known as the Presidi, were placed under Spanish control. A few years later Cosimo obtained from the pope the title of grand duke of Tuscany, thus creating a regime which lasted until the extinction of the line of Medicean grand dukes in the eighteenth century.

Another native state which had only recently been created was successfully brought within the Spanish orbit. In 1545 Paul III made his son, Pier Luigi Farnese, duke of Parma and Piacenza, cities which had long been in dispute between Milan and the Papacy. Pier Luigi was a bitter opponent of Charles V, but his successor Ottaviano was married to Margaret of Habsburg, the widow of Alessandro dei Medici. She, like many other Habsburg women, was devoted to the family interests, and her son Ales-

97

sandro Farnese, duke of Parma, became one of the ablest of Philip II's generals.

THE DUCHY OF SAVOY

Perhaps the most important provision of the Treaty of Câteau-Cambrésis from the standpoint of later Italian history was the reinstatement of Emanuele Filiberto of Savoy in his duchy, after nearly twenty years of military occupation by the French. The duke's position was far from easy, as France retained five of his principal fortresses, including Turin and Pinerolo, while Spain was suspicious of any sign of independence on his part. By successful reorganization of his government and development of his resources he made Savoy a state to be respected. Before his death (1580) he was able to secure by negotiation the withdrawal of the French, leaving him undisputed ruler of the whole of Piedmont. His son Charles Emmanuel, by the Treaty of Lyons with Henry IV of France (1601), exchanged some western provinces of Savoy for the little Marquisate of Saluzzo. The exchange, which involved the sacrifice of rich territory, marked the determination of the house of Savoy to become an Italian rather than a French Power and to retain control over the passes of the Alps as the surest guarantee of its independence.

THE DECLINE OF LIBERTY

The hundred and fifty years of Spanish domination (1559–1713) are perhaps the dullest in Italian history. The country as a whole was exhausted and ravaged by war and burdened by heavy taxation. Spanish policy was conducted on the principle of the minimum of interference, and even in the provinces under the direct rule of Spain it was not unpopular. Yet Lombardy became an armed camp, and Naples was the happy hunting-ground of corrupt officials; everywhere Spanish influence acted as a deterrent to energy or initiative. The influence of the Papacy was no less oppressive. It was the era of the Inquisition, the Index, and the power of the Jesuit Order, when Italians of all ranks were forced to fly the country because of their opinions, when scholars found their studies restricted by authority, and printing was rigidly censored.

The period, however, was by no means one of unmitigated intellectual and artistic decadence. The paintings of the Mannerists now find the admirers that they long lacked, but no revolution in taste has been necessary in respect of baroque architecture or sculpture. The great name here is that of Gian Lorenzo Bernini (1598–1680) and the fortunate visitor to Piazza S. Pietro and Piazza Navona will understand his reputation. In music, the Italians, earlier content to learn from the Flemish, now produced a great composer of church music in Palestrina (1525–94) and the first significant operatic composer in Monteverdi (1567–1643). As for Italian science, it has been well said that it led Europe 'as long as the Inquisition would let it'. Galileo (1564–1642) achieved so much that no brief account can do him justice. He was the first astronomer to make effective use of the telescope and was thus able to confirm by observation the system of Copernicus. His discoveries in mechanics laid the foundations of that science and provided much of the basis for Newton's theories. Above all he was the main founder of the 'experimental-mathematical' method which has characterized modern scientific thinking. Galileo was imprisoned by the Inquisition, but died a free man. Giordano Bruno (1550–1600), the adventurous philosopher who conceived the universe as an infinite plurality of worlds, paid for his courage and perished at the stake, and Tommaso Campanella (1568–1639), the author of a Platonic Utopia, suffered imprisonment for thirty years. Academies flourished in Rome (the *Lincei*) and Florence (the *Cimento*) and smaller centres, such as Padua and Bologna, continued to produce original work. Biology, which then appeared the least controversial of the sciences—its theological implications were to emerge later—was the field in which most advances were made. Of many names that which most deserves record is perhaps Marcello Malpighi (1628–94), who supplemented Harvey's work by discovering the capillary circulation of the blood.

The Medici grand dukes never wholly lost their civic simplicity, nor Florence its air of freedom. One by one, however, the cities were deprived of their ruling families, and with them went the remnants of independence. In 1597 Clement VIII took advantage of the death of Alfonso II d'Este to annex Ferrara to the papal dominion, and the Este capital was transferred to the smaller imperial fief of Modena. Ferrara, for long the home of a brilliant court, became a city of 'grass-grown streets.' Urbino had been immune from attack by Julius II because its duke was a della Rovere, the son of the Montefeltro heiress and himself the pope's nephew. In 1631, on the death of the last della Rovere duke, his state devolved to the Papacy, and the precious library of manuscripts collected by duke Federico in the fifteenth century was taken to Rome.

Undoubtedly the happiest of the Italian states was Venice, better governed, more prosperous, and preserving more of the old spirit of liberty and civic patriotism. Here freedom of thought was still possible, and the Inquisition itself was under state control. In 1606, led by her Servite friar, Paolo Sarpi, Venice successfully defied a papal interdict, in vindication of her claim to be mistress in her own house in ecclesiastical matters. Throughout the period, however, the republic was fighting a losing battle with the Turks. Despite the victory won by Christian arms in the naval battle of Lepanto (1571), Venice was forced to yield Cyprus, and in 1669 Crete too was lost. With her commerce declining and fearing Spain hardly less than she feared the Turk, Venice herself degenerated. The vigilance of the Council of Ten became terrorism, the nobility grew corrupt and idle, and the government stagnated. Like Italy as a whole, Venice was living on her past.

ITALY AND THE FRANCO-SPANISH WARS

The presence of the Spaniard involved Italy in much unnecessary suffering by forcing her to play a part in the long struggle between France and her enemies which culminated in the Peace of Utrecht. France regarded as her own every cause which might serve to weaken the Habsburgs, and she was apt to make a cat's-paw of the Italian states whose interests she appeared to be protecting. In 1627 the heir to the now united duchies of Mantua and Montferrat was half a Frenchman—Carlo Gonzaga, duke of

Nevers. When the emperor refused him investiture, a French army crossed the Alps in his support, but it was powerless to raise the siege of Mantua by the imperial forces. When Mantua fell after a nine months' siege, the sack which followed rivalled that of Rome as an exhibition of Teutonic barbarity. Mantua never recovered and, although for the time being the Gonzaga dukes retained their dominions, these became the cockpit of the battle between the two great European Powers.

With the death of the last Habsburg king of Spain (1700) and the acceptance of the Spanish throne by Loius XIV of France for his grandson, the Franco-Spanish struggle entered on its final phase. In the course of the fighting in north Italy Savoy rose to be not only the leading state in Italy, but an equal of the European Powers; her alliance was courted and her interests were consulted in every phase of the negotiations. This was due chiefly to her situation as a buffer state between France and Spanish-controlled Milan, able to close or open the passes of the Alps to either side. In Victor Amadeus II she had a ruler who enabled her to make the fullest use of her advantages. An able diplomat, at the head of a good army and supported by a united nation, it seemed at moments as if he would win for himself the much coveted prize of Milan. Yet the full triumph of the house of Savoy was still in the future, and the outcome of the War of Spanish Succession was the establishment of the Austrian Habsburgs in the place of the Spaniards as the dominant Power in Italy.

THE PEACE OF UTRECHT

The terms of the Peace of Utrecht (1713) assigned to the Archduke Charles of Austria, who became the Emperor Charles VI, Milan, Mantua, Naples, and Sardinia, that is to say, the major part of the Spanish possessions in Italy. In north Italy Victor Amadeus had to be content with the duchy of Montferrat and a strip of Milanese territory which included Alessandria. In addition he was assigned the island of Sicily with the title of king. By this arrangement the two parts of the Sicilian kingdom were again separated, and the long-established Spanish rule was replaced by that of monarchs who had no traditional associations with southern Italy. The Peace of Utrecht sacrificed Italy to the balance of power in Europe. Her territories were parcelled out, regardless of their history and traditions, in order that neither Austria nor France might gain a preponderating accession of strength, and that the various participants in the war might receive adequate compensation for their efforts. Nevertheless, the very unreasonableness of the changes effected gave hope that they would not be permanent, while the fact that they had been made at all roused Italy from her apathy. Spanish domination enjoyed the advantage of appearing to Italian eyes as the extension of an already existing rule. Austrian domination was new and on that ground alone open to criticism. The lowest point in the political degradation of Italy was the prelude to her rising again.

2. THE EIGHTEENTH CENTURY

As an historical period the eighteenth century may be said to begin with the Peace of Utrecht (1713) and to close with the outbreak of the French Revolution (1789). This period in Italy is divided into two sections by the Peace of Aix-la-Chapelle (1748). The earlier period is characterized by a further resettlement of territory which altered considerably the arrangements made at Utrecht, and the later by a movement of political reform in certain states, and by an increasing infiltration of French revolutionary thought, which was to have a profound influence on subsequent events.

POLITICAL CHANGES

The settlement of Italy in 1713 did not last long. The first change came in the year 1720 when after the failure of an abortive attack by the Spaniards on the island of Sicily the duke of Savoy was obliged to exchange it for the half-barbarous island of Sardinia and to hand over Sicily to Austria. Thus the dukes of Savoy became kings of Sardinia, which title they held until 1860 when they became kings of Italy. Later, by the Peace of Aix-la-Chapelle, in 1748, the kingdom of Sardinia, on withdrawal from the

War of the Austrian Succession, received back Nice and Savoy and advanced its eastern boundary to the river Ticino.

Another change took place in 1734. Elizabeth Farnese, the politically minded wife of Philip V of Spain, was resolved to attempt the recovery of Naples and the Milanese province, handed over to Austria by the Powers in 1713. She dispatched an army to Italy under her son Don Carlos, who, frustrated in his attempt on Milan, turned southward and without difficulty took possession of Naples and Sicily. As Charles III of Naples, he and his descendants after him held the kingdom until it surrendered to Garibaldi and Victor Emmanuel II in 1860. Three years later another change took place. The last of the house of Medici, Giovanni Gastone, grand duke of Tuscany, died in 1737. The duchy now passed to Francis of Lorraine, the husband of Maria Teresa, who became empress of Austria on the death of her father Charles VI in 1740. In 1745 Francis was elected emperor and Tuscany passed to his son Leopold. All these rulers or their successors were destined to be driven into exile during Napoleon's occupation of Italy (1796–1814), but all were restored by the Congress of Vienna in 1815.

SOCIAL CONDITIONS

For half a century, from 1748 to the invasion of Italy by Napoleon in 1796, Italy was at peace, though Sardinia was fighting the revolutionary armies of France from 1793. It was an age of great social contrasts everywhere in Europe, with enormous wealth concentrated in the hands of the few and the masses of the people existing in misery and squalor. Nowhere was the contrast more marked than in Italy, where the rich seemed richer and the poor poorer than in any other country. Rome was the artistic and religious centre of the world. The gorgeous pomp of the Papacy, the sumptuous banquets and receptions of the cardinals and Roman nobility, the treasures of art and literature in the galleries and libraries, and the new interest in archaeology, attracted not only the wealthy cosmopolitan element but the cultured and artistic of all countries. Nor was it only Rome. Venice was the playground of Europe, where in spite of war, visitors flocked to laugh at the comedies of Goldoni and to enjoy all the fun of the Carnival. At Naples the charm of its natural surroundings, the mildness of the climate, and the recent excavations at Pompeii and Herculaneum drew many visitors, even though conditions of the roads, the danger from brigands, and the lamentable state of the inns made the journey southward an ordeal. All this was on the surface, but the splendour of the wealthy classes in Italy was only possible at the expense of the masses. Poverty and crime in Italy were appalling. In Rome, for example, during the pontificate of Clement XIII (1758–69) 13,000 homicides were registered in the Papal States, in a population of under 3 millions, over 4,000 in the city itself, with 160,000 inhabitants. The rich city of Milan, one of the most favoured in Italy, was worse. At Venice in the twenty years from 1741 to 1762 no fewer than 73,000 executions or life sentences to the galleys were recorded, despite the fact that the municipality provided an itinerant court of justice, consisting of a judge, a criminal lawyer, a confessor, and an executioner, together with a posse of police, who patrolled the streets and environs of the city on horseback, with power to arrest, try, sentence, and hang on the nearest tree any malefactor whom they caught.

BENEVOLENT DESPOTISM

Much of this state of things was due to the excessive wealth and worldliness of the Church, the lack of education, and the existence, chiefly in the south, of a medieval system of feudal privilege. To limit the wealth and numbers of the clergy and to break the feudal power of the barons became the principal objective of a series of reforms which continued until the outbreak of the French Revolution. The states in which these efforts were made were those under foreign rulers, Milan, Tuscany, and Naples; elsewhere there was little change in the old system. The most beneficial reform in Lombardy, as the Milanese province now came to be called, was the *censimento,* a fixed tax on land, made after an exhaustive survey. It was moderate in amount and led to the development of an intensive form of cultivation which made Lombardy the most prosperous part of Italy. There was little feudalism in the north of Italy, except perhaps in Piedmont, but Maria Teresa and, later, Joseph II, by the abolition of privileges and exemptions equalized and improved the lot of the smaller proprietors. The Church received more drastic treatment. In 1768, in a population of about one million, there were 290 monasteries for men and almost as many for women. More than a hundred of these were gradually suppressed and the proceeds of the sale of their goods and lands devoted to hospitals and orphanages and to the development of the University of Pavia. By a concordat made with the pope, all ecclesiastical possessions acquired since the sixteenth century became subject to taxation, and privileges and exemptions were abolished. In his later years, Joseph developed a mania for centralization in the Empire, including Lombardy. The Senate was suppressed and the administration handed over to Austrian judges and bureaucrats, and the numerous privileges of self-government enjoyed under Maria Teresa disappeared. But Lombardy was improved and developed. The people were entirely exempted from military service, only a few Austrian regiments being kept, more for the display of imperial dignity and state occasions than from necessity.

In Tuscany the reforms of Leopold (1765–90), the younger brother of Joseph II, were even more thorough. He introduced free trade, abolishing all restrictions on exports and imports. He swept away with a single edict the whole medieval system of trade guilds with their tribunals, rules, and restrictions, and replaced them with a Chamber of Commerce. In 1770 he imposed equality of taxation on all citizens, including the Royal House. He introduced vaccination, reformed the prisons, abolished secret procedure, torture, and the death penalty, exposing the instruments of torture found in the prisons in the courtyard of the Bargello. He suppressed some convents and monastries, curbed appeals to Rome, and sequestrated the incomes from ecclesiastical vacancies for public purposes. He had little use for the army or navy. He sold the two corvettes, of which the navy consisted, to Russia, and disbanded the army, keeping only a garrison in the radical city of Leghorn, substituting civic guards to maintain order. In his last years in Tuscany, Leopold, with the vigorous support of

Scipione Ricci, bishop of Pistoia, entered upon a struggle for the reform of the Church culminating in the famous Synod of Pistoia in 1785, which closed with popular tumults; after which Leopold withdrew his support, the bishop resigned, and the old order was restored.

REFORM AT NAPLES

In the kingdom of Naples the soil was owned by the king, the Church, and the barons. 'If we divide all the families in the kingdom into sixty parts', wrote Genovesi in 1765, 'one of these owns land and fifty-nine have not sufficient to be buried in. Half the soil of Naples is held by the Church and may not be sold, a mortal wound, I know not if it is remediable.' For the spiritual needs of a population well under five millions, this kingdom supported twenty-one archbishops, 165 bishops and abbots, 50,000 priests, and more than the same number of monks and nuns. With an income of nine millions of ducats from land, supplemented by another three millions from masses and other offerings, the Church lived in ease and luxury amid poverty, misery, and squalor. As to the peasantry, the verdict of contemporaries is unanimous. Abject and utterly ignorant, living in hovels and caves, tied to the soil, without rights or defenders, they were like the beasts of burden that cannot eat the food they carry on their backs. The barons, possessing vast areas of land, much of it wild and uncultivated, lived as despotic lords. The earth, the water, the wind, the minerals, the forests, the very souls and bodies of the inhabitants, were regarded as part of their feudal rights. Up to the second French invasion the barons had the right of appointing the judges and magistrates, who, in consequence, gave decisions in their favour. Both the Church and the baronage were exempt from taxation, or, at most, paid an utterly disproportionate contribution of the national requirements, which thus fell almost entirely upon the peasantry, the small proprietors, and the middle class in the towns.

In the city of Naples, the legal profession was most patronized. The Neapolitans were notoriously litigious, and are said to have provided a livelihood for no less than 26,000 members of the legal profession in Naples alone, with another 4,000 in the provinces. There were at least ten codes of law, including Roman, Norman, French, Spanish, and Austrian. Cases were known which had lasted for centuries and the intricacies and contradictions of the existing codes provided endless occupation for the host of lawyers. Some made fortunes, all contriving a living. With a kingdom in such a condition, the task of reform undertaken by Charles III, and after his accession to the throne of Spain (1759) by his viceroy the marquis Tanucci during the minority of Charles's son Ferdinand, was a labour of Hercules. Something however, was done. By a concordat with the Papacy the clergy were rendered liable for half the amount of taxation paid by the laity, though with a long list of exemptions, such as parochial buildings, hospitals, and orphanages. The ratio of clergy to parishioners was fixed at ten per thousand and the number of monks and nuns was controlled.

In his attempt to master the feudal problem Charles had to be circumspect. He endeavoured to attract the nobility to court and relieve the tenants of their presence. He issued an edict permitting the peasantry to sell their produce in the open market, and not to their feudal lords only. He admitted the right of appeal from the baronial to the royal courts. In another edict he limited the numbers of armed retainers, chiefly brigands, protected by the barons and used indiscriminately against exasperated peasants or the royal power, and abolished a number of degrading personal services which the tenants were called upon to render without payment. Tanucci persistently asserted the rights of the throne against the Church, abolishing privileges, insisting on the royal consent before the publication of papal bulls and ordinances, prohibiting the bishops from printing writings until passed by the censor and approved by the Crown, and extracting money from the clergy whenever possible. The pope retorted by refusing to fill episcopal vacancies. Then Tanucci expelled the Jesuits, and ten years later refused to pay the Chinea, an annual gift of a white horse and 7000 ducats, which had been paid since Norman times as a sign of recognition of papal overlordship. In the same way he harassed the barons with new ordinances and restrictions, but he never touched the root of the evil, which required a far stronger hand and much more drastic methods. In 1776 Tanucci retired, and Ferdinand and his masterful wife Maria Carolina assumed the reins of power. The last decade before the Revolution was uneventful. The struggle against the Church and the barons died down. The king hated business and spent his time hunting. The army and navy were both neglected, the former had but 15,000 effectives, while the naval personnel was under 3,000. There was to be a rude awakening for Naples before many years passed.

Elsewhere in Italy there was little change. Venice lay in decay with her medieval Doge and Council of Ten, with no policy but neutrality, and no life but frivolity. One event of great significance took place at Rome, where, under sustained pressure from foreign governments, the pope dissolved the Order of Jesus in 1775. As for Sardinia and Savoy, a despotic king, an ignorant and semi-feudal nobility, a clergy that preserved a rigid censorship, and an active Holy Office, kept the country in immobility. But Victor Amadeus III, who came to the throne in 1773, was a keen soldier determined to defend his country. He strengthened the line of fortifications on his alpine boundary, increased the active army and the reserves, and drilled them incessantly. It was well he did so, for it enabled him to defend his country for three years when war broke out with France in 1793, and he succumbed only to the genius of Napoleon. Thus, on the eve of the Revolution, Italy (Sardinia and Savoy excepted) lay untrained and unarmed, a prey for the first conqueror, with her manhood destined in the coming years to be a fruitful reservoir for Napoleonic armies whose eagles they followed from Madrid to Moscow.

THE MIDDLE CLASS AND FREEMASONRY

All these reform movements were imposed on Italy by their rulers. There was no popular demand for them. The mass of the people lay inert. But Italy was by no means intellectually dead. Eighteenth-century Italian culture was fragmented and provincial, but it was certainly not despicable. One example will suffice to illustrate this: Montecchio (now Treia), a very small town in the March of Ancona, had its own academy which was concerned with improvements in agricultural technique (on which it published a journal), meteorology and the introduction of new arts and crafts. Seventeenth-century Naples had produced the extraordinary lone figure of Giambattista Vico (1668–1744), whose cyclical philosophy of history was too pessimistic—indeed too historical—to be acceptable or even comprehensible in his own day. More characteristic men of the Enlightenment were the economists Galiani and Pietro Verri (1728–97). The latter, a Milanese and the editor of *Il Caffé*, advocated free trade and industrial development: for a time he co-operated in economic reform in Lombardy. The *abbé* Galiani (1728–87), secretary of the Neapolitan legation in Paris, wrote on currency and the grain trade and was one of the best-known figures in Parisian intellectual circles. It was at Naples that Antonio Genovesi (1713–69) was professor of 'commerce and mechanical arts' from 1754, holding what was virtually Europe's first chair of political economy. But undoubtedly the Italian most admired by the French encyclopaedists was the criminologist Marquis Beccaria (1738–94). Applying to crime the criteria of 'reason', his book *Dei delitti e delle pene* advocated the recognition of punishment as a measure of social defence. He was therefore opposed to unnecessarily violent and vindictive forms of punishment.

It was neither from these intellectuals nor from the masses that movement was to come, but from the middle class between them. This class knew by experience the deadening effect of the old absolutism in their business and in their social life, and these were the men to whom the new French thought directly appealed. Liberty and equality were ideas to which they gave a very crude but practical meaning. As the struggle grew more intense in France these ideas spread more widely in Italy. French agents, official and unofficial, were soon to be found in most Italian cities. They found one organization ready made in the Masonic Lodges, which, formed in the first half of the century by travelling English nobility or by those resident in Italy, had spread and prospered despite condemnation by two papal bulls. On the eve of the Revolution France had already adherents and sympathizers all over Italy agitating in secret and preparing the overthrow of the old absolutist system both in Church and State.

3. NAPOLEON AND ITALY, 1796–1814

The French Revolution broke out in 1789. In 1793 France declared war on Austria and Sardinia and an indecisive struggle was waged in the Alps for three years, until the command of the army of Italy was committed to Napoleon Bonaparte. Striking at the point of junction of the two armies, he drove back the Sardinians, and the invasion of Italy began. During the years 1789–96 the governments of the other Italian states did nothing. The efforts of the king of Sardinia to form a confederation of Italian states and oppose a common front to the enemy met with no success. The rulers were content to redouble their vigilance against their own subjects or engage in separate and futile negotiations while awaiting the outcome of events. The royalties viewed with deepening horror the excesses of the revolutionaries. The Church, and with her the masses of the people, were scandalized by the display of sacrilege and atheism. Yet in its early stages the revolution was not without its sympathizers and adherents in Italy. There was evidence among sections of the intellectuals and upper classes of an academic feeling in favour of liberty and equality, caught from the pre-revolutionary aristocracy in France. But the real support came from groups of extremists scattered throughout the country, who were only awaiting an opportunity to take action. Genoa was a hotbed of conspiracy and full of French agents, who found easy access to Piedmont and Lombardy where they collaborated with the restless elements. At Turin three Jacobin clubs were discovered, and there was a conspiracy to create confusion by setting fire to buildings, to seize the citadel, and murder the royal family, while the army was defending the country in the Alps. Three conspirators were executed. In December 1792 the reality of the Revolution was brought home to Naples, when a French squadron sailed into the bay, and under a threat of bombardment, peremptorily demanded complete neutrality, the acceptance of the citizen Mackau as French representative, and the immediate dispatch of an ambassador to Paris. While the terrified government negotiated, the officers and men landed, fraternized with the people, attended a banquet offered by the Jacobin element, and in return gave a reception on the flagship, at which the admiral outlined a scheme for a Jacobin club on French lines. A year later a conspiracy was discovered and the usual sentences of death, imprisonment, or exile followed. Plots followed by executions were unearthed in Sicily and Bologna, while at Rome the French agents, Basseville and Flotte, so exasperated the populace that the mob sacked their residence and killed Basseville.

THE NAPOLEONIC REPUBLICS (FIG. 13)

Such was the state of things in Italy when in 1796 Bonaparte broke through the Sardinian defences, forced the king to sign the disastrous Treaty of Cherasco, and began the conquest of Italy. Three armies in succession, under Würmser, Beaulieu, and Alvinzi, were defeated and the Austrians driven out of northern Italy. After a triumphal entry in Milan, Bonaparte passed on to Bologna and thence to Verona, where a popular rising led to the occupation of Venetia. Behind him republics sprang up like mushrooms. In January 1797 Reggio, Bologna, Ferrara, and Mantua formed themselves into the Cispadane Republic; then Milan, Brescia, and other cities formed the Transpadane Republic, while Genoa converted itself into the Ligurian. On the suggestion of Bonaparte, the Cispadane and Transpadane republics combined as the Cisalpine and secured a constitution. Bonaparte now negotiated terms of peace with Austria, which were signed at Campo Formio in October 1797. By this treaty Venice at last lost its independence and was handed over to Austria, France acquiring the rest of northern Italy. Before the close of the year Bonaparte left Italy for France and thence for Egypt, and during his absence the rest of Italy turned itself into republics. On the departure of Bonaparte the command in Italy passed to General Berthier with headquarters at Bologna. It was not long before, even in Rome, the republican spirit revealed itself. An attempt to plant a tree of liberty led to a riot, and the young French General Duphot, attached to the Legation, was killed. Berthier at once advanced from Bologna, occupied Rome, and instituted a republican government. The pope fled to Tuscany (February

Fig. 13. Italy in 1798

1798), where his arrival at once brought trouble. General Miollis, in command of the French troops at Leghorn, received orders to occupy Florence, whereupon the grand duke fled and a peaceful revolution transformed the duchy into the Etruscan Republic (March). Before the close of the year the fate, not only of Rome and Tuscany but of Piedmont, was settled. Victor Amadeus died in 1796 and the new king, Charles Emanuel IV, weak and pious, was ill equipped to face the situation. Harassed and threatened, in October 1798 he abdicated, and with his wife and brothers left Piedmont for the island of Sardinia. A provisional government was formed and Piedmont, divided into four departments, passed into the orbit of France.

During 1798 the main objective of Napoleon's enemies was to win over Russia to the help of Austria. Lengthy negotiations were successful, and in the late autumn Russian troops were moving into Galicia. In August Nelson had destroyed Napoleon's fleet at the battle of the Nile, and left him penned up in Egypt. Excited by these two successes and urged on by the British Ambassador, Sir William Hamilton, and his wife—the bosom friend of the Neapolitan Queen Maria Carolina and the mistress of Nelson—Ferdinand, the king of Naples, decided to drive the French from Rome. He now had an army of 60,000 under the Austrian General, Mack. In December he marched on Rome. Championnet withdrew to concentrate his troops and Ferdinand occupied the city without opposition. His triumph was brief. A few days later the French attacked, and the Neapolitan army, completely demoralized, fled back to Naples in utter disorder. No one ran quicker than the king, who arrived in time to collect his queen and 20 millions in cash, embark on the British fleet, and sail in safety to Sicily. The occupation of the city, however, proved no easy task, for the *lazzaroni*, loyal to their king and infuriated against the heretic French, fought like tigers and victory cost Championnet dear. When order was at last restored and a provisional government installed, the kingdom of Naples had become the Parthenopean Republic. Thus in the short space of eighteen months the whole of Italy was transformed into a group of republics kept in existence by the presence of French armies. The whole construction was, however, artificial, and the problem of Italian independence was not to be solved on republican lines.

The French conquest and settlement of Italy had been rapid,

but the collapse of the structure was even more so. In March 1799 an Austro-Russian army under Suvarov crossed the Adige and swept the French out of northern Italy. The southern French army, where Macdonald had replaced Championnet, was hastily recalled, but was caught by Suvarov at the Trebbia and severely handled, and with great difficulty joined Masséna at Genoa, the only corner of Italy left in French hands. The allied victories were accompanied everywhere by a wild national rising. Led by priests, and in some cases bishops, armed bands of peasantry harassed and murdered their French oppressors and all who were believed to share their views. In Piedmont, the bishops of Albi, Asti, and Acqui led bands against isolated French garrisons, while thousands flocked to the standard of the 'Christian Mass' led by an obscure individual who called himself Brandaluccio. In Tuscany the countryside round Arezzo took up arms under two peasants, a man and a woman, whom they believed to be S. Donato and the 'Madonna of Comfort'; they harried indiscriminately, and developed into a force calling itself the 'Aretine army' under the 'pious Buglione' and Alessandrina 'the maid of the Valdarno'. But nowhere was the reaction so tragic as at Naples. On the withdrawal of the French troops, Ferdinand at once dispatched Cardinal Ruffo to the mainland with full powers to raise an army and recover Naples. The nucleus of this force was composed of Russian, Turkish, and English detachments, to all of whose governments Ferdinand had appealed for help. Around these, Cardinal Ruffo gathered bands of peasants and brigands, including the famous Fra Diavolo. Then, with some 40,000 men, he attacked the capital. After two days of slaughter, looting, and incendiarism, Ruffo called a halt and opened negotiations to save the city from further destruction. The republican government and garrison surrendered on terms which included a safe conduct and transport to Marseilles. The capitulation was signed by Ruffo and the king's representative, as well as by the commanders of the foreign detachments. At this moment Nelson appeared and, prompted or ordered by the king, rejected the capitulation, handed over those who had surrendered to the royal vengeance, and hanged Admiral Caracciolo, the commander of the republican forces, from the yardarm of his own flagship. The vengeance of Ferdinand and Maria Carolina was savage. More than a hundred of the leaders, 'the flower of Neapolitan virtue and intellect', as an eminent historian has called them, were hanged or shot: 220 were sent to the galleys for life: 312 for definite periods, and some hundreds more exiled. Thus did the king's brutality crown the triumph of Ruffo's 'Army of the Holy Faith'.

NATIONALIST REACTION

The three years of the first French invasion and the reaction that had followed were a bitter disillusion for the Italians. All the French professions of liberty and equality were just a mockery. Italy had been treated as a conquered country, trampled on, looted, and plundered, with a greed and a cynicism that infuriated every section of the community. The brutality and irreligion of the soldiery, the spoliation of the treasures of art which the French 'savants' carried out with such zeal and thoroughness, were only equalled by the insatiable rapacity of the civil and financial experts who followed the victorious army and descended like vultures upon each prostrate government in turn. Hatred of the foreigner was being rapidly bred in Italy, for there was little to choose between French and Austrians, Russians or English. It was at this time, and as a result of this cruel experience, that the secret societies began to appear, the Carbonari, the Raggi, the Adelfi, and others. Offshoots from Freemasonry, but all anti-French and patriotic, they were the first signs of a national conscience, and in their constitutions we find the earliest outlines of a programme and an ideal. The Carbonari, for example, took religion, independence, and constitutional government as their basic principles. Their theatricality and their fantastic symbolism, their fearsome oaths and penalties, had one invaluable result, that no member could ever forget that he had sworn to give his life for the independence of Italy, however little he was prepared to implement his oath. Hundreds of thousands of Italians of all classes passed through one or other of these societies, and slowly inoculated the nation with the determination to drive out the foreigner and govern their own country in their own way.

Fig. 14. Italy in 1810

THE KINGDOM OF ITALY

The triumph of the Allies in 1799 was shortlived. In October, Bonaparte arrived back in France from Egypt. In the following spring he organized a new Italian campaign. Then, in June, while Masséna still struggled with Austria on the Alpine border,

Bonaparte crossed the St Bernard pass, descended into Lombardy in the rear of the Austrians, and crushed them at the battle of Marengo. A year's fighting was necessary before peace was signed, but at the Treaty of Lunéville (February 1801) France obtained the control of northern Italy to the Adige, leaving only the eastern half of Venetia in Austrian hands; for the time being the kingdom of Naples was left alone. There were to be no more great battles in Italy after Marengo. In the ensuing years Italy was slowly organized in three divisions and lay quiet under the control of the emperor, who found it a steady source of financial help and man-power. With the *coup d'état* of the 18th Brumaire, the Directory had disappeared and Bonaparte was now First Consul. After the Peace of Lunéville he reorganized the Cisalpine Republic, summoning 450 delegates to the 'Committee of Lyons', from whose deliberations it issued as 'The Italian Republic' with Bonaparte as President and his stepson Eugène Beauharnais as his representative or viceroy. A little-known feature of the Committee of Lyons was the organization of a special secret society for the purpose of dominating its decisions in the interests of national independence. This society was called the Astronomia Platonica and was divided into Hemispheres, Segments, First Stars, Rays, and Lines under a mysterious leadership known as the Solar Circle. At Lyons they split over the question as to whether or not to oppose the decisions of Bonaparte, and, unable to agree, the whole elaborate structure collapsed. Bonaparte never lost his interest in the Italian Republic. When three years later he became emperor, the original Cisalpine Republic became again renamed 'The Kingdom of Italy' with the emperor as king. Venice was added to it in 1806, and two years later the March of Ancona, which carried its southern border to the Neapolitan boundary; in 1810 the Italian Tyrol was attached (Fig. 14). In the last years of the Empire the kingdom had seven million inhabitants and an army of 100,000 men. Though its government was allowed no initiative and was merely an administrative body taking orders from Paris, Italian writers have always kept a warm corner in their hearts for this Regno d'Italia, as the first stage towards national unity and independence. In its first form as the

Cisalpine Republic it had taken as its flag the *tricolore* which was to be the flag of Italy, the red and white of Bologna and the green of liberty, and this has never been forgotten and still endears the memory of Napoleon's first constitutional experiment.

In 1806 Napoleon decided to settle accounts with Naples. An army was dispatched to the south of Italy. Ferdinand and the court promptly fled once more to Sicily, and Napoleon's brother, Joseph, was installed as king. After two years employed in valuable reforms, Joseph was transferred as king to Madrid, and the emperor's brother-in-law, Marshal Murat, became king Joachim of Naples, where he remained until the empire fell. The remnants of Italy were incorporated in France. Piedmont, Savoy, and Nice had already been absorbed. Tuscany came next (1808), being constituted into three departments, and the following year the remaining Papal States and the city of Rome became part of imperial France. The opposition of the pope was useless: he was arrested and hustled out of Rome, finding a temporary refuge at Savona. Rome was declared the second city of the Empire, and when Marie Louise presented Napoleon with a son, the title given to him was 'king of Rome'. But in the enforced exile of the aged pope, neither flattery nor high-sounding titles, bestowed upon the son of an upstart emperor, could restore the grandeur that was Rome.

The artificial fabric of Napoleonic Italy rose and fell with the emperor, and the final stages were marked by an element of indecision and intrigue which betrayed the insecurity of its foundations. After the disastrous campaign of 1812 in Russia, in which both king Joachim and the Viceroy Beauharnais took part, together with the flower of the army of north Italy, few of whom returned, the fall of Napoleon appeared inevitable. Beauharnais, though he refused to send what was left of his army to the aid of the emperor in the final campaign, remained loyal to Napoleon, but king Joachim intrigued with both sides. At Milan, Beauharnais refused to summon the Electoral Colleges and have himself elected king, and thus to present the Powers with a *fait accompli:* he was content to dispatch a deputation to Paris, asking for the retention of the kingdom of Italy as an independent state

with the viceroy as king. When this was known, the opponents of
Beauharnais organized a demonstration which ended in a riot
and the murder of Napoleon's capable but much hated Finance
Minister, Prina. This gave Austria her opportunity: Marshal
Bellegarde occupied Milan, the Italian troops were disbanded or
sent elsewhere, and the viceroy retired quietly into obscurity. The
fate of the northern kingdom had been as good as settled when, in
a secret treaty signed at Prague, Austria had demanded its cession
to her and England had agreed to support her claim at the Congress. The fate of Murat was more tragic: having refused to give
his kingdom a constitution and thereby alienated public opinion,
he finally made a last attempt to rally Italy to his standard with
the promise of unity and independence. He marched north, but
was defeated by the Austrians and, unable even to defend Naples,
he fled to France. The emperor refused to see him, and at last,
landing in Italy with a handful of followers, he was captured and
summarily shot.

REBIRTH OF NATIONALISM

For fourteen years Italy had been under the rule of Napoleon, and
the benefits she had received were great. It was not only the
material improvements: roads and bridges, buildings and schools
and public gardens. Far more important were the financial reorganization, the efficient French system of administration, and,
above all, the imposition everywhere of the Code Napoléon. By
this the feudal system was swept away, the old-fashioned, complicated system of law simplified, and all citizens, high and low, rich
and poor, equalized before the Law. There were other benefits
more valuable, if less obvious, even than these. It was Napoleon
who at last shook Italy from the long torpor in which she had lain,
since, after the marvellous flowering of the Renaissance, she had
fallen back exhausted into the deadening rule of Spanish and
Austrian viceroys. He taught her men to fight, disciplined the
youth of the country, and gave them a new pride in their manhood. With the obliteration of the old state boundaries the people
began to think of themselves as Italians rather than Tuscans or
Piedmontese, and there began to emerge the outlines of a national

conscience. The very roughness of his handling, and the hatred he inspired, tended in the same direction: it deepened their desire to rule their own country and drive out the foreigner. They had a long road to travel before this aim was realized, but the thought was born and the old Italy of placid acquiescence had gone for ever.

CHAPTER VI

THE UNION OF ITALY

THE RISORGIMENTO, 1815–1848

THE CONGRESS OF VIENNA

THE principles underlying the reorganization of Italy at the Congress of Vienna were twofold: to eradicate French influence and to put a strong power in a position in which it could overawe the Peninsula and form a bridge-head in case of an attack from France. This Power was obviously Austria. She had already stipulated with England that the former kingdom of north Italy should be handed over to her (p. 119). She would have dearly liked to have had Piedmont also, but, from the first, England was firm that this valuable buffer state between the two Powers must remain independent. To eradicate French influence, all claims on the part of Italy to any form of independence were swept aside, the Napoleonic settlement broken up, and the old boundaries and the old rulers reimposed. Ferdinand came back with a new title, as king of the Two Sicilies, Victor Emmanuel I returned from Sardinia to find his kingdom enlarged by the addition of the former Ligurian Republic (Genoa). Ferdinand III of Hapsburg-Lorraine followed his father in Tuscany, and the duchy of Parma was bestowed on Marie Louise, the wife of Napoleon, for whom a lover and later a husband was provided in the person of a dashing one-eyed Austrian general, Count Neipperg. Austria did not get all that she wanted at the Congress. The Papacy recovered all its former possessions. Some Novarese territory, crossed by Napoleon's military road from France to Italy, remained in the kingdom of Sardinia. Thus Austria had to be content with Lombardy-Venetia, together with useful garrison rights at Comacchio, Ferrara, and Piacenza. From the Italian point of view these arrangements were not merely disappointing but disastrous. They wiped out at once all those prospects of a fuller national life that had been opened up by Napoleon. The enlarged administrative experience, the discipline of the military life, the wider economic and social contacts, all disappeared, and the narrow, bigoted absolutism of the small states came back in full force, under an Austrian influence which was strong in the north and centre, and recognizable everywhere. It was a return to the mentality of the eighteenth century. In some places even—notably in Tuscany—the restored régime was less enlightened than the one which had existed before the arrival of Napoleon.

THE AGE OF CONSPIRACIES

The first period of what is generally known as the 'Risorgimento' by which Italy became a united, independent kingdom under the house of Savoy, with a constitutional parliamentary government, extended from the Congress of Vienna to 1848 and ended with the First War of Independence and defeat by Austria. The Congress of Vienna left Italy at the mercy of Austria, who possessed her two richest provinces, Lombardy and Venetia, together with satellite dukedoms at Florence, Modena, and Parma. The policy of Austria was in the hands of Prince Metternich, Foreign Minister until 1821 and afterwards imperial chancellor. His aim was peace, but it was a static peace in opposition to the whole spirit of the age, and flouted the three great movements of thought which were then active in Europe—nationalism, romanticism, and industrialism. All of these were dynamic and, in a limited sense, revolutionary. Nationalism was a reaction against Napoleonic despotism, which, after appearing in Spain, Russia, and Germany, was finally active in Italy in the formation of secret societies. Romanticism was mainly a literary movement, a reaction against the restrictions and conventions of the eighteenth century, and against the limitations imposed on the freedom of the human spirit by the deadening materialism of the Napoleonic period. Industrialism, as yet in its infancy, was an unknown factor, but was already transforming England and bringing in its train immense problems of world-wide import.

The policy of Metternich was based on the support of the Quadruple Alliance—England, Russia, Prussia, and Austria—

pledged to maintain order in Europe, if necessary by armed intervention, for which purpose periodic meetings were to be held for a general survey of Europe and the solution of particular problems. Metternich desired an alliance, if possible, with all the restored rulers, the unqualified support of absolutism, the prevention of any movement towards constitutional government, and the suppression of the secret societies. Naples and Tuscany accepted the alliance, undertook not to alter their forms of government without consulting Vienna, and promised aid to Austria if attacked, but the pope and Piedmont both refused. To the proposal for alliance Metternich attached an innocent-looking request for a Postal Convention, by the terms of which the foreign correspondence of each state was to pass through Austria. What this meant in practice was that the correspondence was dealt with by Metternich's special Bureau, which opened, copied, and resealed it, forwarding to the Chancellor all that was deemed of interest. The Papacy, Tuscany, and Piedmont refused. Austria had the most elaborate and effective police system in Europe and Metternich found no difficulty in obtaining, in police matters, the collaboration of the Italian rulers. By this means the whole population of Italy was, in effect, kept under police supervision. This network of espionage extended from the Austrian minister at each court, who had his private spies and political agents, down to the miserable informers who haunted the public places, cafés, and restaurants, and reported private conversations and the gossip and rumours of the street.

In the face of this organized system of repression and detection, the people of Italy were practically defenceless. The armed forces were at the disposal of their rulers, behind whom stood Austria and the Quadruple Alliance. Yet nothing that Austria could do had power to repress the national feeling nor lessen the deepening hatred for her government and her methods, and those of her satellite princes. To police and armies Italy replied with conspiracy. These Italian conspirators were an extraordinary type. Men mostly of the middle classes, with a sprinkling of the lesser nobility, inspired partly by hate but more by patriotism, they organized the most hopeless rebellions in the face of overwhelming force and treachery within and without, for vague objectives which they themselves can scarcely have comprehended. Yet these victims of the prison and the scaffold did a vital work for Italy. They stood for the new ideals and kept alive the spirit of opposition: they prevented their country from falling back once more into the old mentality of acquiescence.

With the fall of the empire the secret societies received large additions to their numbers. Thousands of demobilized officers and men from Napoleon's armies, unemployed civil servants from the former kingdom of Italy, and many of those who had served France in Naples or in the incorporated Italian states, flocked to swell the army of the sectaries. Italy was honeycombed with disaffection. The Carbonari in the south, the Federati and the Adelfi in the north, and in the Papal States other strange societies like the Spillo Nero (the Black Pin), the Latinisti, and the American Bersaglieri, were all alike plotting upheaval. Early in 1817 a rising at Macerata in the Papal States was nipped in the bud by the police. It came to nothing, but the leaders went to the galleys. This minor rising was a prelude to a more serious attempt elsewhere.

REBELLIONS OF 1820–1831

Just at this time the Austrian garrisons were recalled from Naples, and the government, in an attempt to deal with brigandage, authorized a new system of militia to be organized by the generals commanding military divisions. In organizing his contingent of 10,000 men at Avellino, General Pepe soon found that the only suitable material were almost to a man Carbonari, and without hesitation he enrolled them. Pepe was a strong Constitutionalist but not a Carbonaro, and with this force at his disposal he proposed to march on the capital and demand the Spanish Constitution of 1812. In March 1820 news reached Naples of the Carbonarist rising in Spain and the grant of a constitution. At once the kingdom was in a ferment. Two lieutenants raised the standard of rebellion at Nola, in Pepe's district, and he at once mobilized his militia, and putting himself at their head, marched on Naples. The king, terrified, took to his bed, appointed the Hereditary

Prince as vicar-general, and agreed to everything almost before he was asked, but at the same time he wrote imploring help from Austria. The Spanish Constitution was proclaimed and sworn to by the king, together with freedom of the press and other reforms, and parliament met on the 1st of October. During these months Naples was in the hands of the Carbonari, and had it not been for Pepe, whose influence was very great, there might easily have been a reign of terror. The hated Minister of Police, Giampietro, was indeed brutally done to death, but this was the only real outbreak of ferocity.

The Powers were already planning to meet to deal with the events in Spain, when they heard of the revolution in Naples. Ferdinand appealed to them for help. Meeting first at Troppau, and then at Laibach, they invited him to attend the Congress in November. As the consent of Parliament was necessary, the king asked permission to go to Troppau on the grounds that he would try to persuade the Powers to accept the Constitution. Nothing was farther from his mind, but Parliament believed him and let him go. At Laibach, the king went hunting while the Powers decided not only to reinstate him unconditionally, but to abolish the Constitution, and for this purpose to dispatch an army to Naples at once. When news of these decisions arrived at Naples Parliament, under pressure from the Carbonari, decided on resistance. Elaborate defence measures were taken, two armies mobilized, one under Pepe in the Abruzzi, the other under Carascosa. The Austrian army marched south. Only one clash occurred, at Rieti, where, after a desultory action, Pepe's troops first retired, then, seized with panic, disbanded. Carascosa's army followed suit, and the Austrians occupied Naples practically without fighting. Ferdinand followed at a safe distance, bringing with him as minister of vengeance the infamous prince of Canosa. Safe again on his throne with an Austrian army round him, Ferdinand executed justice with his usual brutality. Hundreds were flung into prison, flogged, hanged, or shot, while some thousands more were exiled or left the country to save their lives. So ended the revolution in the south.

At the moment when the Austrian troops were approaching

Naples yet another rebellion broke out, this time in Piedmont. This was the work of a group of aristocratic officers led by the count Santorre di Santarosa. The troops at Alessandria and Vercelli mutinied, demanding war with Austria and a constitution. The government were paralysed, and the king, faced with civil war or a constitution, abdicated in favour of his brother Charles Felix, then at Modena, and appointed the heir presumptive, prince Charles Albert, as regent. Charles Felix at once applied to Austria for help, troops were sent, and together with the loyal regiments of the Sardinian army scattered the rebels near Vercelli, and occupied Turin. The rebel leaders fled abroad. The complicating factor in this outbreak was the position of Charles Albert. All the rebel leaders were his friends and they believed that they had his consent and support. When the crisis came he tried to act as mediator, to postpone the outbreak, and at the same time to induce the king to grant a constitution. He failed in both attempts and was regarded by both sides as having betrayed them. Appointed regent, he yielded to the force of circumstances and promulgated the Spanish Constitution of 1812. His action was hotly repudiated by the new king and he was exiled to Florence. As in Naples, several thousands of actual or potential rebels fled abroad. Two only were executed, but there was a drastic purge in the circles suspected of disaffection and a long list of imprisonments.

Suspecting collusion with the rebellion in Piedmont, Metternich set his police to work in Lombardy, and soon unearthed the threads of a similar plot. For three years, urged on by Metternich, the investigation continued, with the primary object of getting evidence against Charles Albert and discovering the source of Carbonarist activity, but in both these objectives he failed. While this was taking place in Lombardy, the States of the Church were in a condition almost of civil war. The Papacy had enrolled in its support an organization known as the Sanfedisti, and between them and the secret societies was waged a ceaseless struggle of assassination and outrage. To end this state of things the pope dispatched Cardinal Rivarola, who, after a preliminary investigation, condemned out of hand to exile or forced works over 500 citizens. Some hundreds more were subjected to police surveillance, compulsory monthly confession, and an annual relegation to a 'retreat' chosen by the bishop. In spite of this the struggle went on sporadically and the 'Twos and Threes' (i.e. the papal colours red and white and the liberal colours red, white, and green) and the 'Cats and Dogs' murdered one another in an endless vendetta.

After 1821 Austrian garrisons, and the imprisonment or exile of the most active liberal elements, kept Italy outwardly quiet for some years. The real effect of the policy of force and oppression was, however, to transfer the centre of activity from Italy to Paris and London, where international committees were now organized to plot against Austria and absolutism. But even in Italy the lull was only momentary. In 1826 a young Modenese lawyer named Henry Misley began a fresh and more elaborate conspiracy. His plan was to form a central Italian Kingdom to be extended to absorb the whole peninsula. By a process of elimination he arrived at the conclusion that the only ruling prince sufficiently firm, wealthy, and ambitious to occupy the new throne was the Archduke Francis IV of Modena. This bigoted little tyrant was the most hated ruler in Italy. He had distinguished himself in 1821 by combing his little duchy for suspects and eventually hanging a priest and sending many victims to the prisons or galleys.

For nearly four years Misley worked unceasingly. He organized rebellion in the Romagna, roused Hungary to make trouble for Austria, and obtained promises of help through the Czar's agent Capodistria, who was anxious to make complications for Austria while Russia made war on the Turks. Misley then explained his scheme to the Paris committee, by whom the duke was loathed, and who agreed to accept him only if he gave a guarantee of good faith. The duke was actually persuaded by Misley to give a free pardon, a safe conduct, and a personal interview, to a member of the London Committee, Camillo Manzini, whom he had previously condemned to death. The duke acted with diabolic cunning. He kept completely in the background, committed himself to nothing, and was equally prepared to accept the throne or to crush the conspiracy according to the requirements of his personal safety. The arrangements were nearly completed when the July Revolution broke out in Paris, and Louis Philippe, who was in close touch with the international committee, became king. His Cabinet at once announced the doctrine of non-intervention, which meant that if Austria sent troops to quell a rising in an Italian state not under her jurisdiction, France would oppose her by force. Armed with this guarantee the order to rise was given, but the duplicity of the duke had not been reckoned with. Informed of everything, he allowed the conspirators at Modena a free hand until the last minute, and then he surrounded the house where the final arrangements were being made and arrested them all. When, in spite of this, Bologna rose, he fled for safety. Then Austria, defying France, marched in troops and crushed the rebellion. Louis Philippe gave way, changed his Cabinet, and forgot the principle of non-intervention. The duke returned, seized and burnt all compromising documents, and resumed his role as a loyal absolutist.

At this point France interfered, and declaring that the whole trouble arose from papal misgovernment demanded a scheme of reform. A conference of ambassadors met in Rome for this purpose. The pope did not want reforms and was supported by Austria, anxious to check French influence. England and Prussia worked conscientiously and finally produced a memorandum of suggested improvements, while France pressed for the evacuation of the Austrian troops from papal territory. In the end the scheme was accepted and then quietly shelved; the Austrian forces were withdrawn, and the Papacy made some inadequate changes in the administration. But no sooner were the Austrians gone than the trouble began again and Austrian troops reoccupied Bologna. France promptly occupied Ancona, where her troops remained face to face with the Austrians at Bologna for six years.

After the events of 1830-31 there was a threefold change in the situation. First, new rulers were on the thrones—Ferdinand of Naples died in 1825, his son Francis in 1830, and his grandson Ferdinand II came to the throne (1830-59). There was a new pope, Gregory XVI (1831–46), and a new king of Sardinia, Charles Albert (1831–49). Second, the rebellion of 1831 caused the collapse of the old secret societies as a political force. The Carbonari, the Federati, and their cognate societies now sank into insignificance and were replaced by Mazzini's Young Italy, a secret society of a different type. Third, the revival of French power in Europe was a check on Austrian influence in Italy; the Quadruple Alliance no longer existed; England had withdrawn and now leaned towards friendship with France. In an emergency Russia and Prussia still supported Austria, but they were no longer aggressive.

THE REBELLION OF THE INTELLIGENTSIA

The remarkable feature of this new period 1831–46 was the appearance of a patriotic literature. There was, in short, a literary conspiracy, with the double purpose of rousing national feeling and discrediting Austria; and it was very effective. Everything was influenced by it: journalism, poetry, history, fiction, drama, even painting and music. It focused national opinion, created an atmosphere, and absorbed and redistributed in Italy the romantic, industrial, and national ideals which were transforming Europe.

The first and by far the most potent of these literary men was Giuseppe Mazzini. The son of a Genoese doctor, he became an active Carbonaro when very young, but was soon disgusted with the ritual and theatricality with which it was impregnated. Arrested on suspicion of complicity by the Austrian police, he was exiled and went to Marseilles. Here with a few companions he founded his society of Young Italy and began the publication of the journal with the same title. It was a youth movement with an age limit of forty. Mazzini's motto was 'Thought and Action', which meant 'Education and Rebellion'. To the current aims of liberty and independence Mazzini added a third, unity. Italy must be free, independent, and united, under a republican form of government seated at Rome. He rejected monarchy as implying inequality, and federalism as tending to weakness rather than strength. But Mazzini realized from the first, what others did not, that power implies responsibility, which in its turn depends on education, and he set before the youth of Italy a high moral standard of conduct, both individual and national. He urged them to be worthy of their destiny and to make of Italy the leading nation of Europe. Mazzini was the first, not only to give an ethical content to the national movement, but to teach the Italians that they must rely on their own strength, and not, as they were so ready to do, look to France to save them from their own weakness. The teaching of Mazzini reached the middle classes, he never had success with the peasantry, nor did he influence the upper classes or the nobility. The poverty of his resources, and the profound secrecy in which his propaganda had of necessity to be conducted, limited his success, but all over Italy were groups of men who absorbed his teaching and accepted his ideal. Mazzini's campaign of action began with an appeal to Charles Albert, on his accession, to put himself at the head of a great nationalist effort against Austria. When this was ignored, he plotted to dethrone him, but the activity of the police unravelled the whole design, which was crushed with such severity that for the rest of the king's reign Piedmont was undisturbed.

Simultaneously with the work of Mazzini a literary form quite new to Italy began to interest the nobility and upper classes. This was the historical novel. Beginning with Manzoni's master-piece, 'The Betrothed' (*I promessi sposi*), a series of books of this kind were published. They were romantic in spirit and derived from Sir Walter Scott, but they had a political purpose. They were all written round some striking event or personality in the past, and were intended to arouse patriotic feeling by contrast with the submissive spirit of the present. Though Spain instead of Austria was usually represented as the oppressor, their purpose was unmistakable and they met with great success. It was the same with the drama. The theatre was very popular everywhere in Italy, and the dramatic authors of this period were as outspoken and as patriotic as the novelists. When, for instance, Niccolini's drama *John of Procida*, based on the Sicilian Vespers, was performed at Florence, the French Minister, who was present, was most indignant at the cheers which greeted the lines directed against his countrymen, but the Austrian Minister quietly remarked, 'Don't take it badly: the envelope is addressed to you but the contents are for me!'

In all the intellectual activities at this time are found the same desire to express in some way the national feeling. Music was no exception. Rossini found a patriotic theme in *William Tell* and an early Verdi opera was *The Lombards of the First Crusade,* and whenever the popular note was struck it was applauded with such fervour that sometimes the performance could not be continued until it was repeated, and afterwards it would be sung and whistled in the streets. In the same spirit painters took battles and kindred subjects for their canvasses. Giusti's epigrams and satires were passed on by word of mouth to those who could not read. Poetry glorified liberty and justice and denounced tyranny, drawing, too, a bitter picture of Italy's sufferings. The most curious feature of all this activity is the underlying note of optimism. There is, of course, anger and bitterness, but there is no despair. It is as if the Italians were convinced beyond all doubt that, with their cause based on the great principles of truth and liberty and justice, it could not be defeated.

The more thoughtful of the people could not be satisfied with quoting epigrams and reading historical novels, and there now began, as any form of political activity was impossible, a great interest in social and economic reform. For some years there had been a journal, *Gli Annali* ('The Annals'), edited in Lombardy by one of the greatest Italian intellects, G. D. Romagnosi. Though nominally a trade journal, the skill and ingenuity of the editor had contrived to leaven it with a patriotic spirit, eulogizing every reform, stimulating trade by facts and figures from other countries, stressing the dead hand of Austria and urging Italy on the path of progress. Romagnosi died in 1835, but his work continued and spread, and other journals on the same lines like the *Politecnico* and the *Rivista Europea* followed where he had led. They drew contributors from other states, from Piedmont and Tuscany, thus getting in touch with the progressive element all over northern Italy. The idea of a possible solution of Italy's future by reform, rather than war, began to gather strength and was supported by all those disgusted with the sacrifice of life in futile risings and vendettas. Thus was formed a party known as the 'Riformisti' opposed to the republican doctrine of Mazzini with its aim of conspiracy and upheaval. They believed in co-operation between rulers and people and the development of some kind of Italian federalism. Their schemes for railways, banks, schools, and a common monetary system were in reality unitarian, and tended to the weakening of the power of the rulers. This in its turn strengthened the position of those who believed that Austria must be fought, that only Sardinia could take the lead, and that in Charles Albert lay the real hope of Italy; these became known as the 'Albertisti'. Thus in the early forties there were three currents of thought, Republican, Federalist, and Monarchist.

It was at this moment (1843) that the great book of the Abbé Gioberti appeared in Italy, 'The Moral and Civil Primacy of the Italians', commonly called the *Primato*. It was the work of a philosopher and a theologian not a statesman, and the political solution it put forward was a federal Italy under the presidency of the pope, with a kind of super-cabinet composed of the ruling princes. The existing systems in the different states were to remain intact. It created tremendous excitement and was at first enthusiastically received, even in the sanctuaries of absolutism, for Gioberti had spared no pains to propitiate everyone. Gioberti had, however, posed the political problem, and his book was followed by others offering both criticism and alternatives. But the one inescapable fact which quickly emerged was that Austria meant to fight to the death for her Italian provinces. The wordy warfare of Republicans, Federalists, and Monarchists was in full blast when the pope died (1846), and to the delight of Italy and the consternation of Austria, the new Pope Pius IX was hailed at once as a liberal and a reformer.

TOWARDS THE YEAR OF REVOLUTION, 1848

The period that now follows, from the election of Pius IX (June 1846) to the outbreak of war in March 1848, is intricate and confused. The Austrian emperor, Ferdinand I, was mentally deficient and a mere figure-head, and since 1835 the empire had been governed in effect by Metternich and Count Kolowrat, who managed the internal administration. There was trouble within the empire in Hungary, where Kossuth, stimulated by Mazzini, was leading a movement for independence. Abroad the situation was complicated. England was friendly to Austria on principle, as being the state best calculated to keep Russia in check, and also because both wished to preserve the settlement of 1815.

To Italy England gave a moral support for reforms, but would not help to drive Austria out of Italy or upset the detailed settlement of 1815. The policy of France was equally two-sided. She would not at this date oppose Austrian aggression in Italy, but she would view with favour any upset of the arrangements of 1815 which arose without her interference.

The real difficulty for Metternich lay in the probability that, if a constitution was granted in any one state, it would at once be demanded everywhere in Italy; the demand would then spread to Austria, the whole structure of which might collapse, whereas England was already advocating reform as the panacea against revolution. His one consolation was that Austrian action would not be an immediate *casus belli* with France. The danger lay in the Papacy, for whatever reforms could be won from the pope would be demanded in the other states, and military action against the Papal States would create an uproar in Italy, especially in the one state with an effective army, Piedmont, whose king would turn crusader.

Both the personality and the policy of Charles Albert, the new ruler of Sardinia, were a profound enigma. Ascending the throne deeply distrusted by both liberals and royalists for his attitude in 1821, his personal abhorrence of Louis Philippe had thrown him at once into the arms of Austria, with whom he had signed a military convention in case of attack by France. Since then for fifteen years he had ruled as an absolutist; he had crushed the Mazzinian rising of 1833 with excessive severity, rejected every suggestion of political concessions, and supported all the absolutist attempts in Europe: the duchess of Berry in France, Dom Miguel in Portugal, and Don Carlos in Spain. Yet his Foreign Minister, who watched him closely for twelve years, declared that his king had one absorbing obsession, to drive Austria out of Italy and to found a strong northern kingdom in her place, and then to restore the glories of the medieval Papacy. Charles Albert had no vices. He lived a life of religious asceticism, and worked long and conscientiously as a ruler, though afflicted by a painful malady which caused him intense suffering. There is no doubt that he hated and distrusted Austria like all his house, but he was morally weak, though physically brave to a fault. Held back by the Austro-clerical party, urged forward by the liberals, he took refuge in an enigmatic silence which effectually masked his designs from both sides. But soon after 1840 Metternich detected a slow but disconcerting change in his attitude. Between the two countries there were a number of disputes, a question of wines, another of the transit of salt to Switzerland, and above all, railways. On all of these questions Charles Albert became difficult, refusing to compromise and even keeping them deliberately alive, as if to make further openings for trouble. Diplomatic pressure from Vienna was ignored, a strong letter of warning read to the king was merely acknowledged, and the usual reply 'my policy is unchanged' gave small satisfaction. At home the king's popularity increased with every sign of firmness.

With the election of Pius IX the excitement was redoubled. The election of the gentle priest, then bishop of Imola, to the papal throne as Pius IX was preceded by risings in Bologna, Calabria, and Rimini, which may have influenced him to make reforms. He began his reign with a political amnesty, an unheard-of concession, which at once endeared him to all Italy, and opened a vision to the eyes of the people of a liberal and reforming pope. For a time the reforms went on, commissions were appointed, railways planned, legal and judiciary improvements projected, and questions of social and economic reforms brought into review. There was tremendous enthusiasm and endless public demonstrations of loyalty. All this meant very little, but in the course of the first twelve months three important reforms were granted, freedom of the press, a *consulta*, and a civic guard. To obtain them an ingenious form of pressure was brought to bear. Approval was shown by organized demonstrations and cheers and vivas, disapproval by silent crowds interspersed by groans or cries of condemnation. Pius IX, vain and sensitive, was thus subjected to a constant war of nerves, and steadily pushed farther than he meant to go.

It was the last of these reforms, the civic guard, that brought Austria into the picture. Metternich did not worry over administrative measures, but putting arms in the hands of the people was dangerous and required a counter move. So, on the anniversary of the pope's election, a force of all arms was marched into the papal town of Ferrara. This provocative action roused a storm of protest, and united the liberals and the papalists in joint defence of Italian soil, and it quite failed to intimidate the Papacy. From now on the public demands rose steadily higher. Tuscany demanded a free press and a civic guard. Piedmont, the most undemonstrative state in Italy, broke out into crowds and vivas and papal rosettes. Genoa, always a radical city, took the lead with deputations to the king for reforms, and in October Charles Albert issued a long list of reformative measures including freedom of the press. This concession, as everywhere else in Italy, simply provided a mouthpiece for extreme demands for a constitution. It was the South that gave the final blow to the old order. Sicily broke into rebellion and drove out the Neapolitan garrison; the movement quickly spread to the mainland, and in January 1848 the king granted a constitution. Within a month Sardinia and Tuscany followed suit and, a little later, Rome.

THE RISING IN MILAN

All these movements were subsidiary to the great problem of driving Austria out of Italy. It was in Lombardy that action was first taken. Reports of reforms and constitutions elsewhere in Italy roused the Lombards. There were clashes between civilians and soldiers. In Milan the Austrian officers were boycotted at social functions, and the enthronement of a new archbishop, an Italian, gave the people an opportunity for a patriotic demonstration. For some time conspiracy had been afoot, arms were being smuggled across the border and plans made for a rising in the city. Austria had nearly 70,000 men in the two provinces and some 13,000 in and around Milan, and with such a force the city seemed secure enough. Then the third week in February Paris flared into insurrection, on the 24th Louis Philippe abdicated, and the provisional French Government proclaimed the Republic. The news spread like wildfire across Europe. Revolt broke out all over Germany, on 12 March Vienna rose, and the next day Metternich resigned and fled to England. News of the revolution at Vienna reached Milan on 17 March, and the next day began the famous 'Five Days' of struggle which ended on the 23rd with the withdrawal of the Austrian troops from the city. On the 19th Count Arese reached Turin from Milan with the first account of the fighting, but it was not until the 23rd that Charles Albert received a formal request for help from the provisional government. On the 26th the Sardinian army crossed the frontier in pursuit of the retreating Austrians and the first War of Independence began.

THE FIRST WAR OF INDEPENDENCE, 1848–9

The most optimistic Italian could hardly have devised a more propitious situation for driving the Austrians out of Italy than that of March 1848. Austria was in full revolution, Metternich was gone, and the Austrian army in Italy, scattered over two provinces, was no larger than that of Piedmont at full strength. When Marshal Radetzky withdrew from Milan he retired eastwards, and took up his position in the famous Quadrilateral,

Mantua-Peschiera-Verona-Legnago, one of the strongest positions in Europe.

By the end of April Charles Albert had won only minor successes, but was receiving reinforcements. Reserves from Piedmont were followed by 5000 Tuscan volunteers. A little later 7000 papal troops crossed the river Adige behind the Austrians and joined the Venetian troops at Vicenza. Early in May the first contingent of the Neapolitans (40,000 had been promised) arrived at Bologna under General Pepe. But on 15 May there was a counter-revolution at Naples. The king promptly recalled the troops from the north and suppressed the constitution. Half the 12,000 men at Bologna returned, but those that remained went with Pepe to Venice, and took part later in the siege. At the end of April the pope, in a private consistory, had announced the impossibility of declaring war on Austria. This was a bad blow to the national enthusiasm and was taken as separating the Papacy from the cause of Italy. In June and July the Austrians received reinforcements, and in spite of occasional moments of triumph the Piedmontese were finally defeated. On 7 August the king's army was back on its own soil. The War of Independence had been lost.

ARMISTICE AND DEFEAT

The Armistice of Salasco, which closed the fighting, was, however, only a pause in the struggle for freedom in Italy. English and French mediation, while it kept the Austrians out of Piedmont, did nothing to reconcile the country to its failure, and not only here, but in Tuscany and the States of the Church, the democratic spirit surged up for a renewal of the fight for freedom. 'The war of the kings is over; the war of the people begins' was Mazzini's summary of the situation. In Piedmont two moderate governments had to give way in turn to a democratic Cabinet under the Abbé Gioberti, amid a rising demand for a denunciation of the armistice. The army was reorganized on democratic lines, discipline was relaxed, quality was sacrificed to quantity and, with the introduction of politics among the rank and file, the old spirit of loyalty was sapped at the source.

Charles Albert was removed from his command of the army, and, after France had refused to provide a commander-in-chief, a Polish general—Chrzanowski—whose name nobody could pronounce and who spoke no Italian, was given the post of 'General-Major'.

When Gioberti became Premier, being a convinced federalist he tried to form a confederation with Tuscany and Rome, where a republic had been declared by a democratic Assembly and the pope expelled; but both were too jealous of Piedmontese ambitions. Then he thought of restoring order in Tuscany and strengthening the hands of the grand duke by means of Piedmontese troops. All this he did without consulting his Cabinet and this led to his fall. Accused of sending Italians to fight Italians, he resigned. With the disappearance of Gioberti the last chance of peace was removed. On 12 March the armistice was denounced and on the 21st hostilities began. It was all over in a week. In a fierce day's fighting before Novara, Charles Albert's army was completely beaten. That evening he abdicated in favour of his son, Victor Emmanuel, duke of Savoy, and passing unrecognized through the Austrian lines, made his way across France and Portugal to Oporto, where he died four months later.

THE REPUBLICS OF VENICE AND ROME
AND THEIR DEFENCE

Italy's effort had failed; Lombardy was in Austrian hands; Piedmont was crushed; Tuscany by the end of July was again in the hands of the grand duke. All that remained in arms was Venice amid her lagoons and the Roman Republic. The Venetians had secured an almost bloodless revolution in March 1848, without outside assistance. The Austrian military and civil governors had behaved in a more civilized fashion than Radetzky had done in Milan. They had meekly abandoned Venice where an independent republic—the Republic of St Mark—had been founded, with Daniele Manin, an Italo-Jewish lawyer, as president. Manin hoped that Italy would eventually be united as a republic, but his methods were moderate. He prevented the Mazzinians from gaining control of the Venetian revolution. When the revolutionary assembly which had been elected in Venice voted for union with the Piedmontese monarchy, Manin accepted the majority decision and advised other republicans to do likewise. One day, he hoped, a constituent assembly would be called for the whole of Italy, and there would then be opportunity for republicans to support their opinions in a constitutional manner. Ironically, the Venetian decision for union with Piedmont was reached only a week or two before Charles Albert's defeat, after which the independent Republic of St Mark was hastily restored.

After the defeat of Piedmont, Venice survived for many months in a state of siege. Food became desperately short, cholera broke out, and in the terrible summer of 1849 the Austrians started to bombard the city. The defence of the two republics of Venice and Rome forms the most admirable chapter in the history of the 1848 revolutions in Italy. The Roman Republic was ruled by a triumvirate whose dominant figure was Giuseppe Mazzini. For the first and only time in his life Mazzini was able to govern an Italian state. He proved that he was not simply a political visionary, but capable of running an administration in a surprisingly enlightened and tolerant spirit. Surrounded by bitter enemies inside and outside the city, Mazzini refused to muzzle the press or to imprison political opponents. The Roman revolution had been concerned as much with social aims as with nationalist, unifying ones. It had been more universal and classless in character than revolutions had been elsewhere in Italy.

Mazzini's government tried to help the more wretched of the pope's former subjects—the urban poor and the shepherds and peasants whose already low living standards had been declining in recent years. The tax on grain was abolished and other taxes were eased. Justice was made cheaper, and so available to the poor for the first time. The revolutionary assembly took over ecclesiastical houses and property, and distributed the land to the poorer farmers. In the towns unemployment was eased by a programme of public works, and in this context the need for the manufacture of arms could be utilized. Workers for the government and the men in the army were handsomely paid. Reductions in tariffs enabled an appreciable improvement in the general standard of living, but antagonized the middle class whose wealth had depended on economic protection. A forced loan further alienated the richer Romans from the regime. Politically the Republic was based on universal suffrage, and the assembly rather than the triumvirate was the sovereign body. It was unlikely that so radical a regime would be allowed to survive in the Europe of 1849.

Garibaldi, as commander of the forces of the Roman Republic, had at his disposal a little army of some 10,000—a hardly adequate force to resist the disapproval of all the Powers, and the active hostility of more than one of them. The restoration of the pope had now become a European question. Spain proposed a congress of Catholic Powers and sent an expeditionary force to Italy. Naples moved troops to her northern frontier, while Austria seized Bologna. But it was republican France under her president, Louis Napoleon, who claimed the right to crush a sister republic and replace the pope on his throne. In April, General Oudinot landed with 10,000 men and advanced on Rome, but his two divisions were both soundly beaten by Garibaldi and he was forced to retire and await reinforcements. On 3 June he advanced again, this time with 30,000 men, but even then it took him a month before the defence was finally broken. The French entered the city on 3 July. The day before Garibaldi and the remains of his small army had left Rome to retreat across Italy. His troops slowly disbanded, and he himself, after hairbreadth escapes, recrossed the Apennines and found safety in Tuscany. In August, after a heroic defence, Venice surrendered and once again all Italy lay at the feet of Austria.

Italy had failed in 1848 because of external causes: the ability of the government in Vienna to send reinforcements in the north and the decision of the Second French Republic to intervene. The only regular force available in Italy had been the Piedmontese army. All the other forces which fought Austria—

Tuscan, Papal, Venetian, Lombard and Neapolitan—had been inadequately armed and trained. The pope's change of heart and the counter-revolution in Naples had further weakened the Italian effort. The high hopes of March 1848 had come to nothing. Enthusiasm, intelligence and vision had proved no substitute for guns.

2. THE RISORGIMENTO, 1849–1861

When Italy took stock of her position there seemed but one thing saved out of the wreckage, the Constitution in Piedmont. This was the celebrated Statuto granted by Charles Albert. It included such elementary guarantees of liberty as security of person and property, equality before the law, parliamentary control over taxation, a free press, right of public meeting, and the formation of a citizen army or National Guard. A collection of constitutional maxims rather than a constitution, it supplied, nevertheless, a very fair basis on which to build up a free government. From it arose the Constitution of United Italy which remained in being until the advent of Fascism and of which the main organs were:

1. *The King.* A constitutional monarch, exercising supreme executive power but acting always on the advice of a responsible minister.

2. *Parliament composed of two Chambers:* (i) The Senate, consisting of men over the age of forty who had held high office or achieved distinction in any sphere, nominated by the king for life. Members of the royal family from the age of twenty-one were senators by right; (ii) The Chamber of Deputies elected every five years, or following a dissolution of Parliament by the king, by male citizens over the age of twenty-five and who were literate. Money bills could only originate in this Chamber. The consent of both Chambers and the royal assent was required for the passing of any bill into law.

3. A council of ministers consisting of the heads of the chief departments of government and a president or prime minister,

who might or might not hold another portfolio. All ministers were members of one or other Chamber of Parliament.

Despite the pressure brought to bear upon him at the moment of defeat, the young King Victor Emmanuel was loyal to his oath and the Constitution was preserved. The politically conscious middle class tended to look now to Piedmont for national leadership. Gioberti's federalism was forgotten and Mazzini's influence declined in the 1850s. The two Italian Republics had survived longer than Piedmont in the struggle against the foreigners in 1849, and it might have been expected that the Savoy monarchy would have been discredited. But the existence of constitutional government in Turin meant that positive leadership could be found only there. The initiative was to be siezed by Cavour in 1852 and retained by him until the early months of 1860. Conspiracy alone had proved insufficient. Cavour was often to play the game of revolutionary conspirator, and often less successfully than Mazzini, but his real role was that of the diplomat. In 1848 he had believed, like Charles Albert, that Italy should rely on her own efforts. But the events of 1848 and 1849 had shown him that the belief was no longer tenable. He now realized that the help of at least one of the Great Powers must be solicited. The history of Italy from 1852 to 1859 was to be more closely integrated with the history of Europe.

CAVOUR

By the 1848 Constitution the government of Piedmont was in theory responsible to the Lower Chamber. In practice, until 1852, nothing resembling a parliamentary regime existed in Turin. Governments did not always have majorities behind them in the Lower Chamber, and when they left office they did so for reasons having little to do with the wishes of the Chamber. The king had an unconstitutional influence, and Massimo d'Azeglio as prime minister avoided the rough-and-tumble of debate in the Lower Chamber, where the democrats were apt to get out of hand, and preferred the calmer atmosphere of the Senate. He found, fortunately, a very capable lieutenant in the young Count Camillo Cavour, who after a short ministerial career replaced him as premier in 1852. Cavour was then forty-two. A liberal from boyhood, his political creed was summed up in his phrase 'an honest *juste-milieu*', opposing, that is, the reactionaries on one side and the democrats on the other, and to this position he remained loyal for the ten remaining years of his life. He was a man of strong character, firm of will, clear-sighted, knowing his own mind and what he wanted, and generally how to get it. As a young man his liberal ideas had led to his resignation from the army. He had taken up farming, and by the application of machinery and modern methods made a handsome fortune out of the family estates. He was interested in finance, in banking, and in many industrial concerns. He had travelled extensively in France and England studying agriculture, social conditions, and especially political life, for he had been a student of European politics almost since his schooldays. He had met many of the leading men in France, and some in England. He was unusually well equipped for the post he now occupied. When the freedom of the press was granted, he became a journalist and was editor of *Il Risorgimento* when he first entered the Chamber of Deputies.

One of the remarkable qualities in Cavour was the early maturity of his policy. It may be said with some truth, that from the moment he entered the Cabinet as Minister for Commerce, generally considered the least important post, he took charge of the national policy. Friendship with England and France, especially the latter, was the keynote. To achieve this, he did not hesitate to sign a disadvantageous commercial treaty with France, and justify so doing by insisting that good relations with France were essential, even at the cost of some economic sacrifice. This was the first and least satisfactory of a series of treaties which practically committed the country to a policy of free trade. Then, as Minister of Finance, he floated a loan in England, paid off the Austrian indemnity, rescued the national finances from the grip of the House of Rothschild, and used the balance for the railway from Turin to Genoa. In the next three years the army was reorganized, important judicial changes carried out, and a stimulus given to industry, which set the country on the path of economic progress with an expanding trade and a diminishing adverse balance at the Treasury. No less remarkable was the development in parliamentary efficiency. Under Cavour the Chamber played its full role for the first time. Cavour was a great admirer of the English Constitution though he prevented the growth of a two-party system at Turin. Of the four groups which could be distinguished in the Chamber, Cavour united the two centre parties and the combination gave him a steady majority throughout his tenure of power. He abolished the rostrum and made members speak from their seats, which rapidly deflated the Italian love of oratory and turned the Chamber into a practical, businesslike body, much praised by the English minister at Turin.

Cavour had been in office only a year when he broke his first lance with Austria. A revolt organized by Mazzini broke out in Milan. Thereupon Austria sequestered the goods of the Milanese *émigrés,* many of whom were now Piedmontese subjects. Cavour protested, but received only angry replies from Vienna: the question was, however, well handled, for Cavour was prompt, firm, and dignified. He put Austria in the wrong and kept her there, and in the end Piedmont gained more than she lost. He drew up and circulated amongst the Powers a memorandum which put the illegality of Austria's action in full light. Thus the first step was taken to discredit Austria and win the moral support of Europe for Italy. Cavour's ultimate objective was war with Austria, in alliance with France and if possible England.

THE CRIMEAN WAR

When France and Britain went to war with Russia in 1854 it was at once apparent that the Italian Question would be affected in one way or another. Until quite recently historians have depicted Cavour as arranging, virtually single-handed, for the intervention of Piedmont, as part of a master-plan for the ultimate unification of Italy. But the truth is never quite so tidy as this. It is now clear that Britain and France first exerted pressure upon Piedmont to persuade her to send forces to the Crimea.

Cavour's achievement lay in the realization of the danger facing Piedmont. If Austria became an active ally of the Western Powers while Piedmont remained neutral and isolated, hopes for even the slightest improvement of the situation in Italy would have to be abandoned. Rather than face such a possibility Cavour accepted the idea of intervention, without a subsidy from Britain and with no guarantees for the future. Had he not done so, Cavour would have been dismissed by Victor Emmanuel, who had firmly decided on intervention, if necessary with a government of the Right. In the spring of 1855 some 18,000 Piedmontese troops left Italy for the Crimea. Cavour had had difficulty in winning the consent of Parliament and the country to the alliance. To the Piedmontese there was only one enemy to fight—Austria, and only one place to fight in—the Lombard plain. The idea of sending the flower of the army to die of cholera in the Crimea and to fight an enemy with whom they had no quarrel, appeared suicidal. But a minor victory went far to appease the public. The Piedmontese went into action at the Tchernaia and fought well, and La Marmora, who commanded them, became a national hero. Cavour knew how to make the most of the congratulations he received from his allies and a wave of pride swept over Italy. In 1856 the peacemakers met at the Congress of Paris. Cavour represented Piedmont. He had already established the myth that he alone had been responsible for intervention in the Crimea.

THE CONGRESS OF PARIS

Few statesmen have had a more difficult task. Not only was he the representative of a small and unimportant state, but he had set himself the problem of adding to the agenda of the Congress a most controversial subject that had nothing to do with the purpose for which the Congress was summoned. Regarding himself as the spokesman for Italy, he was determined to bring the Italian question to the forefront, and, if possible, to obtain a condemnation of Austrian policy in Italy. He wanted also to obtain some increase of territory, the Duchy of Parma, if possible. Cavour worked unceasingly, but he failed completely to get any additional territory. Every attempt was blocked by the veto of Austria. 'Austria will give way on nothing', Napoleon said to Cavour; 'she would go to war sooner than let you have Parma.' So Cavour concentrated on bringing up the Italian question. He had a strong case. After the collapse of Italy and the triumphant re-establishment of absolutism in Europe, the reaction of the restored rulers was brutal. Austrian troops kept order with the bayonet in Tuscany and the Papal States, occupying the Romagna and enforcing the reactionary policy of the Papacy, for there was no longer any taint of liberalism in Pius IX. Napoleon was disgusted at his refusal to make any adequate reforms, yet, for fear of throwing him completely into the arms of Austria, he was obliged to keep the pope on his throne by French bayonets. In Naples, Ferdinand filled the prisons with liberals of all classes. It was estimated that no less than 40,000 suffered for their political opinions. Gladstone, who was in Naples in 1851, studied the situation at first hand, and in his two famous letters to Lord Aberdeen stigmatized the government of Ferdinand as the very 'negation of God'.

It was not always easy during the Congress for Cavour to get information direct to Napoleon, but, foreseeing this, the emperor had, on his own initiative, arranged a private channel of communication, so that all Cavour's information reached him safely. Cavour's best ally was, however, the English representative, Lord Clarendon. As Cavour's information was put before him, his disgust and anger grew intense, and when at last the Italian question was brought forward, as a kind of supplementary problem upon which the French Emperor was anxious to have the opinion of the Congress, it was Lord Clarendon who spoke first. The vigour of his denunciation of both the papal government and that of Naples gave the conference a shock. 'He charged', wrote Cavour's secretary, 'like Lucan at Balaclava.' It was precisely what Cavour wanted. It put the Italian question before Europe with a vigour and an accuracy which could not be overlooked. The reaction of the delegates to Clarendon's indictment was what was to be expected. All were surprised that a subject so alien to the purpose of the Congress should be discussed at all. All disclaimed any instructions to deal with it. Cavour himself drove home the points of Lord Clarendon's speech, but with tact and moderation. No resolutions were made, and the Congress closed without further reference to Italy. When the Congress was over Cavour had confidential talks with both Clarendon and Napoleon and made it clear that in his opinion no solution of the Italian question was possible except by war with Austria. After a visit to London, which cooled his opinion as to English help against Austria, he returned to Piedmont, where he was received with gratitude and enthusiasm.

CAVOUR AND NAPOLEON III

On his return from Paris, Cavour was convinced in his own mind that Napoleon was set on war with Austria. Upon this his policy was henceforth based. Towards Austria he adopted a correct but stiff, defensive attitude, disregarding her susceptibilities, but giving no cause for open hostility. At the same time his domestic policy became Italian rather than Piedmontese. Large sums were voted for the fortifications of Alessandria, towards which, to Austria's intense annoyance, the Lombards opened a subscription to present 100 cannon. The naval base at Genoa was moved to Spezia, and more money was spent on the army. Piedmontese hospitality and assistance was offered to political refugees from other states in Italy, and a secret national propaganda was spread over Italy by the National Society with the motto 'Italy and Victor Emmanuel'. Strict order was kept in Piedmont and no encouragement was given to premature outbursts elsewhere in Italy. But Cavour had some awkward corners to turn, especially in January 1858, when Felice Orsini and two or three associates hurled three bombs at the French emperor and empress on their way to the opera. Bitter threats and recriminations followed, but once again the tact of Cavour and the courage and firmness of Victor Emmanuel weathered the storm. At last in July the results of Cavour's diplomacy, initiated two years before at Paris, began to appear, when an invitation reached him to meet the emperor privately at

Plombières. At this historic meeting of the two arch-conspirators in Europe, Napoleon laid all his cards upon the table. Austria was to be driven out of Italy and a new kingdom formed for Victor Emmanuel 'from the Alps to the Adriatic'. Prince Napoleon, the emperor's cousin, was to marry the king's daughter, and the price to be paid was Savoy and Nice for France. It was left to Cavour to find the *casus belli,* which must be such that France would be justified in coming to the help of Piedmont. In other words, Austria must be goaded into declaring war and thus become the aggressor.

Although there was as yet no treaty, and he was entirely dependent on Napoleon fulfilling his word, Cavour on his return at once began preparations for war. In the last year or two the Austrians had gone far to appease the population of Lombardy and Venetia. In the beginning of 1857 an amnesty had been offered for political prisoners. Statues had been raised: to Leonardo da Vinci in Milan and to Marco Polo in Venice. Radetzky, having reached the age of ninety-one, had been replaced as governor of Austria's Italian provinces by the liberal archduke, Maximilian, who was to become emperor of Mexico and to have his life cut short by a firing squad. Maximilian's record in Italy was a fine one. The education system in Lombardy was superior to that elsewhere in Italy, even though literary subjects were to some extent played down in favour of scientific and technical ones, presumably to discourage pride in the national past. The thaw in Austrian administrative methods in Lombardy made it all the more necessary for Cavour to act with speed. He was anxious that as far as possible the Piedmontese army should assume an Italian complexion, and with this end in view he began to recruit a volunteer force from all over Italy, for whom as a leader he destined Garibaldi. Though this irregular force was looked at askance by the Piedmontese generals and savoured far too much of the revolutionary element to be acceptable to Napoleon, Cavour valued it from the national standpoint, as giving an Italian rather than a purely Piedmontese aspect to the coming struggle. Napoleon on his side was busy clearing up points of difficulty in Europe.

Russia was friendly and could be relied on for a benevolent neutrality and a probable effective check on Prussian anti-French activity. England would be averse to war but was unlikely to intervene. Though suspicions and vague rumours began to circulate in the European chancelleries, the year 1858 closed with no more than uneasiness as to what lay behind. In January 1859 Prince Jerome Napoleon arrived at Turin (bringing with him the treaty of alliance) and was married to the king's eldest daughter, the Princess Clothilde. The marriage completed and the treaty signed, all thoughts turned to war. Cavour hoped for a loan from France, but it proved impossible; Italy, however, rose to the occasion and the 40 million lire he asked for were provided. As it was scarcely practicable to begin operations before the end of April, Europe had still three months in which to prevent war from materializing. The lead was taken by England, whose Foreign Secretary was indefatigable in his efforts for peace. Personally sympathetic to the Italian cause, Lord Malmesbury was afraid that war in north Italy might spread to the Balkans. He insisted that the settlement made at the Congress of Vienna could be altered only by negotiations between the Powers. Austria pretended to have great respect for the sanctity of the 1815 treaties, but she had already broken them herself by her annexation of Cracow. She put more trust in soldiers than diplomats, and poured troops steadily into Lombardy, to which Piedmont replied by calling up reservists.

The situation of Napoleon was even more difficult than that of Cavour, who, at least, had the country behind him, for the emperor was almost alone in his desire for war. His Foreign Secretary, Count Walewski, was pro-Austrian and did all he could to spoil Napoleon's plans. The stocks fell on the Bourse, the bankers could find no money, trade and business were all for peace. Even the army hesitated at a war with Austria. To gain time, Napoleon accepted a Russian proposal of a congress, which Cavour opposed and Austria ruined by stipulating impossible conditions for her acceptance. Then Lord Malmesbury proposed disarmament. Cavour accepted, provided Austria disarmed first. Austria, of course, refused. Napoleon would not consent to coerce Cavour. Every kind of pressure was brought to bear at Turin, but so long as he did not receive a collective note from the Powers, Cavour would not disarm. At last Napoleon gave in, and provided that Piedmont was admitted to the Congress, agreed to join England in a joint note for immediate Sardinian disarmament. Cavour had to yield, but the patience of Austria was by now exhausted, and, ignoring all efforts for peace, she dispatched an ultimatum to Turin giving Sardinia three days to choose between disarmament or war. The conditions of Plombières were fulfilled, Sardinia was attacked and the French alliance came into force.

THE SECOND WAR OF INDEPENDENCE, 1859

Upon Cavour's rejection of the Austrian ultimatum, Marshal Gyulai at once invaded Piedmont. The weather was atrocious and the whole countryside was under water. After advancing to within twenty miles of Turin, the Austrians retired, recrossed the Ticino, and remained inactive until 20 May. In the meantime the French army poured into Piedmont. Napoleon arrived at Genoa on 12 May, and soon after the general advance began. The whole campaign was comprised in two pitched battles, Magenta and Solferino, and the Peace of Villafranca which ended hostilities was signed exactly two months after Napoleon's arrival at Genoa. After the French victory at Magenta on 4 June, the Austrian satellite princes fled. The grand duke of Tuscany had already departed and the duchess of Parma and the duke of Modena both withdrew to safety. Cavour at once sent commissioners to hold the vacated states for Victor Emmanuel. When, a little later, Austria was forced to withdraw her garrisons from the Romagna and the populace demanded union with Piedmont, Cavour sent the Marquis d'Azeglio to Bologna as Royal Commissioner.

While all this was taking place the second and decisive battle was fought at Solferino. It was a repetition of Magenta, and the Austrians, beaten on the field, retired to the safety of the Quadrilateral, but were still capable of resistance. Napoleon was now faced with the same problem as Charles Albert in 1848, how to force the Quadrilateral, and the prospects of success were not very bright. His losses were serious, and reinforcements were not forthcoming. The failure of the commissariat, the intense heat, and the horror of the carnage, depressed and discouraged him. He was incensed at Cavour's prompt action in the duchies and the Romagna, and the little support received from the rest of Italy. Alarming news of the Prussians massing on the Rhine decided him to make peace. Without consulting Victor Emmanuel, he sent General Fleury to offer an armistice; then he told the king.

THE PEACE OF VILLAFRANCA

A few days later the two emperors met at Villafranca and drew up the terms of peace. Lombardy was surrendered to France, who would give it to Victor Emmanuel, but Venetia was to remain with Austria. Italy was to be a confederation under the Papacy. The princelings were to return, but no force was to be used for their restoration. A few days later Napoleon returned to France. The Peace of Villafranca was a bitter blow to Italy. Austria was not driven out, unity was replaced by federation, even the gain of Lombardy, with the fortresses in Austrian hands, was almost an illusion, and would only be held on sufferance. Cavour resigned, but not before he had sent orders to Florence, Bologna, and Parma to hold on and refuse to take back their old rulers. Two men saved the situation. At Florence, the Baron Bettino Ricasoli held Tuscany in a grip of iron; he refused to let the grand duke return and declared the grand duchy united to Piedmont. At Bologna, Luigi Carlo Farini became Dictator of Parma, Modena, and the Romagna, and did the same.

On leaving Turin Napoleon had said to the king, 'You will pay me the expenses of the war and we will say no more about Nice and Savoy.' He was now in a quandary. He had failed in his promise, had not driven out Austria, had exasperated the Italians by the peace treaty and brought France nothing but glory. He was pledged to an Italian federation which he could not implement, and to the return of the dispossessed princes which he could not enforce. What he really wanted was Nice and Savoy. As usual, he proposed a congress, but this suggestion was coldly received; he then dropped the idea of federation and hinted that he would be glad to take Savoy and Nice as payment for expenses. But La Marmora's government at Turin was too timid or too patriotic to entertain such an idea and things remained as they were. There was only one person bold and clever enough to solve the deadlock, Cavour, and in January 1860 he came back to power. Knowing that Napoleon owed his position to a plebiscite, and that he could not refuse to accept a verdict given on that basis, he ordered Farini and Ricasoli to hold plebiscites at once, and a similar vote was to be given in Nice and Savoy. The result was a foregone conclusion—Nice and Savoy voted themselves into France, Tuscany and Emilia into the Sardinian state. To regularize the vote, Cavour brought a bill into Parliament; this was little more than a matter of form since Napoleon had already seized his coveted prize. The debate provoked much bitter opposition, but created little excitement outside Parliament. The eyes of all Italy were looking south, for Garibaldi and the Thousand had sailed for Sicily.

GARIBALDI AND CAVOUR

The expedition of the Thousand illustrated all the divergencies in the Italian nationalist movement: the conviction felt by Mazzini and his more active disciples that Cavour was a traitor to the Italian cause, Cavour's own reluctance to help any movement of unification unless it could be accomplished under the Savoy monarchy, and Garibaldi's distrust of parliaments and diplomats. In 1860 the unification of Italy was to result from the conflict between Cavour and Garibaldi—to emerge sooner than Cavour intended and in a shape of which neither Garibaldi nor Mazzini could approve. But in the spring of 1860 Cavour had lost the initiative, and, like the rest of Europe, could do nothing but watch the amazing achievements of Garibaldi.

THE CONQUEST OF SICILY

Conspiracy and rebellion were endemic in Sicily. With their long tradition of independence and their hatred of the Neapolitans, there were always elements among the Sicilians ready for an outbreak. After Magenta there had been a popular movement, but the police were on the watch and it was easily stopped. Since then another effort was in course of development, organized by Mazzini's agent Nicola Fabrizi, and the stormy petrel of conspiracy, Francesco Crispi, one day to be premier of Italy. A Sicilian, La Farina, who was the secretary of the National Society, also had agents active in the island working for Italy and Victor Emmanuel. In April 1860 Sicily was again seething with rebellion, and though a rising at Palermo was quickly crushed, the whole countryside took up arms. When news reached Genoa, an appeal was at once made to Garibaldi to lead an expedition to help. Garibaldi hesitated. There was much conflict of evidence as to the real situation. There were over 20,000 troops in the island and the chance of success seemed remote. For a month the indecision continued, while the volunteers gathered at Genoa and arms and ammunition were collected, mainly from the National Society. At last on 5 May the 1100 volunteers, crowded on to two old merchant ships, sailed from Quarto, and six days later disembarked safely at Marsala on the western extremity of the island. The expedition had a narrow escape when landing, for two Neapolitan cruisers, arriving just too late to catch the two ships at sea, started to bombard the harbour, but the protests of the captains of two English vessels intimidated them and they withdrew.

The troops at once took the inland road which led north-east across the island to Palermo. At Salemi, the first town, Garibaldi proclaimed his dictatorship over the whole island in the name of Victor Emmanuel. Continuing his march, he found the road blocked at Calatafimi by a Neapolitan force double his own strength, strongly posted on the summit of a terraced hill. The fate of the whole expedition was at stake. In the intense heat of the afternoon the Garibaldians stormed the hill, terrace by terrace, relying more on bayonets than bullets. As the last terrace was rushed, the enemy, still greatly superior in numbers, broke and ran. Victory was won. By 18 May Garibaldi, at Renda, was within sight of Palermo, where he received news that the entrance from the west was defended by the bulk of the Neapolitan army 20,000 strong. He turned south and by a circuitous march through the mountains finally reached Gibilrossa, where La Masa joined him with 3000 Sicilians. He was now on the opposite side of Palermo, where he was least expected. On the 27th he seized the Porta Termini by a night attack and the struggle for the city commenced. The citizens rose against the garrison, erected barricades, and fought beside the Garibaldians, while the Governor Lanza bombarded the city by sea and land, causing more damage to buildings than loss to the enemy, until the English admiral, Mundy, induced him to ask for an armistice. Terms were arranged and the 12,000 Neapolitan troops were withdrawn from the city, leaving Garibaldi victorious.

THE CONQUEST OF NAPLES

With the surrender of Palermo Sicily was practically in Garibaldi's hands and political issues came to the fore. Cavour wanted immediate annexation to the new kingdom, but Garibaldi refused, and Francesco Crispi, his political adviser, became pro-dictator. Cavour then sent La Farina to urge annexation, but Garibaldi shipped him back promptly to Genoa. At this time Garibaldi was bitterly resentful over the surrender of Nice, his birthplace, to France, and it was almost sufficient for Cavour to make a proposal for Garibaldi to reject it. On 20 July came the final battle for Sicily at Milazzo, after which Garibaldi's intention was to cross the straits and conquer Naples. Reinforcements had now reached him and he had a relatively large force under his command. Garibaldi had no political sense, he completely ignored the international reactions to what he was doing and had no notion how much the unification of Italy must depend upon French friendship. It was his fixed determination not only to conquer Naples but to go on to Rome, turn out the French garrison, and proclaim Victor

Emmanuel king of Italy on the Campidoglio, and he made no secret of it. But Napoleon had never wanted Italian unity, and now urged upon England the division of Italy into two parts, north and south, and for this purpose proposed a joint patrol of the straits to prevent Garibaldi from crossing. The British Whig Government rejected the plan. On 18 August Garibaldi crossed to the mainland, welcomed on all sides, and his journey to Naples was a triumphant procession. On 6 September King Francis II fled, and the day following Garibaldi, miles in front of his army, entered the city amid wild enthusiasm.

The amazing rapidity and completeness of Garibaldi's success and his obstinacy in refusing to permit annexation until his work was finished by the seizure of Rome created a most awkward situation for Cavour. He had already fathered a conspiracy to drive Francis from Naples by means of an internal rebellion in Naples itself, in order to be in the city before Garibaldi got there, but it had been a complete failure. Now, the only alternatives appeared to be either an unexpected check to the dictator's success, by the effective resistance of the remains of the Neapolitan army on the Volturno, or the dispatch of the royal army through the Papal States to bar the road to Rome. It was a combination of the two that saved the situation. The battle of the Volturno, though a victory for Garibaldi, was sufficiently costly to ensure a long delay before the army was ready to advance once more, and this gave time to send the royal army south. The papal troops were beaten at Castelfidardo, and with Victor Emmanuel at its head the royal army advanced on Naples until, at Teano, king and dictator met and the unification of Italy was a fact. A few days later they drove together through Naples, and then, refusing all rewards, Garibaldi returned to his rocky home at Caprera.

THE DEATH OF CAVOUR

Cavour was now anxious to cover as quickly as possible the methods of revolution with the aegis of constituted authority, by calling together the first national Parliament of Italy and proclaiming Victor Emmanuel its king. The elections took place in

January 1861, and on 18 February Victor Emmanuel opened Parliament. The session was brief. A short bill legalized the position of the new king of Italy and all that now remained outside his sway was Venetia, still occupied by Austria, and the Patriarchate of St Peter, a narrow rectangular strip of territory running north and south of the city of Rome. The royal session over, Cavour plunged into the mass of problems confronting the new country, but above all stood the question of Rome. It was vital to try to find a *modus vivendi* between Italy and the Papacy, and Cavour believed that a solution was possible along the lines of his famous phrase 'a free church in a free state'. He offered in exchange for the surrender of the Temporal Power a spiritual liberty and a financial security such as the Papacy had never known in Italy. He hoped also to induce Napoleon to withdraw his garrison from Rome and remove the stigma of foreign bayonets from the new kingdom. But to the consternation of Italy, with scarcely a warning, Cavour collapsed and died the first week in June. While Cavour was still living, in a debate in the House of Commons, Lord Palmerston uttered these words: 'In regard to the Italian statesman who has so often been censured during this debate—Count Cavour—I limit myself to say that Italy, present and future, will regard him as one of the greatest patriots that have ever adorned the history of any nation. I know no country that owes so much to any of its sons, as Italy owes to him.' It was a worthy tribute.

The death of Cavour was a grievous loss to Italy. His great qualities as a statesman, his profound knowledge of European politics, his friendship with Napoleon, and his diplomatic abilities, were irreplaceable. But there was one aspect of his genius, seldom noticed, which would have been, perhaps, more valuable still, his gifts as a constitutional minister and as a great parliamentarian. For some years, until Italy was firmly on her feet, safety first must be her motto, and she was very unlikely to indulge in an adventurous policy. What Italy wanted above all was political education and organization to enable her new constitutional system to take root in the country. A democratic form of government was too often regarded as a self-acting panacea, which once installed required no further attention. That the country had to learn to work a parliamentary system was an idea which no one seemed to realize. In Cavour Italy had found a leader with not only a profound grasp of democratic principles and with ten years of experience in parliamentary procedure and practice, but one with a real gift for handling a difficult Chamber, who understood the party system, set a high standard of purity in public life, and realized that parliamentary life must be the true expression of the will of the people. Had he lived, he might have trained Italy as he had trained Piedmont, and made democracy a success; as it was, after fifty years of endeavour, democracy failed, and was replaced by Fascism, and election from below gave place once more to nomination and selection from above.

3. UNITED ITALY, 1861–1870

THE NEW STATE

The Piedmontese Constitution had been extended to Italy with the minimum of revision. One of its weak points was the narrow franchise. Illiterates were debarred from voting. This had not been so great a drawback in Piedmont, where the standard of literacy was relatively high, but when extended to the Papal States and the South less than three per cent of the population had a vote. On top of this came the papal *non expedit,* that Catholics must be neither electors nor elected. Adding to this the inevitable percentage of those who through ignorance or negligence never voted, the 443 members were actually elected by some 300,000 voters out of 20,000,000, or less than 700 per seat. The great majority of the nation had no direct political interest at all, and the electors were little more than a clique in each constituency. Another difficulty was that Parliament met at Turin. The expense and inconvenience this caused to the members from Sicily and Naples, in a country with inadequate railways, must have been excessive. Inevitably, contact between members and constituents was possible only at long intervals, which tended still further to lessen the national interest in the new form of government.

When the first national Parliament met, the majority

Fig. 15. The unification of Italy

belonged to the Right. The core of this was the solid block of Piedmontese, around which gathered adherents from every part of Italy. For fifteen years the electorate unfailingly returned this party, although during that period there were thirteen different ministries and eight different premiers. Six were Piedmontese, one a Tuscan, and one from the Papal States. It seemed as if the electors were determined, in spite of the differences and quarrels within the party, that Italy should be settled on the Cavourian tradition, and that the influence of the south should not be allowed to predominate, until the basis of the new parliamentary system was firmly laid. 'The Left' consisted of a group of ex-republicans, Mazzinians mainly, and an amorphous collection of Garibaldians of all shades, from whom was collected the Party of Action, bent upon the recovery of Rome and Venetia as quickly as possible, and by irregular means if necessary. In the last months of his life Cavour had enunciated certain principles which he believed should guide the national policy. The first of these was that Rome must be the capital of the kingdom and the seat of government, but its acquisition must come either by consent or negotiation, not by force. For Venice, he said, Italy must wait. It would be some years before the army and navy would be fit to challenge Austria and until then they must have patience. Friendship with France and the emperor was likewise a principle of his policy, both from a sense of gratitude and from the more practical standpoint as an offset to Austrian provocation.

For two years there was no trouble and the Government went ahead with the great work of reorganization. The administrative question was settled by the creation of fifty-nine provinces, each under a prefect, on the model of France. Piedmontese civil and penal codes of law were introduced elsewhere, except that Tuscany was for the time being permitted to retain her own penal code, which was in some respects more enlightened than the Piedmontese model. In Tuscany the death sentence had been abolished for all crimes, and it would clearly have been repugnant to the civilized Florentines to have it reintroduced. The educational system was also standardized under the state. Roads were built. The secret police disappeared, the press was free, and the internal customs barriers were abolished. The reorganization of the army and navy was taken in hand and a uniform system of weights and measures and coinage was devised. But over all forms of progress hung the spectre of financial instability—unity had been very costly. The debts of seven separate states had to be taken over and the result was an appalling deficit. In Quintino Sella, Italy found a Finance Minister who was ruthless in taxation and cut down expenditure wherever possible, but it was only after fifteen years of effort that a balance of expenditure and receipts was obtained, and then it was only momentary. The situation, difficult as it was, was rendered worse by the condition of Naples, where brigandage had assumed the proportions of a semi-religious guerrilla war. At the time of Garibaldi's conquest of Naples, Cavour had desired to keep the Neapolitan army intact, transport it to the north, and use it to strengthen the depleted forces in Lombardy. But Garibaldi had disbanded the soldiers who had surrendered to him, and many now joined the brigands in preference to rejoining the army. It took five years of bitter conflict and a ruthless application of the severest penalties, employing an army of regulars and Garibaldini, before brigandage was crushed. A few disappointed Garibaldini themselves joined the guerrillas.

With all these pressing tasks on hand the Government had neither time nor thought for the organization of political parties. The national tendency was for the deputies to group themselves on a regional basis, as Piedmontese, Tuscans, and Neapolitans, though this regionalism was later complicated by groups who followed individual leaders. The absence of party discipline on broad lines inevitably led to the recurrence of the old inter-state jealousies. In the Chamber of Deputies this appeared in the outcry against 'Piedmontism'. A movement was initiated in the press to advocate the removal of the capital elsewhere. This attitude caused much bitterness and threatened to break up that sense of national identity upon which so much depended.

THE ROMAN QUESTION

In the meanwhile the Government, by the pressure of widespread agitation, was being forced to try to find some solution of the problem of Venice and Rome. Cavour, towards the end of

1860, had opened negotiations with Rome, but after a promising beginning the Vatican had abruptly broken them off, exiling Cavour's intermediary. Ricasoli, Cavour's successor, tried to reopen them, but was also rebuffed, and after nine months of office he resigned. Nor would Napoleon negotiate the withdrawal of the French troops from Rome. The king then chose as premier the lawyer, Urbano Rattazzi. His advent at once put heart into Garibaldi, who once said 'one can always do something with Rattazzi', and he began without delay to plan an incursion into Venetia. But the Austrian Government and army was a very different proposition from that of Naples, and on a hint from Vienna, Rattazzi, who had shut his eyes to what Garibaldi was doing, suddenly sent police and troops, broke up the bands collecting at Sarnico, and sent him back to his island of Caprera. Suddenly in 1862 Garibaldi reappeared at Palermo, and, as the honoured guest of the governor, began to make speeches and rouse enthusiasm for an expedition to seize Rome. Volunteers flocked as usual to his standard, assured that there was some secret understanding between Garibaldi and the Government. This time warning came from Napoleon, and again orders were given to stop the movement. But the admiral at Palermo looked the other way, and Garibaldi, with some thousands of ill-equipped troops, landed in Calabria and set out to march for Rome. On the Aspromonte near Reggio they were surrounded by the royal troops, and in the ensuing exchange of shots Garibaldi was wounded in the heel and taken prisoner, but eventually set free. The wounding of the national hero was felt as a bitter humiliation, and the Rattazzi Ministry resigned.

Unknown to his ministers, Victor Emmanuel was already following a secret policy of his own, and was in touch with both Mazzini and Garibaldi. Mazzini, who was planning an internal rising in Venetia to be followed by its occupation by the royal troops, was far too impatient and resented the king's constant insistence that they must wait until the army was reorganized. No less actively than Mazzini, Garibaldi was enrolling recruits and collecting arms, but kept absolute silence regarding his objective. This appears to have been an intrigue in Galicia, in which his collaborators were Polish and Hungarian agents acting with the knowledge of Victor Emmanuel. The ultimate purpose was the seizure of Venetia whilst Austria was occupied with a Hungarian and Galician revolt. Rumours of what was being prepared reached the party of action (p. 159), which strongly disapproved of a movement that separated Garibaldi from Italy and was concerted without its sanction and co-operation. In July 1864 the party published a disclaimer in the columns of *Il Diritto,* condemning the proposed expedition and dissociating themselves from a movement 'ordered by princes and which must serve their interests rather than those of the people'. The exposure of Garibaldi's secret mission offended both Garibaldi and the king, but it achieved its object, and the idea was abandoned. Urged on by these revelations of un-authorized royal political activity, the Cabinet, in great secrecy, made a convention with Napoleon, and in September an official notice announced that France had agreed to withdraw her troops from Rome within two years, Italy guaranteeing the papal territory from any attack from without, while in a protocol the Government pledged themselves to move the capital from Turin to Florence. No reason was given for this, perhaps on purpose, for it enabled the Italians to claim the transfer as a half-way house to Rome, and the French to interpret it as the definite surrender by Italy of Rome as the capital.

The Convention of September, as it was called, had little to commend it. It improved relations with France for a time and satisfied to some extent the national dignity, but it exasperated the Piedmontese and angered the Roman authorities, who well knew what to expect once the French garrison was recalled. Three months after the signing of the Convention the pope issued an Encyclical, accompanied by a 'syllabus of modern errors'. It had been some years in preparation and it was only by chance that it appeared so close to the Convention of September, but it was so apt that it seemed to be the papal reply to the threat to Rome. It was an uncompromising restatement of the claims of the Papacy, and a violent onslaught on the principles of secular government. Politically it was a shrewd blow, for it was aimed directly at the liberal Catholic movement, which, in Italy, was anxious for compromise with the State in order to find a *modus vivendi* between the secular and spiritual powers. This refusal of the Church to come to any accommodation with the State was never relaxed, and not until the Constitution was swept away by Fascism did Rome come to terms with the civil power. The syllabus exasperated still further all those in Italy who demanded Rome as the capital, and convinced them that all negotiation was futile and that the Vatican would yield only to force, and, in the event, they were right.

THE THIRD WAR WITH AUSTRIA

In 1864 Austria had been inveigled by Bismarck into a joint seizure of Schleswig-Holstein from Denmark, but the allies soon quarrelled and were likely to fight. If Italy allied herself with Prussia in order to get Venetia, Austria would be faced with a war on two fronts and a divided army. If Italy made a bargain with Austria, Prussia would have to meet the undivided strength of the Austrian army. Never, perhaps, was the genius of Cavour so missed as in the ensuing negotiations. The premier, La Marmora, was an honest soldier but no diplomat. In August 1865 the Prussian Minister at Florence raised the question, What would the attitude of Italy be, if Prussia declared war on Austria? La Marmora's reply was cautious. Napoleon must be consulted. The reply from Paris was to the effect that the emperor was favourable to Italy's acquisition of Venetia, but that if alliance was contracted with Prussia, Italy would make war on Austria on her own responsibility and without help from France. Bismarck, however, by a personal visit to Napoleon at Biarritz secured French neutrality and a free hand with regard to Italy. General Govone was then sent to Berlin with instructions that, if Prussia was prepared to sign an offensive and defensive alliance, Italy would do the same, but that, otherwise, Italy would not pledge herself. Bismarck cared little for the fate of Venetia and was not prepared to fight Austria in defence of Italy. All he wanted was that the Italian army should immobilize as large a proportion as possible of the Austrian forces.

In the end Bismarck gained his object. On 27 March La Marmora received the terms of the proposed alliance. Italy was to declare war immediately after hostilities commenced between Prussia and Austria. There was to be no separate armistice or peace. Italy was to get Venetia, and Prussia territory equivalent in population. The Italian fleet was to go to the Baltic if the Austrians sent theirs from the Adriatic. Full powers were then sent to General Govone, and the treaty was signed on 8 April. As Austria realized the double threat, she made one last effort to detach Italy. It came through Paris, and was an offer to cede Venetia to France and then to Italy. It was a sore temptation, but La Marmora kept his word to Prussia, and refused. England, France and Russia now intervened with the well-worn specific of a congress, but, as in 1859, it was wrecked by Austria, who would accept only on absurd conditions. On 16 June war was declared between Prussia and Austria and by Italy four days later.

Of the campaigns fought by Italy for her independence, the last was the least costly and the most humiliating. In 1866 she was beaten not by a superior force after a brave struggle, nor in a single disastrous battle, but through sheer incompetence of the high command, and defective intelligence and staff work, by an army half the size of her own, largely because she was unable to bring her full strength into the fighting line. The Battle of Custozza, fought on 24 June, was an indecisive one, but resulted in an Italian withdrawal.

News of an Italian setback spread quickly across Europe, but its effect was neutralized when the Prussian victory of Sadowa was known. Even before this, Napoleon, regardless of Italian feelings of national honour, had telegraphed suggesting an immediate armistice, as the emperor of Austria had offered to cede Venetia to France, to be retroceded to Italy. The next day came news of the Prussian victory. Napoleon had expected the war to be long and end in an Austrian victory. As it was, it was amazingly short and Prussia was the winner. His policy was now to prepare the ground for a Franco-Austrian alliance against the victor. But Italy was indignant at the idea of receiving Venetia at second hand and under the shadow of defeat.

Ricasoli, who had succeeded La Marmora as premier, urged immediate action by land and sea. It was decided to invade Venetia, and to attack the Austrian fleet. But the naval phase of the war was no more successful for Italy than the land phase had been. In the Battle of Lissa an Austrian fleet defeated an equally large, more modern and better armed Italian fleet.

THE CESSION OF VENETIA

A few days after the battle of Lissa, Bismarck signed the preliminaries of peace with Austria at Nikolsburg. He did this without consulting Italy, disregarding the terms of the alliance. No sooner was the armistice signed than Austria rushed all available troops to Trieste and the Isonzo, and Italy found herself faced by an army of 300,000. Unable to carry on the war alone, she negotiated, but neither Bismarck nor Napoleon would support her claims to the Tyrol or the Trentino, and she had to be content with Venetia and to leave the strategic boundary which she coveted in the hands of Austria. In October peace was signed. Although Italy had at last gained Venetia, she could not but feel humiliated over her part in the war and the manner in which her spoils were won. She had been beaten both by land and sea, and also diplomatically. She had had to bend to the will of Bismarck and Napoleon, and accept Venetia at second hand. The incompetence revealed in the high command of both services was a cruel disillusion after the great expectations of victory which the country had cherished.

THE ROMAN QUESTION, 1867–70

After a brief period of excitement over the return of Venice, the country turned back once more to wrestle with its chronic internal troubles. All thoughts were now focused on Rome. France had fulfilled the terms of the Convention of September in the letter, but not in the spirit. She had withdrawn her garrison from Rome, but at once had permitted the enlistment of regular officers and men for service under the pope in a new force known as the Legion of Antibes. This, together with the papal troops and some half-disciplined regiments of ex-brigands, made up the army of 10,000 men which the Papacy was entitled to enrol. At the same time the Italian Government announced its firm intention to keep its word and to prevent all attacks on papal territory, but had soon to admit that, after the drastic reduction in the army, which for financial reasons was carried out after the war, it was practically impossible to patrol the whole boundary.

As to how Rome could be won, the country was divided. The Government and the majority of the Right held still to the Cavourian tradition that Rome must come to Italy not by force but by 'moral means', and in spite of past experience, kept their belief that the Papacy would respond in the end. The party of action, the Garibaldini and the Left generally, believed that Rome would yield to nothing but force, and agitated for action. To assist negotiations Ricasoli proposed a Free Church Bill. The Bill was based on concessions, and the feeling against it was so hostile that Ricasoli decided upon a general election before introducing it. The election was fought with great bitterness. Garibaldi was enlisted to speak against the Bill, and toured the country denouncing priests and pope with his usual vehemence. The new Chamber proved adverse, and Ricasoli resigned. The king now recalled Rattazzi. This last premiership of Rattazzi, which lasted only six months, was accompanied, as both his previous tenures of power, by an orgy of intrigue followed by a national humiliation. His majority in the Chamber was comprised of a scratch collection of votes from various parties on both sides, Left and Right, which made a consistent policy impossible. He did his best to persuade Napoleon to give Italy a free hand if the Papal States were invaded, and at the same time he blew hot and cold on the volunteers and Garibaldini gathering on the boundary for invasion. To Napoleon the Roman question was a nightmare. He would gladly have got rid of it, but he was in the hands of the uncompromising clericals.

GARIBALDI AND MENTANA

In the meantime Garibaldi, Mazzini, and the party of action were rousing the country to fever heat. The attitude of the king was doubtful, and the old republican party was raising its head.

Rattazzi was faced with a terrible decision. To throw himself into the arms of Garibaldi meant a breach with France and perhaps war: to use force against him might mean a revolution. In September the preparations for an attack on Rome were so obvious that Napoleon threatened to embark troops at once, and to save the situation Garibaldi was tactfully arrested and deposited once more at Caprera, with half a dozen warships to prevent his escape. A few weeks later he was back in Italy in spite of all precautions. Raids into the Papal States had already begun. The regular troops sent to watch the frontier fraternized with the volunteers and looked the other way. Feeble attempts at insurrection in Rome itself were crushed by the police. Garibaldi put himself at the head of the movement, while Napoleon embarked a division for papal support. Garibaldi seized Monte Rotondo, but had to retire on Tivoli. At Mentana the French and papal troops intercepted him, and after a brave resistance Garibaldi was well beaten, and what was left of his force recrossed the frontier.

INTERNAL DIFFICULTIES

The exasperation in Italy after Mentana was intense. Napoleon's action was bitterly resented and the tactless remark of the French general that the 'chassepots (the new French rifle) had done wonders' made things still worse. Internally, Italy was sinking into the very slough of despond under the crushing burden of taxation, and the revelations of political ineptitude and financial jobbery. A tobacco scandal, in which it was said that ministers and even the Royal House were implicated, reduced the country almost to despair. The two years that separated Mentana from the Franco-Prussian War were a most dangerous period for Italy. The monarchy was discredited, and republicanism, under the stimulus of Mazzini, seemed to be taking hold in the country, penetrating even into the army. Poverty, cholera, and bad harvests added their quota to the discontent, until it seemed that the very basis of the new kingdom was giving way. But Italy struggled on and despite all her troubles she never took her eyes from Rome.

Since the death of Cavour the relations of Church and State had grown steadily worse. The suppression of monasteries and nunneries hardened the Papacy in the assertion of its spiritual claims and intensified its bitterness at the forcible seizure of its temporal heritage. Moreover, recalcitrant priests and even bishops had been flung into prison and insulted. Accordingly, while France supported him the pope would not yield. Nor was the spiritual armoury of the Papacy yet exhausted, and so after Mentana came the Doctrine of Papal Infallibility. It was not new, but in conjunction with the syllabus, it had a dangerous significance, for it meant that opposition to modern civilization might become binding on all Catholics, and the papal claim to be supreme over temporal sovereigns develop into an article of faith. But the proclamation of the dogma had an unexpected result. It revealed Rome as the enemy of every Catholic Government, and thereby helped to reconcile Europe to the occupation of Rome by Italian forces.

THE OCCUPATION OF ROME

The Franco-Prussian War had long been regarded as inevitable and more than one approach to both Austria and Italy had been made by Napoleon for an alliance, but neither Power would commit themselves. When at last it was seen to be unavoidable the emperor appealed directly to Italy. Victor Emmanuel, out of gratitude for the past, would have willingly gone to the help of France, but the condition of the army and the state of the finances made it impossible, and Italy stood aside from the struggle. The French troops in Rome were soon recalled, and with the disaster of Sedan, the fall of the emperor and the proclamation of the Third Republic, all obligations to France ceased and Italy at last had a free hand. A final demand was made to Rome, but the Vatican would yield to nothing but force, so force was applied. The army marched on Rome, breached the walls, and entered the city. Only then did the pope submit, requesting that the Leonine city should be occupied by the Italian troops and the pope safeguarded from possible outrage. Many streets throughout Italy are named 'Venti Settembre'

(20 September); this was the date of the entry into Rome in 1870.

A plebiscite, overwhelmingly in favour of union with Italy, was taken in October, and after half a century of effort Italy's unity was achieved. All that there remained to do was to define the relations of Church and State and clarify the position of the Papacy. This was accomplished by what is known as the Law of Guarantees. By this the Papacy was left in possession of the Vatican, the church of St John Lateran (the mother church of Christendom), and the summer residence of Castel Gandolfo. The pope was confirmed in his rights and prerogatives of sovereignty, his person declared inviolable, and an annual grant (£129,000) put aside for his maintenance. He had his own postal and telegraph service and correspondence with the ecclesiastical and Catholic world was free. But the State retained the power of the purse and a right of veto over the temporalities of Italian sees and benefices and of inspection over seminaries. The clergy became subject to the civil law of the nation. The pope in reply refused to accept the government subsidy, launched the greater excommunication against all who had taken part in the fall of the temporal power, and declared himself 'the prisoner of the Vatican'. For fifty years no pope passed outside its walls.

The transfer of the Italian seat of government to Rome commenced before the close of the year. In December the Chamber of Deputies opened a new session in the palace of Montecitorio. In May the Law of Guarantees was published and a few weeks later the king took up his permanent residence in the palace of the Quirinal. The Law of Guarantees did not close the breach, as hoped, between the State and the Church. It was a unilateral settlement carried through by the Government without consultation with or the co-operation of the Church, and the Vatican ignored it. But the two powers had to live together and though outwardly the *dissidio* remained as acute as ever, a *modus vivendi* was gradually reached. Behind the scenes many points of differences were amicably arranged but without prejudice on either side, so that the fundamental problem of the juridical position of the Vatican and the delimitation of the exact spheres of action and influence of both Church and State remained unsolved until the Lateran Agreements of 1929.

The year 1870 was a watershed in the history of the Papacy in the spiritual sense as well as the temporal. In the first half of the year a General Council of the Church had met in the Vatican, and proclaimed the dogma of papal infallibility. All the pope's *ex cathedra* utterances were henceforth to be considered as divinely revealed and beyond the power of any subsequent Council to reject or modify. A few liberal Catholic scholars were antagonized by the dogma. The breach between the Church and the secular world of liberal reformism, the world of which the young Kingdom of Italy was a part, now seemed complete.

CHAPTER VII

MODERN ITALY

1. THE RULE OF THE RADICALS, 1870–1915

WITH the signing of the Law of Guarantees and the settlement of Italy, the work of the Right was accomplished. They still remained in office until 1876, carried foward by the momentum of fifteen years of continuous government, but their power was exhausted. They had unified Italy, made Rome the capital, defined the relations of Church and State, and, broadly speaking, kept alive the two-party system. Their leaders had set a fine example of purity in public life and maintained the Piedmontese tradition. They had been nurtured on that lofty idealism which had lifted the earlier struggles of Italy on to so high a level, and given it that element of romance and poetry which won the admiration of all lovers of adventure and high endeavour. Where they failed was in a certain narrowness and rigidity, and economically in their inability to compensate for heavy taxation by any stimulation of trade, or to satisfy the many social needs of the newly created nation.

NEW-STYLE POLITICS

The men of the Left who now came to power were of smaller calibre. Followers of Mazzini, ardent Garibaldians, many of them southerners, they had been nourished on plots and conspiracies, fighting more often against than with constituted government. Unlike their predecessors, they were not so much liberals as democrats, with a wider and vaguer conception of liberty, more prone to overlook popular excesses, and with a more decided anti-clerical spirit. Many of them, only too familiar with the corruption rampant in the south, carried into parliament a lack of scruple and a readiness to let the end justify the means, which boded ill for the future of public life. They quickly revealed a tendency to split into factions, to work for their own ends in little groups, and to ignore the value of party discipline; unfortunately, none of the three men who dominated parliamentary life in Italy for the next thirty years, Depretis, Crispi, and Giovanni Giolitti, made any effort to establish real party government, preferring to secure support by manipulation of groups and sections, with the inevitable sequel of favours and rewards. The advent of the Left to power was the first real test of Italian parliamentary life. If they had proved a homogeneous body with a clear-cut and definite programme, with the defeated Right as an effective opposition, the new form of government might have been firmly established. But the Left inherited no such tradition, and Agostino Depretis, who remained premier, with short interludes, from 1876 to 1887, effectively destroyed the party system.

DEPRETIS AND 'TRASFORMISMO'

The name of Depretis will always be associated with his political system known as 'trasformismo'. When he came to power he found a Chamber already splitting into groups. The old Right had disintegrated, the new Left was amorphous. There were two methods of assuring a majority, either to reconstitute the old parties and discipline them, so that members would vote for and with the party, no matter what their individual opinion might be of any particular bill, as in the English system, or to adopt the simple method of making it worth while for a sufficient number of members to vote with the Government. The second method was adopted by Depretis. In some way discipline must be established. A Chamber of 500 members with each voting according to his private judgment on every bill, would make it impossible for any government to carry through a programme. Depretis covered his scheme with the specious argument that its purpose was to get the best men from all parties in the Ministry. In practice, it meant that as soon as a member or a group became dangerous to the passage of a government measure, or made themselves sufficiently objectionable, they were bribed. Sometimes the leader of a group was offered a seat in the Cabinet, a government post, or it might be inside information of financial value, or a decoration. Sometimes the end could be obtained by promising a school or a railway station to a member's constituency. The methods varied, but the end was the same. Once when Depretis proposed a most unpopular tax on sugar everyone expected that it would be thrown out, but it passed with the greatest ease. The mystery was solved when a few days later the official *Gazette* published a list of no less than sixty members, who had voted for the Bill, given the rank of Commendatore. This system was never abolished, and its results were manifold. It accounts for the constant changes in the ministries, and for the steady loss of interest in Parliament throughout the country. A constituency could never be sure that its member would not vote contrary to his electoral policy, and the interest of members in their constituencies, when once elected, was apt to wane. The system entailed an enormous amount of lobbying and manipulation, in which Depretis was an expert, but it ruined party government.

The Italy of 1876 was a rapidly changing country. The old order was passing and a new generation was coming to manhood, which had never known what it was, in Giusti's bitter phrase, 'to taste Austria in their bread'. Mazzini died in 1872, and the same year saw the passing of Manzoni, the most famous of Italian writers. Rattazzi and Napoleon III died in 1873, and Garibaldi, now old and crippled, took no further part in public life. A few years later Victor Emmanuel and Pius IX were dead. The new Italy was looking forward, not back, and before long, new forces would be in action, new ties would be formed, and fresh influences would be moving the national thought. The new premier, Depretis, signalled his advent to power by a general election, to confirm his party's position and to assure, and, if possible to increase, his majority. The control of a general election in Italy was not, as in England, in the hands of party organizations, who chose candidates and organized voters, apart from all government interference, but was managed by the Minister for Internal Affairs, that is, the Home Secretary. The division of the country into provinces, each under a prefect and a sub-prefect, with syndics or mayors in all the towns and larger villages, all of whom were government officials, put an enormous power in the hands of the Minister concerned. This, in 1876, was Nicotera, a violent man, who had been wounded in 1857 in a revolutionary expedition against Naples and had subsequently spent three years in a Bourbon prison. Inured to extra-legal methods, he had no scruple at all about using government influence, and the result was a shameless exhibition of official pressure. By threats of dismissal and promises of favours, by orders and injunctions, or even the removal of recalcitrant officials, he achieved a resounding success, and four-fifths of the 500 members of the new Parliament professed loyalty to the Government. When Parliament met it was soon obvious that, despite its many electoral promises, the Government had no programme of its own, but had adopted the measures left unpassed by the preceding Chamber. This at once caused endless confusion; the government measures were supported by the opposition, and opposed by its own stalwarts. As an inevitable result, the majority quickly split up into groups and sections and the passage of bills became a matter of manipulation.

FRANCE AND TUNISIA

Very shortly after the accession of King Humbert in 1878, the retirement of Crispi, who had succeeded Nicotera as Minister for Internal Affairs, brought about the fall of the Government. The new premier was Benedetto Cairoli, a name very dear to Italy, for he was the one survivor of five brothers, all the rest of whom had given their lives for Italy under Garibaldi. It was the year of the Congress of Berlin, called to settle the affairs of Europe after the Russo-Turkish War, and marked Italy's first appearance as a great Power in the concert of Europe. Her debut was unfortunate. Count Corti, the Foreign Minister, who represented Italy, was neither a clever diplomat nor a persuasive speaker. His efforts to induce Europe to restore the Trentino to Italy were politely ignored, and Italy got nothing. With Bismarck acting as 'honest broker', England came back with 'peace with honour' in Disraeli's phrase, but also, with Cyprus. Austria occupied Bosnia and Herzogovina, while

France got permission to regard Tunis as her 'sphere of influence'. Italy was angry at Cairoli's failure. Tunisia was already an Italian interest and at this time Italian immigrants formed the only large body of European colonists. Cairoli's ministry fell some weeks later.

Worse happened in 1881. Assured, after the Congress of Berlin, that there would be no serious opposition to her further intervention in north Africa, France had been waiting for a suitable excuse for extending her hold over Tunis. She found it in the real or pretended depredations of some native tribes. At once troops were dispatched, the principal places occupied, and by the Treaty of Bardo (1881) signed with the bey, Tunis was proclaimed a French protectorate. Public opinion in Italy was exasperated, and on both sides of the French frontier there were incidents which increased the growing bitterness between the two countries.

THE TRIPLE ALLIANCE

Bismarck's policy after the defeat of France in 1870 had been to assure peace in Europe, and to guard Germany from any attempt at revenge on the part of France by an alliance of the three emperors of Germany, Austro-Hungary and Russia. There had followed an exchange of royal visits and the preliminaries of discussion. But the Czar Alexander did not approve; such a combination would not only upset the European balance of power, but might easily lead to an enforced neutrality on the part of Austria and Russia, while Germany again attacked France in a 'preventive' war, before she had fully recovered her strength. Never quite able to trust Russia, Bismarck turned to Italy. Between Italy and Germany there was little difficulty, but to bring together Italy and Austria was no easy matter. The difficulty was Italy's 'irredentist' aspirations in the Tyrol and the Trentino where a large Italian population with a German-speaking minority was in Austrian hands. But Bismarck persevered, and in 1881 King Humbert and Queen Margherita visited Vienna and were very well received. After that there was little trouble, and in May 1882 the Triple Alliance was signed.

It could be interpreted as a wise move on Italy's part, for it guaranteed her against attack from either France or Austria and committed her to little. It could equally be interpreted as an attempt to bolster up the Italian monarchy by an alliance with the monarchies of central Europe against republican France. It lasted until the war of 1914–18, being several times renewed after 1882.

THE GROWTH OF VIOLENCE, 1887–97

When Depretis died in 1887 he left the country in a most unsatisfactory state. In addition to the general depression and disappointment arising from the defeats of 1866, and the inglorious manner in which Rome had been acquired, there was the failure at Berlin and the disappointment over Tunisia. A more disturbing symptom of the social *malaise* was, however, the recrudescence of violence. The first wave of revolutionary Socialist doctrines, emanating from the Russian anarchist Bakunin, was already gaining sections of Italian thought, and unchecked propaganda soon gave way to action. The attempted assassination of King Humbert at Naples, as he drove through the city with the queen and Cairoli, was a terrible shock to Italy. It was the first time in the eight centuries during which the house of Savoy had ruled in Italy that such an attempt had been made, and provoked from the queen the bitter words 'the poetry of the House of Savoy has been destroyed'. At Pesaro an attempt was made to seize the barracks where arms were stored. Bombs were thrown in Florence and Pisa, and elsewhere in Italy the same unbridled spirit of violence resulted in bloodshed and loss of life. The pusillanimity of the Government encouraged republicans and 'internazionalisti' alike to rail against the monarchy, and loyal subjects heard with profound disgust the warm defence by Zanardelli in Parliament of the Mayor of Rimini, who had vetoed any form of memorial to Victor Emmanuel. In addition the intrigue and corruption with which government circles were contaminated raised bitter protests and denunciation even in the Chamber itself. On the death of

Depretis the nation turned to the strong hand of the new premier, Francesco Crispi, to restore order and self-confidence in the nation.

CRISPI AND SOCIAL REFORM

Crispi was nearly seventy when he became premier. A Sicilian by birth, a republican by conviction, but now a loyal monarchist, he had been a conspirator all his life. With a natural tendency towards dictatorial methods, born of his immense self-confidence and belief in his own ability, as a parliamentary leader he failed in tact, suavity of manner, and the spirit of compromise. His motto was 'energy', a striking contrast to the cold inertia of his predecessor. About all his policy there was a want of balance. He was too apt to go to extremes. Always impetuous, he saw plots everywhere, and rushed to conclusions upon unreliable information, in a way that sometimes made him almost ridiculous. However, he quickly infused a new energy into parliamentary life. His first measures were excellent. The Bill on Communal and Provincial Administration, giving regional self-government, afforded general satisfaction and lessened the perpetual government interference in local affairs which so irritated the country districts. An admirable law on sanitation and hygiene was a real benefit to public health, and the new penal code, the work of Zanardelli, revealed a liberal spirit which was badly needed. But this good beginning was somewhat marred by the severity of a law on public order, giving the authorities power to prohibit meetings and processions, which, though perhaps salutary at the moment, was not in keeping with the professed liberty of association. In the construction of his Cabinet Crispi kept for himself the portfolios of both Internal and Foreign Affairs, which the Chamber in general, and aspirants to those offices in particular, resented, as savouring too much of dictatorial methods. Crispi characteristically ignored all comments and spoke of exceptional times requiring exceptional methods. Equally typical was his sudden and mysterious departure for Germany before he had been in office a month, to consult Bismarck, for whom he had a great admiration.

In the previous December (1886) the Italian Parliament had rejected the commercial treaty with France, which had been in existence since 1881. In so doing they merely anticipated the rejection already decided upon by the French Chamber of Deputies. The Italian Government, however, at once opened fresh negotiations for a new treaty, realizing the loss that Italy would suffer commercially. Crispi's visit to Bismarck did nothing to improve the chances of success; it merely emphasized the fundamental cause of hostility, Italy's inclusion in the Triple Alliance. The result was that, after long secret negotiations, all hope of a new and more favourable treaty had to be abandoned. The true reason was bluntly expressed by the French commissary when he said to the Italian representative, 'as long as you remain in the Triple Alliance, no commercial agreement between France and Italy will be possible'. It was part of the price that Italy had to pay for security. The logical results followed: France imposed a prohibitive tariff on Italian exports, Italy replied in kind, and economic warfare began. Italy was, however, the chief sufferer. The obvious hostility of the French Chamber and press drove Crispi into one of his panics. On the unsupported reports of spies and secret agents, he declared a French attack on Italy to be imminent, and kept urging his Minister for War to prepare immediately for all eventualities. There was no foundation for such alarm, and after a while Crispi steadied himself again. But the fear of such an attack kept Crispi meticulously loyal to the Alliance. Irredentist agitation in the Trentino was put down with a firm hand, to the intense irritation of the extreme Left and their supporters. Italy was, in fact, at this time divided into two factions. Though the Alliance was undoubtedly not popular, one section, through fear of France, supported it on the grounds of political necessity. The other section wanted friendship with France, opposition to Austria, and the non-renewal of the Alliance, from an instinct based on traditional sympathy; for in spite of their rivalry, there has always been a racial and cultural affinity between France and Italy, but with Teutonic Germany there is none.

After four years of office Crispi's dictatorial handling of the chamber brought about an unnecessary adverse vote, and in January 1891 he resigned. During the three years of growing unrest before he returned as Premier, the Marquis Rudinì and Giovanni Giolitti both held office for short periods.

ECONOMIC CRISES AND SOCIALISM IN 1893

The unhappy results of the commercial struggle with France produced a violent outbreak of disorder in Sicily. Fostered by the new Socialist ideas reaching the island from the north, the discontent and misery of the labourers broke out in open rebellion. The Government, engrossed with its own trouble, failed to realize the seriousness of the revolt. With the fall of Giolitti's Ministry there was a general call for Crispi as the one man strong enough to restore order, and in December 1893 he became premier for the second time. As usual, in moments of excitement, Crispi went to extremes, this time seeing in the violence of the peasantry the sinister hand of Russia. Large forces of troops were drafted into the island, a state of siege proclaimed, military tribunals set up, and the movement suppressed with an unnecessary excess of zeal and punishment. Shortly after, similar methods were adopted in the Carrara district, where the marble workers broke out into violence. The heavy sentences delivered by the military tribunals disgusted all those who realized the economic suffering of the peasantry and exasperated the more violent section. Bombs were thrown in Rome, an attempt was made on the life of Crispi himself. At Leghorn and Rimini there were other outrages. In the face of these dangerous symptoms, Crispi decided to take drastic steps against the whole Socialist movement. But his method was wrong. Instead of investigating the causes underlying the outbreak, and seeking the remedy, he dissolved all the Socialist societies and associations of workers—no less than 271, of which 55 were in Milan alone. The result was not what he expected, for he merely aroused the general but unexpressed sympathy with the Socialist ideals, and the movement rapidly increased instead of diminishing. The general public rightly regarded the punishment meted out as excessive, a view shared by the king himself, who reduced the sentences, and in some cases quashed them altogether. The opposition to Crispi in Parliament intensified, but he was quite undeterred. He balanced the budget, improved the relations of Italy with France, and was not unsuccessful in an attempt to soften the hostility of the Vatican, to whom Crispi's fight against Socialist influence was very congenial.

CRISPI AND ABYSSINIA

Crispi had always big ideas, and not the least of them was his vision of a great colonial empire. In 1882 Italy had acquired a station at Assab Bay on the Red Sea coast of Africa. In 1885, with good wishes from England, the Italians extended their hold on the coast by occupying the harbour of Massawa. A few years later the slaughter of an Italian column at Dogali revealed for the first time the difficulties and dangers of colonial enterprise. Since then, occupied areas had been further extended, partly by force and partly by negotiation with the native chiefs. Crispi had formed these acquisitions into the colony of Eritrea, and had acquired a new outlet for Italy in Somaliland. When Menelik became king of Abyssinia he professed great friendship for Italy, signing the treaty of Uccialli in 1889. Next year Crispi announced to Europe that Abyssinia was henceforth an Italian protectorate. His troubles were, however, only beginning. Menelik was treacherous and untrustworthy, and as Italy penetrated deeper into the country, there were clashes with independent chiefs. Two or three successful actions of this kind convinced Crispi that a vigorous forward movement would be necessary, and Baratieri, the general in command, was recalled to Italy for consultation. On his return, he found a changed situation. Menelik was now hostile and in alliance with chiefs hitherto friendly to Italy. Urged to decisive action by the impatience of Crispi, Baratieri in 1896 took the offensive and marched on Adowa, where on 1 March the Italian army, greatly outnumbered, was cut to pieces. The crushing defeat at

Adowa was not only the end of Crispi's colonial dream but of his political career. Driven from power by popular clamour, when news of the disaster was made public, Crispi, now nearly eighty, retired from political life, to end his days in poverty and obscurity. His unstable and theatrical policy had brought suffering at home and abroad.

SOCIALISM, DISORDER, AND REACTION, 1897–1900

The last four years of the nineteenth century brought the social unrest in Italy to a tragic climax. It was the most violent phase of the struggle. On one side were the welter of new ideas grouped together under the name of Socialism; on the other were the old conservative and reactionary elements, which had their roots far back in feudalism, together with the capitalists of the new industrialism. The movement was in no sense peculiar to Italy, for the problem of capital and labour was exercising the minds of every industrial community in Europe. There were two schools of thought in Italian Socialism. There was an active extremist element, the anarchists and 'internazionalisti', and to their subversive methods were due the bomb-throwing and assassinations which terrorized the public. They were a very dangerous body, but they were only a minority. The main stream was led by a group of intellectuals whose influence spread rapidly. They believed in legal methods, organization, and agitation for social reform, aiming at better industrial conditions and an increase in the standard of living. They had their own press, *Critica Sociale,* founded in 1891 by a group whose most prominent figure was Filippo Turati, *Lotta di Classe,* and *Avanti!*, all of which were good-class papers. The movement was a great success, and when, after much hesitation, it was widened to embrace agricultural workers as well as the industrial element in the north, it assumed the proportions of an imposing national party. They held annual congresses in order to clarify their aims, and in 1895 they formulated their 'Minimum Programme', which included adult suffrage for both sexes, payment of deputies and local councillors, government neutrality in industrial disputes, factory legislation, old-age pensions, feeding of schoolchildren, and a progressive income tax.

The movement alarmed the landowners and the industrialists, and their pressure on the Government had resulted in Crispi's attempt to suppress Socialism by decree. But the excessive use of force had only roused a widespread sympathy and strengthened rather than weakened the movement. The year after Crispi's fall there was a fresh recrudescence of violence, promoted by the extremists. There were riots in Rome and symptomatic movements elsewhere, and another attempt was made to assassinate King Humbert. In 1898 the whole country broke out into disorder. It began in the south where the peasantry in Apulia, goaded beyond endurance by unemployment, bad harvests, and hunger, committed all kinds of outrage. It was suppressed by General Pelloux, who, to his credit, refused to declare a state of siege and pacified the province without military law. But this was only a prelude. In April, risings broke out in the Marches, in the Romagna, and in Tuscany. Thence it spread to the north. In thirty out of the fifty-nine provinces the civil government was suspended and replaced by the military. The climax, however, was reached in Milan, where in a series of wild disorders the military fired on the crowd and even used artillery. Nearly a hundred civilians were killed, and several hundred wounded. Only two soldiers lost their lives. Martial law was proclaimed, hundreds, including several deputies, were arrested, newspapers suspended, and the city patrolled for days. In other cities, such as Florence and Naples, martial law was proclaimed. The whole country, in fact, was a prey to this outburst of long-repressed misery and bitter dissatisfaction with the existing conditions of life and the failure of the Government to deal with the problem.

When quiet was restored in the country, the military courts proceeded to pass sentences on the long list of arrested civilians. However, most of the sentences, which were very severe, were later remitted. The Government resigned in July and another was formed by General Pelloux, which contained no less than three other generals besides the President. At first the new

Ministry professed moderation, but, before long, pressure from the reactionaries and the assassination of the empress of Austria by an Italian anarchist produced a reaction. A series of 'political provisions' was introduced which empowered the Government to dissolve any organization whose object it considered to be subversive of public order or dangerous to the Constitution. These provisions were opposed by the extreme Left as too restrictive, and with such obstinacy were their obstructive methods maintained, that the Bill was held up for months. Pelloux then prorogued the Chamber and announced that the Bill would come into effect by Royal Decree (*decreto legge*). But when the Chamber met in the autumn, matters were no better, and the Government dissolved Parliament and appealed to the country, believing that the new Chamber would be more amenable. In this they were wrong, and when the High Court declared the *decreto legge* to be unconstitutional, Pelloux resigned. A whole year of parliamentary work was wasted in this struggle. The attempt made by a Cabinet of Generals to rule the country on authoritarian lines had failed. The country was sick of military rule; the brutal methods of General Bava-Beccaris against the unarmed civilian population at Milan had disgusted everyone. Nothing had revealed more clearly the unreasoning panic which had seized the authorities than the bestowal of the Grand Cross of the Order of Savoy on the 'victor' of Milan, accompanied by a eulogy on his great services in saving the country. A Cabinet of conciliation was now formed by Saracco, the President of the Senate, and the country turned with profound relief to a period of quiet. But the century was not to close without one final tragedy, when in July 1900 on a visit to Monza, King Humbert was assassinated and the throne passed to the young Victor Emmanuel III, who was to reign throughout the fascist era.

GIOLITTI AND THE DECLINE OF PARLIAMENT

From 1901 to the eve of the Great War the presiding genius in Italian political life was Giolitti. Giolitti was a bureaucrat who by hard work and genuine ability had risen to the highest posts in the civil service, chiefly on the financial side. His career had given him much patronage, and he had used it wisely for his own advantage. No one was more familiar with the personnel of parliament or had more direct influence over officials whose advancement was due to himself. A deputy said in the Chamber, with truth, that Giolitti in his long career had 'nominated nearly all the Senators, nearly all the councillors of state, all the prefects and all the other high officials in the administrative, judicial, political and military hierarchy of our country'. With this power behind him, he combined great skill as a manipulator of groups and parties. He was one who preferred the reality of power to the continuous burden of office. Rather than face a critical situation and the probability of defeat, he would retire, taking care that his successor should be dependent on a majority of which he himself had the control, so that he could replace him at the selected moment. This 'happy art of leaving a sinking ship', as a socialist writer put it, helped greatly to prolong his political life, for someone else was always left to face the dangerous situations.

There were other premiers between 1901 and 1914, but they all held office by the support of a majority controlled by Giolitti. To keep this subservient majority was his constant preoccupation, and to do so he was prepared to come to terms with all parties. A new feature in political life was the clerical element. Dread of Socialism had at last induced the Papacy to rescind the *non expedit* (p. 157), and Catholics could now give their votes openly. In 1913, when his majority appeared threatened, Giolitti had no hesitation in making terms with the Clerical party, whose leaders afterwards boasted that the Catholic vote had assured the election of government candidates in two hundred seats.

Giolitti's government was liberal, and as such opposed by the Socialists, but the premier stole their thunder by absorbing much of their programme into current legislation, without adopting their principles. At the same time, he kept the opposition of the conservative element in bounds by his support of the armed forces, again in spite of Socialist opposition. Giolitti's clever and unscrupulous handling of parties preserved his majority, and enabled him to carry out a long programme of valuable social legislation. But his methods carried a stage further the decline initiated by Depretis, sapped parliamentary life of virility, and took all interest in politics from large sections of the electorate. For centuries the Italian people had been ruled by absolute monarchs and had taken no interest in politics. They had regarded their governments as necessary evils, paid their taxes, obeyed the laws or revolted against them and paid the penalty, and lived their own life. Now, if constitutional government, when it came, was to be a success, this scepticism towards political life must be exorcised and a new interest created and sustained; for popular interest is the essence of parliamentary government. The policy begun by Depretis and continued by his successors failed because they did not recognize this fact. Parliament became isolated from the national life. Once the novelty of the new system had worn off, the old scepticism returned, the people became indifferent, and when opposition came, as it did with Fascism after the war, the nation dropped the parliamentary system without an effort to save it. This isolation had an equally disastrous effect upon Parliament itself. It led to stagnancy. The same set of ideas propounded by the same men circled round year after year. Political intrigue was so absorbing that the wider issues of the national life were too often lost sight of, and men grew old and narrow within the charmed circle of Montecitorio.

PROSPERITY, SOCIAL REFORM, AND THE DECLINE OF LIBERALISM

The first decade of the new century was a period of real advance in Italy. The country had at last turned the corner. For the first time the Treasury knew what it was to have a balance in hand. Industry was making rapid strides owing to the development of cheap electricity through the use of water power. Foreign trade rose from 124 millions sterling in 1901 to 213 in 1910, which, though still a modest amount in comparison with richer countries, was a great improvement. Wages were likewise rising, owing in part to the official policy of non-interference with strikes and labour disputes, but chiefly to the flourishing state of industry. Emigration was on a large scale, reaching its maximum of some 870,000 in 1913. Although this wholesale exodus depopulated wide areas of the country districts, especially in the poverty-stricken south, it found compensation in the substantial sums returned to Italy by the successful emigrants abroad, and it was not sufficient to affect the population, which rose steadily from $32\frac{1}{2}$ millions in 1901 to $34\frac{1}{2}$ ten years later.

The general improvement in the material conditions of Italy was accompanied by a movement in national thought, which helps to explain developments in twentieth-century Italy. It was the tragedy of Italy that just when she had won her unity and independence, the whole basis of Liberalism upon which it rested was crumbling throughout Europe. Two new influences were at work in Europe, and both had their source in Germany. The first was Marxism, with its doctrine of economic materialism and its revolutionary theory of the class struggle. The modified form of Socialism, which appeared in Italy, was international and pacific, but economically aggressive, aiming at industrial expansion and higher wages, which in turn required new markets and raw materials. The second influence was Bismarckism or the cult of force. Three successful wars of aggression, followed by the millions of the French indemnity, had inoculated Germany with a fierce materialistic greed. Bismarck's creed of 'blood and iron' was in due course developed into a whole series of theories expounded in books and lectures: the idea of the Superstate and Superman, the Race theory, Aryanism, the Nordic type and pan-germanism, with its latent anti-semitism.

Both these movements had reactions in Italy, but with opposite effects. Socialism was not only a success: it was beneficial. It gave the people what they had hoped in vain to get from the Government, a clear-cut programme of social reform. It attracted the intellectual youth and up to the close of the century the Socialists were the most influential force in the kingdom. Their success was seen in the reforms carried by Giolitti, which included manhood suffrage and a scheme of social legislation about public health, accidents to work-people, child labour, health insurance, and old-age pensions. After this, Socialism declined, and the rising generation was instead attracted by the new nationalist or imperialist creed, derived from the new theories in Germany. To the great majority of the Italians the successful achievement of unity and independence brought the national effort to a definite close. They now wanted peace and quiet and no further adventure.

THE NEW NATIONALISTS AND IMPERIALISTS

There was a minority which thought very differently from the normal Italian. These men regarded unity, not as the end, but as the beginning of the new Italy. They now dreamed dreams and saw visions of a great and powerful kingdom, with a wide colonial empire, feared and respected throughout Europe. In support of this, they quoted and misinterpreted Mazzini's 'third Rome' and Gioberti's 'Italian Primacy', reinforced by a conception of Crispi and his policy, which saw in him the precursor of a new Italian world power. Yet Italy was not an aggressive nation. Except in Piedmont, there was no military tradition. Nor was she a promising subject for state control, which Italians had always hated; nor for collectivism, since her genius had been always strongly individualistic. Divided for centuries into small states, separated by trade barriers, local customs, varieties of dialect, and inter-state jealousies, she was not even yet fully conscious of her unity as a single people, and the idea of mass movement was completely alien to her way of thinking. Yet the primary objective of the new nationalism was precisely to change all this and turn Italy into an aggressive military Power under an all-pervading State control. This meant a revolution not merely in the politics but in the mind of the nation.

The movement soon had a press, of which the most important paper was Corradini's *L'Idea nazionale;* others were of a more jingoistic, popular type, such as *Il Tricolore* and *Grande Italia.* Corradini advocated state control, militarism, and colonial expansion which should absorb emigration and retain for the homeland the colonists now benefiting other countries. Against the spirit of individualism Corradini stressed

187

the inevitable collectivism of modern industry, maintaining that from the national point of view the individual was of no more importance than the fallen leaf in relation to the forest. He sought to rouse the spirit of adventure, to combat the pacifism of Socialism with a eulogy on the 'moral value' of war. In short, he voiced the whole creed of power-politics. Corradini's views appealed strongly to the restless, unsatisfied element, particularly youth, and were welcomed by the industrialists in need of markets and materials.

LITERARY PROPAGANDA

A more subtle and indirect influence, but no less national in spirit, was that of poetry, which has always been associated with political thought more closely in Latin countries than in England. The poetry of the earlier period had been idealistic and patriotic, but after 1870 the spirit of it changed. It was now positive and practical, dealing with concrete problems like poverty or even politics and clothing its ideas with a simplicity of form and language that varied little from prose. The fine flower of this new school of poets, known as the *Veristi* or Realists, was Gabriele d'Annunzio. D'Annunzio was a great artist, with a deep sense of the dramatic, an exquisite lyrical touch, and a superb mastery of language. But the character of the man was below that of the artist. A voluptuary and a hedonist in his private life, he was one to whom the joys of life were physical, and this innate sensualism pervaded all his work. Allied to this materialistic view of life went a strain of ruthlessness and cruelty. D'Annunzio was greatly admired and very widely read, but his influence was far from wholesome. He intensified the craving for pleasure and excitement, already an unhealthy symptom amongst the younger generation. He deepened the restlessness of the time, and its dissatisfaction with life, hymning the joys of material pleasure to the exclusion of all the higher spiritual aspirations of men, and urged his country forward on the perilous road towards *grandezza*.

The Nationalist propaganda received valuable support from various other sources. The historical work of Alfredo Oriani, which later became a popular text-book of Fascism, expressed with great force the expansionist views of the author, his demand for an African empire and the belief in 'greatness as the end and heroism as the means'. Less conspicuous, but more practical, was the work of a group of economists under the leadership of Mario Alberti, who surveyed the ground and laid down the principles of future Italian economic penetration, especially in the Near East, Russia, and the Balkans.

From these converging channels of thought, a strong imperialist current emerged, urging upon the Government a forward policy of *grandezza*, to rescue the heroic spirit of the nation from the pettiness and misery of existing conditions of life.

CONQUEST OF LIBYA

More powerful motives than clamour in the press were urging the Government to fulfil the aims of the nationalists. Italy had already the consent of England and France to the acquisition of Cyrenaica and Tripoli. Careful preparations were made in due time, and in September 1911 an ultimatum was sent to Turkey, followed by a declaration of war and the dispatch of troops to Libya. The war made all Italy nationalist, and once again the ringing notes of Garibaldi's Hymn resounded throughout the country. The Nationalist press, who claimed the war as their own, displayed the wildest extremes of enthusiasm and patriotic ardour. D'Annunzio fanned the flames with his poems on the heroism of the fighting forces, and it seemed as if, at last, Government and people were fused in a new unity. But the war lasted too long, and the nature of the fighting hardly lent itself to sustained popular excitement. The interference of France and Austria to prevent a naval attack on the straits, or the infliction of serious damage on Turkey in Europe, robbed the war of spectacular incidents. Peace was concluded in October 1912, and with it came the inevitable reaction, as Italy recognized that Tripolitania was unlikely to offer to emigrants the financial attractions of America, and that for many years her new colonies would be no more than an additional burden on the Treasury.

After the war the Nationalist party, in spite of defections and divisions, remained sufficiently homogeneous to put forward its aims and programme. *L'Idea nazionale*, its chief organ, was now a successful daily paper, which began to advocate a wholesale educational reform. The rising generation should be brought up to realize that they belonged to a nation that 'aspires to conquer for itself the largest share in the rule of the world'. They should no longer be educated in the old ideals of Liberalism but rather in 'the morality of men that do things'.

THE FALL OF GIOLITTI AND SOCIAL DISORDERS, 1912–14

Socialism, on the other hand, had declined, until from a national party it had become a matter of groups in single constituencies. At the close of 1912, however, the editorship of *Avanti!* passed into the hands of a certain Benito Mussolini, and a new force came into Italian Socialism. At this time Mussolini was a whole-hearted revolutionary, going back to the uncompromising doctrines of Karl Marx. With the extreme section of the party his leaders in *Avanti!* and his speeches had great influence, and he was later thanked for the new energy and interest he had created in the movement. More moderate, middle-class leaders of Socialism, like Turati and Bissolati, were losing the confidence of the workers.

In 1912 Parliament passed a bill giving universal suffrage, which increased the electorate from $3\frac{1}{2}$ to 8 millions. In the year following there was a general election, and the country awaited the result with great eagerness, for there was much speculation as to the direction in which the new electors would vote. The general election of 1913 was Giolitti's political *chef d'œuvre*, but he overreached himself. Not only had he compounded with the clericals and used pressure on the constituencies up to the limit, but he had extended government support to any candidate who gave nominal adherence to his programme. The result was a majority containing every shade of political opinion. It was impossible, even for Giolitti, to keep together such mutually antagonistic elements, and in March 1914 he resigned again, and for seven years held no office, though he continued to control a majority of deputies in the Chamber.

During the last few months before the outbreak of the war in 1914 there were many further disturbances. Giolitti had left behind him an epidemic of unsettled strikes, a deficit of over 20 millions on the budget, due to the Libyan war, and an impending strike of railway men. Early in June a series of disorders broke out in the Marches of Ancona and the Romagna; in some places 'republics' were set up, in others the soldiers were besieged in their barracks. There was great nervousness in the public, but there was no organization behind the movement, and in a week it collapsed. It was due, at least in part, to the most extreme views expressed in Mussolini's paper *Avanti!*, and the disorders of 'Red Week' gave the editor and his supporters every satisfaction.

DECLINE OF THE TRIPLE ALLIANCE, 1903–14

The Triple Alliance had been renewed in 1902, but with important additional clauses about Austria. These stipulated that in case one of the members, not being attacked first, declared war on another Power, the other two would maintain a benevolent neutrality. There was also a clause relating to the Balkans, in which it was provided that Austria and Italy should give each other full information regarding their own or any other Power's intentions in that area, and further, that if either Power was obliged to change the *status quo* in the Balkans, the Adriatic, or the Aegean, such change should be made by mutual agreement and on condition of compensation to the other Power. The significance of this lay in Italy's desire for expansion towards Trieste and Albania, as well as her anxiety for her Balkan trade, where her motor-car industry was already finding a profitable market. The Triple Alliance was never popular in Italy. It was directed solely against France, for it was clearly understood by all three parties that England was excluded from its scope. Yet Italy was obviously tending to friendship with France and England and might even have withdrawn from the Alliance if it had not been for the Socialist hatred of Russia, the ally of France since 1894. The king and President Loubet exchanged visits, and

Italy supported France against Germany at the Algeciras Conference in 1906. Commercial relations were restored, and Italy recognized the claims of France in Morocco, and in return, France admitted Italy's interest in Tripolitania. Italy had thus become a very weak link in the alliance, and it is doubtful if either of the other two partners put much trust in her support.

In the first part of 1914 relations with Austria, never good, deteriorated. The action of Prince Hohenlohe in ordering the dismissal of Italians employed by the municipality at Trieste had led not only to clashes in Trieste itself but to sympathetic demonstrations in the Trentino. The protests from Italy produced no results, for Austria intended to treat her Italian subjects as she pleased, but the bitterness of Italy towards Austria was deepened and all thought of an active alliance between the two nations made almost impossible. Such was the condition of Italy at home and abroad when on 28 June the Arch-duke Ferdinand and his wife were assassinated and four weeks later came the Austrian ultimatum to Serbia.

NEUTRALITY AND INTERVENTION, 1914–15

If there had been any doubt regarding the real opinion of Austria and Germany as to the value of Italy as the third partner in the Alliance, it was set at rest by the invasion of Serbia. It was a rude shock for Italy. The terms of the Alliance had been contemptuously flouted. Italy had not been either informed or consulted, and she was, in consequence, perfectly at liberty to announce her neutrality. This she did on 2 August. It was received with tactful approval by France and as obviously correct by England. But for Italy the matter did not end here. She was still a partner in the Alliance, which contained clauses stipulating clearly that any increase of territory by Austria in the Balkans should be met by an equivalent compensation for Italy. The Italian Foreign Secretary at once wrote to Vienna that the only territory Italy would accept was that situated in the Italian provinces held by Austria, which meant the Trentino. Austria curtly refused even to discuss the matter.

Whilst diplomacy was thus engaged, opinion in the country was dividing itself into 'neutralists' and 'interventionists'. In the early stages of the war the former were by far the largest section. The Conservatives and the Catholic party, many of the Liberals, industrialists dependent on German capital, and those who took their opinions from Giolitti, were all for neutrality. On the other side stood the friends of France, Republicans and Freemasons, a group of Socialists led by Mussolini, the Irredentists, and above all, the Nationalists. To the non-political majority 'intervention' meant alliance with France and England, for to fight on the side of Austria was now unthinkable. The Nationalists, however, who were all for war itself, no matter with whom, favoured Austria and Germany, until, finding no support, they changed over to become warm advocates of the Entente.

In any case an immediate decision was impossible. The Libyan war had revealed great deficiencies both in military organization and equipment. The army was totally unprovided for a winter campaign in the Alps. Nothing could be done before the early summer of 1915. Equally important, and far more difficult, was the task of rousing the nation to face the appalling sacrifices which intervention implied in a spirit that would carry them through to victory. Great assistance came from the press, which was almost entirely pro-Entente, and they were helped by the superiority of the Allied propaganda; for the methods of Germany were so clumsy that the authorities, in some cases, refused to publish the material supplied by Berlin. The struggle in the country was reflected in Parliament, but in the Chamber the neutralist element was strong, because so large a proportion of deputies were still under the spell of Giolitti, and he, always a pessimist, was fearful of disaster, distrustful of the army, and inclined to peace almost at any price.

While the sympathies of the nation were veering steadily towards the Allies, the Chamber remained neutralist; but to the Ministers the wisdom of permanent neutrality was growing more and more doubtful as its dangers became more apparent. There was nothing to be hoped for from Germany and Austria if they won, and the Allies were not likely to prove generous to Italy if she did not help in the hour of need. One more attempt was made to induce Austria to satisfy Italian aspirations, but it only met with an uncompromising refusal. Then Salandra, who had followed Giolitti as premier, turned to England and France. Secret negotiations were opened, and continued in an atmosphere very sympathetic to Italian aims.

THE TREATY OF LONDON

On 26 April 1915 the secret treaty with the Allies was signed. The terms were all that Italy could ask for. She was to have the Trentino and a defensive frontier on the Brenner pass, Trieste, Istria, and a part of the Dalmatian coast, the port of Valona, and special rights in Albania; Rhodes and the Dodecanese, and certain islands in the Adriatic. If Asia Minor was divided, she was to have Smyrna, and territory in Africa, if there was a further redistribution in that continent. Secret treaties of this kind, signed in the midst of war, are seldom reliable documents. However, in May Italy publicly announced that she had withdrawn from the Triple Alliance, and the last phase of the conversion of the country to war was carried through in an atmosphere of tense excitement and delirious enthusiasm. D'Annunzio, in a series of fervid speeches as a private citizen, roused his varied audiences to wild demonstrations of patriotic ardour and was an important factor in bringing Italy into the war. The popular clamour raised by his activity made it impossible for Giolitti to maintain his neutralist majority in the Chamber, and on 24 May the king declared war on Austria.

2. ITALY IN THE WAR, 1915–1918

The outbreak of the European War found Italy utterly unprepared for action. It was mainly a question of money. Expenditure on the army was never popular. Great indignation in military circles had been caused when the Finance Minister had classified the Army Budget as 'unproductive expenditure', and when, after the war had commenced in 1914, the War Minister demanded £24,000,000 to put the army on a proper war footing, it was indignantly refused and reduced to one-third. The deficiencies revealed by the Libyan campaign had, in consequence, never been made good. There was a grave shortage of artillery. But the Italian commander-in-chief, General Cadorna, was a great organizer, and in the months of neutrality planned an offensive on the Austrian mountain frontier. From May until August 1915, the Italian offensive went well all along the front, the four Italian armies advancing slowly into Austrian territory. Austrian resistance was toughest on the eastern end of the front, where the battle of the Isonzo raged in October. In the spring of 1916 the Austrians launched in the Trentino their first major offensive, but were held by appreciably smaller Italian forces. Once the danger towards Vicenza had passed, Cadorna promptly returned to the attack on the Isonzo front. In August an Italian offensive was launched in the region of Gorizia. The fighting in the summer of 1916 in the dry, limestone hills of the Carso was grim and costly for both sides, and summer was followed by a severe winter along the whole mountainous front. In 1917 the tide turned against Italy. The collapse of Russia released the full resources of Austria for action on the Italian front. Fighting in the spring brought enormous casualties. For the first time, during the May campaign, a failure in morale and a weakening of the offensive spirit was observed amongst the troops. A massive Austrian offensive in October on the Isonzo front was stiffened by German divisions. The Italian line crumbled, and with it the morale of the troops. Cadorna, although not alone responsible for the failure, was a hard and unpopular man. After the disaster of Caporetto, he was replaced by General Armando Diaz. Italy's allies quickly realized the scale of the defeat at Caporetto. Six French and five British divisions were sent to Italy, but before they reached the front the Italians had alone stabilized the position. In the battle of the Piave twenty-nine Italian divisions halted fifty Austro-German divisions, and the arrival of the French and British did something to restore the balance in numbers. A final spring offensive by Austria on the Piave in 1918 met with total failure, and in the autumn the Italians and their allies sealed their victory in the battle of Vittorio Veneto. On 4 November an armistice was signed between Austria and Italy, a week before the armistice on the Western front. In the three years and six months of fighting Italy had mobilized 5,230,000 men, 14.4 per cent of her population, and lost 680,000 killed.

3. ITALY AND FASCISM, 1918–1940

The Armistice found Italy facing the same problems as other countries: demobilization and the reabsorption of man-power into civil life; a feverish demand for goods of all kinds due to war shortage, which created a temporary boom in industry; the switch-over from war production to peace requirements; high prices, trade restrictions, and government control. There was also the problem of high wages, inflated staffs, and innumerable special posts. Italy was hampered more than other countries by lack of coal and raw materials and the shortage of shipping, and like her Allies she had an enormous budget deficit.

THE PEACE CONFERENCE

The Government had scarcely time to take the first steps to deal with this complicated series of problems when the Peace Conference opened in Paris. From the first Italy found herself at a disadvantage. Her war effort was not fully appreciated. The fact that she had only been opposed by the Austrian army, and that the one occasion upon which she had measured herself against German troops and generalship had resulted in Caporetto, depreciated her stock in the eyes of the Allied leaders. It was overlooked that she had had to conduct an offensive on a terrain of immense natural strength, already strongly fortified before the war, and developed with skill and care during the months of her neutrality. She was also taxed with being 'imperialist', a charge based more on the persistent nationalist propaganda of the pre-war years than on a general knowledge of the terms of the secret Treaty of London, upon which her claims were based. Then, too, she had committed a bad diplomatic blunder in neglecting to inform America of the terms of the Treaty of London before the issue of Wilson's 'Fourteen Points', which spoke only of a 'rectification of frontiers', meaning the Brenner line. This mistake was repeated when Wilson arrived in Rome and was allowed to leave Italy without a discussion of Italian claims in the light of the London Treaty. Again her case was badly presented. Orlando, though a man of high intelligence, had the lawyer's facility in seeing both sides of the question, which proved a weakness in dealing with a man like Clemenceau, who saw only one. Finally, Italy's position suffered from her lamentable internal condition, with disunion and bitter quarrels in the Ministry, dissatisfaction, strikes, and dislocation in industry, and a widespread *malaise* throughout the country.

The secret Treaty of London (p. 194), signed with Italy upon her entrance into the war in 1915 by England and France, promised Italy the Brenner pass as her northern frontier, Trieste, Pola, and the Istrian peninsula, the northern part of Dalmatia with some Adriatic islands, and the Port of Valona with a narrow hinterland. Her interest in Asia Minor was recognized, and she was promised also compensation in Africa if either France or England increased their African possessions. The American experts, however, upon whom Wilson relied, were markedly adverse to the claims of Italy, even that of the Brenner line, and President Wilson himself, though firm about the Brenner, refused to recognize the validity of any 'secret' treaty such as that of London. The Allied experts were, in fact, much more interested in the formation of the new countries, such as Czechoslovakia and Yugoslavia, than in enlarging Italy's sphere of influence or providing her with an empire. The settlement of Asia Minor is a good illustration. In 1916 a body of French and English experts produced what is known as the Sykes-Picot Agreement, which divided Asia Minor, regardless of the Treaty of London, between France, Great Britain, and Russia. Against this Italy protested vigorously, and in 1917 Asia Minor was again divided, on paper. This time Italy was to get Smyrna, Konia, Adalia, and Itchili, provided the consent of Russia was obtained. But the collapse of Russia made this impossible, and later, making use of the absence of Russia's signature, France and England repudiated the treaty (known as that of St Jean de Maurienne) and allocated Smyrna to Greece.

The claims of Italy were circulated in the Conference by a long memorandum, explaining the cultural and racial aspects of the questions involved as well as their strategic necessity. They included the Brenner line on the north and the watershed of the Julian Alps on the east, which meant the inclusion in Italy of Julian Venetia. Farther south they embraced Istria and northern Dalmatia with the coastline between Zara and Šebenik. No demand was made for lands beyond the Adriatic. A long section was devoted to Fiume, the fate of which was one of the knotty points of the Conference. In opposition to the Italians, Pasic, the Serbian Premier, circulated another memorandum claiming a frontier beginning about 15 miles from the Isonzo and embracing Trieste, Pola, and Fiume, together with all Dalmatia and a large portion of northern Albania. Italy was furious over the opposition to her claim to Fiume, which in a plebiscite had declared unmistakably for union with Italy. In the heat of the struggle Orlando and Baron Sonnino returned to Rome to get parliamentary support. The visit proved unfortunate, for during their absence the mandates for Africa and the East were allocated and Italy got nothing, which still further embittered Italian feeling against her Allies. Soon afterwards Orlando was defeated in the Chamber and Nitti, with Tittoni as Foreign Minister, took over the Government. In Paris the treaty with Austria was signed at St Germain-en-Laye by which Italy acquired the coveted line of the Brenner. This was followed by a settlement of the Libyan border, France surrendering to Italy a chain of wells and oases, and England giving to Italy an area in Jubaland between Kenya and Italian Somaliland.

ITALY AND YUGOSLAVIA

In January 1920 the Treaty of Versailles was ratified, leaving the rival claims of Italy and Yugoslavia still unsettled. In September 1919 d'Annunzio at the head of a collection of fanatics had seized Fiume, and inaugurated a crankish regime which anticipated the later Fascist organization of Italy. When Giolitti became premier in April 1920 he sought to reach agreement with the Yugoslavs. His first move was to recall the troops from Albania and evacuate Valona. Later in the year the 'touring company' of premiers and statesmen, who had replaced the Peace Conference in an endeavour to settle the still outstanding difficulties, met at Rapallo (November 1920). Here at last Italy and Yugoslavia composed their differences over their frontiers. Italy gained the line of the Julian Alps, including Monte Nevoso, Istria with Pola, Trieste, and Julian Venetia. Fiume was made an independent state, but when this proved unworkable the town passed to Italy (1924), whilst Sušak, across the river, went to Yugoslavia, with Port Barôs and the Delta. This necessitated the removal of d'Annunzio. Troops were sent, but there was little opposition and the incident closed. Italy had now attained nearly all she had demanded except northern Dalmatia, where she acquired only the enclave of Zara on the Dalmatian coast.

Italy thus emerged from the resettlement of Europe with a substantial increase in territory (the Trentino and Istria), a fine strategic boundary both north and east, and a firmer grip than before over the Dalmatian coastline. But she had acquired neither mandates nor colonies, because the oases in the Libyan desert and the strip of territory in remote Jubaland gave her neither raw materials nor an outlet for colonization. The politicians professed to be satisfied, but there was no disguising the fact that while England had added $2\frac{1}{2}$ million square miles to her Empire and France a million, Italy had but 100,000 square miles to show, mostly desert. An unfortunate feeling remained, deeply impressed upon the more thoughtful classes, that Italy had not been generously treated, that her Allies had been grasping in their own interests, and that there was little to be expected from them in the future, unless Italy was strong enough to act independently.

THE DISINTEGRATION OF PARLIAMENTARY DEMOCRACY, 1918–22

Italy's domestic condition throughout the three years after victory had grown steadily worse. The Socialists had at first been an inspiration to Italy, and many of their proposals had been adopted with benefit to the working classes, but already in the years before the war their outlook had narrowed. They had devoted themselves largely to municipal control; nearly half the towns of Italy, especially in the industrial north, were in their hands. They were also strongly represented in the trade-union movement, which was said to have 2 million members. During the war Socialism, while active in pushing up wages and indulging in reckless municipal extravagance, had revealed a spirit of pacifism which had had a bad influence on the troops when on leave, and contributed, it was thought, to Caporetto. In the very difficult social and economic situation which followed the war, with the relaxation of discipline, demands for immediate demobilization, and impatience for a return to normal conditions, there ensued everywhere an increase of crimes of violence.

It was at this moment that Italian Socialism came under Russian influence. There was no central organization, nor did any such figure as Bela Kun emerge, but there was an ugly outbreak of violence against disabled soldiers and officers in uniform, especially those wearing medals or ribbons. The extreme Socialists took the title of 'Maximalist', the equivalent of 'Bolshevik', and adopted the hammer and sickle for their emblem. In the Romagna, notably at Bologna, their leaders inaugurated what their opponents described as a reign of terror. All over Italy an orgy of strikes, sometimes for economic reasons and sometimes for political, reduced the social services to a state almost of chaos. Trains and telegraphs and postal arrangements became totally unreliable; industries went on strike at a moment's notice, and a widespread failure of social discipline, coupled with an orgy of extravagance, threatened the country with industrial and financial collapse. The high-water mark was reached with the seizure of the factories by the employees and the attempt to make the management run them for the benefit of the workers. This was a complete failure.

In the face of disorganization and violence the weakness and *noncuranza* of the Government was lamentable. The worst offender was Nitti, and his term of office from June 1919 to April 1920 saw a steady deterioration in the country's condition, which his successor Giolitti did little or nothing to improve. Nitti systematically gave way to the Socialist demands. He amnestied the deserters, which infuriated the army; he published the report on Caporetto the moment it was completed, with its adverse findings on generals, officers, and men, thus giving the Socialists an admirable weapon with which to castigate the army; when officers were beaten up or even murdered in the streets, all he could do was to confess his inability to protect them and advise them to wear mufti when not on duty. Holding the view that this state of things was the inevitable result of the war and would work itself out in due course, he steadily refused to use force to suppress violence and maintain order. He would not even put the law in action where it existed and prosecute the ringleaders of illegal strikes.

Towards the end of 1919 Nitti resorted to the expedient of a general election, the result of which at the same time merely strengthened the opposition, the Socialists winning 156 seats. A new force emerged, the *Partito Popolare,* founded by the Sicilian priest, Don Sturzo. Trying to reconcile modern social and democratic ideas with the ancient faith of the Catholic Church, the *Popolari* were the political ancestors of the present-day Christian Democrats. In 1919 they appealed to the peasants by advocating the break-up of the big estates. In their first election they won 101 seats.

From the elections of 1919 until June 1920 a further wave of strikes and riots swept the country, including a sit-down strike of 600,000 workers. The Socialists would not participate in government but were not sufficiently energetic or constructive to carry out a revolution. The strikes eventually settled themselves, and by the autumn of 1920 any genuine 'red menace' had disappeared. A sign of the weakening of Socialist influence was their loss of many seats at the municipal elections. It was inevitable that a reaction would develop to this state of things. Already there had been attempts at strike-breaking and volunteers had come forward at a crisis to carry on essential services, but they had been local and spasmodic and had received nothing but discouragement from the Government. However, at the end of 1920, when the real crisis was over, the *Squadristi,* irregulars of the Fasci or 'Groups' of Mussolini, began to appear in numbers.

THE RISE OF FASCISM

It was in March 1919, in the office of his paper *Popolo d'Italia* at Milan, that Mussolini formed the first *Fascio di Combattenti* or Battle Band. There were present some 150 young men. Most of them were ex-soldiers, some were to go with d'Annunzio to Fiume, and all of them were full of ardour to crush the so-called 'Reds'. They were not the only body with this aim. The Nationalists—natural allies of the Fascists with whom they eventually coalesced—had already formed similar groups, of which the most prominent were d'Annunzio's *Arditi,* mostly very young men who were frustrated because the war had ended before they were old enough to fight. Fasci sprang up all over Italy, financed by some of the great manufacturers. Other sums were raised by the methods of the racketeer; the nervous and the fearful bought 'protection' or immunity from the bludgeon and the castor-oil bottle. Quickly organized, before the end of the year the Fasci were in vigorous action; in fact, for the next two years Italy was in a state of civil war. The Government did nothing, the carabinieri had no instructions, and looked on without interference while the Fascists sacked and burnt the Socialist headquarters. The Fascists soon won the sympathy of the middle and upper classes and the beneficent neutrality of the military, who allowed them to commandeer civilian and army lorries for their raids. They had the special advantage that whereas formerly Nitti had tolerated the Socialists, Giolitti now tolerated the Fascists as a counter to the Socialists. Their vigorous methods soon proved effective. In November the city and province of Bologna, a stronghold of the Communists, was subjected to a violent attack, their power completely broken, and 'order' restored. With unscrupulous determination the Blackshirts, now fully armed and organized, bludgeoned and burnt and sacked wherever the Socialists held the upper hand. They in their turn replied with bombs and ambuscades. At Milan the Fascists seized the municipal buildings, ejected the council, and took possession of the archives. Local fascist dictatorships began to replace the socialist monopoly in municipal affairs. Farinacci as 'ras' or boss of Cremona boasted that he had compelled (by castor oil and the blackjack) the resignation of 64 local councils.

At the elections of May 1921 Fascists won thirty-five seats and Mussolini entered Parliament. Though the Liberals still had a majority, the predominating influence was that of the Partito Popolare, who threw out Giolitti and supported Bonomi as premier. In the autumn Mussolini called a conference of his party at which he announced the formation of the Partito Nazionale Fascista and set out its programme. Social reform, national prestige abroad, rigid economy at home, the restoration of the authority of the State, financial equilibrium, the cessation of strikes, and arbitration of difficulties between capital and labour, were the principal points. What is most surprising about Mussolini's speech on this occasion was the calm assurance which pervaded it that the Fascist party would before long be in control of the State, and the plain indication that it had a complete programme ready and every intention of carrying it through. At this time the enrolled Fascists numbered about 152,000, of whom 62,000 were working-class or proletarian and about 90,000 were independent or professional people, small tradesmen, landowners, and proprietors of businesses large and small.

Further parliamentary troubles, in which the Popolari were the only staunch supporters of the Government, led to the resignation of Bonomi in February 1922. Facta, a Giolittian representative supported by the wealthy Conservatives, succeeded him. Facta's taking over of office was the signal for further strikes and disorders. On 19 July Facta fell and Turati, the Socialist leader, expressed his readiness to abandon the principle of non-co-operation and to form a government. It was probably too late to put down the Fascists unless the monarchy and the army could be induced to move against them. In any case the Socialists were divided, and many of the rank and file—as was also the case with the Popolari—did not realize the imminence of the danger and were dissentient. Facta's weak Government resumed office.

The March on Rome. On 1 August the Alleanza del Lavoro (an organization supported by Socialists, the General Confederation of Labour, Republicans, and some Liberals) planned a general strike. Not only were the Fascists able to break the strike by running the essential services themselves, but the strike itself served as a final excuse for seizing control of key points. By 18 October the Fascist *quadrumviri*—Bianchi, Balbo, De Vecchi, and De Bono—were ready for a *coup d'état* under Mussolini's orders. By the 28th Fascist forces had occupied the lines of communication from the north of Italy to Rome. Consternation reigned, but there was no effective or unified opposition. On the evening of 29 October the king invited Mussolini to Rome and asked him to form a cabinet.

MUSSOLINI IN POWER

The national policy of Mussolini, which he was now in a position to enforce, was based upon certain fundamental aims to the realization of which all his legislation was henceforth directed. The first was the unquestioned supremacy of the State in every department of the national life; the second was 'no opposition'; and the third 'Empire'. He was hampered by no moral scruples. 'All things are lawful for me, but all things are not expedient' was his motto. These aims were of course concealed or camouflaged according to the needs of the moment, but sometimes they flashed out with unexpected candóur. These aims were not new. They were but the logical expression of the teaching that the Nationalists had drawn from Germany. The one novel feature was the organized use of propaganda, by the press, radio, and cinema, to dope the people at home, and to create abroad whatever impression was considered most desirable.

Mussolini's first Cabinet was designed on a wide basis, containing four members of the Partito Popolare, three Nationalists, two Liberals, and two Social Democrats. One new office was created, that of Director-General of Public Safety, a title not devoid of a latent hint of warning; it was filled by General De Bono, already Commander-in-Chief of the Fascist *squadre,* who had shown his capacity in organizing and controlling the March on Rome. There was no immediate vindictive or retaliatory action on other parties. With his armed Fascists, who now numbered 300,000, Mussolini was in complete control of the country and could afford to be generous. Besides, he was no doubt anxious to get an unprejudiced estimate of the national reaction to his *coup d'état.* The newspaper offices of adverse opinion which had been occupied by Fascists, were handed back (where not wrecked) to their editors, except for a few extremist organs, like Nitti's *Il Paese,* which were suppressed. Socialist and Communist municipal offices, likewise occupied, were evacuated, and the various Camere del Lavoro (such as had not been burnt or sacked) were once again occupied by their owners. The result of this wise forbearance was justified, for the majority both in the press and the municipalities became cautious and moderate and not a few quickly turned Fascist.

The Fascists had not the least intention of becoming one party amongst others in the Chamber. Like the Roman Church, they admitted no compromise. In the spring of 1923 the Partito Popolare held a congress. Their attitude to the Government proved ambiguous. The members of the Party in the Cabinet were promptly summoned, and after an interview with Mussolini their resignations were offered and accepted. This split the party, one section turning Fascist and the other hardening in opposition, but they were now sufficiently weakened by defections to be innocuous. A similar breach opened with the

Social Democrats, whose leader the duke of Cesaro resigned after Mussolini's refusal to contract an alliance with the Party. Mussolini devised a new electoral method which would effectively abolish the old party system and prevent the possibility of a Fascist defeat. By a law of 1923 the country was divided into fifteen large constituencies and each party submitted a national list of candidates. The party gaining the largest number of votes became entitled to two-thirds of the seats in the Chamber (356), the remainder (179) being divided in proportion amongst the other parties. A general election was held in April 1924 under the new system. The Fascists and their allies secured 65% of the votes cast, and the other parties were reduced to impotence.

THE ELIMINATION OF OPPOSITION

The parliamentary situation came to a head with the murder, on 10 June, of the popular Socialist deputy Giacomo Matteotti. Mussolini himself, or at least the Fascists, were blamed for the murder; there was a wave of popular indignation throughout the country, and the crisis shook the Government from top to bottom. The opposition parties left the Chamber as a protest, and moved to the Aventine. They demanded the abolition of the Fascist militia and new elections. Even the ex-service men wavered. The Government was helped, however, by a vote of confidence in the Senate.

The crisis marked the beginning of a new wave of Fascist terrorism which quickly led to the liquidation of any serious semblance of democratic government. Mussolini announced at the beginning of 1925 that 'force' would 'solve the problem of the Aventine'. Roberto Farinacci, now Party Secretary, was the principal instrument of this force, and with the use of bludgeon and castor-oil he encouraged the leaders of the anti-Fascist parties to go into exile. The freedom of the press was destroyed and special tribunals established for the persecution of the remaining opponents.

Trade Unions. The Fascists had their own trade unions or 'syndicates' and other social or economic organizations. To these no rivals were to be permitted. To deal with 'unreliable' or recalcitrant associations, especially those of a political complexion, of which inevitably there were a great many in Italy, a series of decrees were issued which subjected them to steadily increasing pressure. In January 1924 they were put under the surveillance of the prefect, who could inspect their books, install a state commissioner to administer their funds, and eventually dissolve them and use their assets for other purposes. In 1925 all associations were ordered to submit the names of members and officials to the police whenever requested to do so. Finally, in November 1926 a communiqué to the press announced that 'all political associations of an anti-fascist character, all political parties and others regarded with suspicion, have been dissolved'.

Press. The subordination of the press was essential, but there was a tenacious tradition of independence of thought. With many papers there was little difficulty, but others stood firm. The treatment of the *Corriere della Sera,* one of the leading Liberal papers in Italy, reveals the methods of the Government. The editor and proprietor, Senator Albertini, was a persistent but cautious critic of the Government. Being a person of too much influence for summary dismissal, he was bought out by a group of capitalists and the policy of the paper changed. In 1924 there were 3300 journalists in the Italian press, three years later the number was less than half, and over 100, many of whom had previously exercised great influence, had been dismissed and forbidden to write.

Lawyers. The prolonged opposition of the lawyers, the representatives of justice and personal freedom, forms the strongest indictment of Fascism. In every Italian province there were two associations, one for barristers and one for solicitors. These were left alone, but a third, an association of Fascist lawyers, was formed in each province, and supported by the Government. The struggle between the Fascists and their opponents continued for years, and some idea of the exasperation which the prolonged opposition provoked may be gleaned from the fact that in 1931 the names of over 2000 lawyers were struck off the list of those allowed to practise.

THE ESTABLISHMENT OF THE TOTALITARIAN STATE

From the moral point of view the murder of Matteotti and its consequences shook the power of the Fascists from top to bottom, but from the only standpoint which Mussolini regarded as important, that of force, it was a triumph. It made clear not only the political weakness of the opposition but likewise the absence of any effective reaction in the country to the policy of brute force upon which the Government relied. These events had convinced Mussolini of the need for further repressive legislation. By a law on the press he 'sought to abolish the subversive press' (1925). Some controlling legislation was needed, for in Italy there was no law of libel protecting public men and no penalties for contempt of court. But it is easy to realize how a press law would be used by Fascism. Henceforth the press must be pro-Fascist. Another law abolished secret societies; this was aimed at the Freemasons, and owing to the extreme secrecy of their methods may not have led to their complete extinction, but henceforth no Fascist was allowed to be a Mason and the lodges were dissolved. A law on public safety after the first attempt on the Duce's life enacted the severest penalties for such attempts, and a special tribunal for the defence of the State was set up (1926). The Secret Police (OVRA— Opera volontaria repressione anti fascista) produced the victims.

Three further laws put still more power into the hands of the Fascists. The first (December 1925) defined the powers of the Head of the Government, i.e. of Mussolini himself. Ministerial responsibility and parliamentary control of the Government disappeared. No bill could in future be brought in without being first submitted to him, he had sole responsibility, and that not to Parliament but to the Crown. Subsequently he acquired power to issue decrees which would have the force of law, without consulting the other powers of the State. The second law remoulded (or killed) the vigorous municipal system by replacing the local mayors and elective councils with nominated officials (*podesta*) and councils. The third basic law made the Fascist Grand Council into an organ of State. As the result of this legislation the political and administrative machinery of the State was in the hands of the Party, which made full use of every repressive measure. Direct force was applied by a large police force.

ECONOMIC CONTROL

Fascist syndicates or unions had been formed to represent the two sides, employers and employed. For these the Government claimed a gross membership of 2 million, but this was an imaginary figure. When, for instance, in April 1925, the 18,000 Fiat motor workers voted for a council connected with the firm's benefit society, not a single Fascist was elected or even nominated, though over 90 per cent. of the workers voted. In 1925, by the Vidoni Palace Pact, representatives of both employers and workers agreed that they should be represented solely by Fascist unions. This agreement was legalized by the Law of 3 April 1926, which abolished the right to strike. After subsequent changes the final position of industry was as follows:

The whole national industry was grouped into nine *confederations*, four for the employers, four for the workers in industry, commerce, banking, and agriculture, and one for the professional classes, by themselves. In each of these confederations the Government only recognized individual *federations* controlled by Fascists. But there was one difficulty in this absolute control of Fascism over the national industry. Italy was a participator in the International Labour Office at Geneva, and was pledged to recognize 'the principle of freedom of association'. Therefore, into the charters of the confederations there was inserted Article 12 which provided that those employers and employees who did not wish to join the legally recognized organizations could form what were called *de facto* unions. Some of these were formed, but they were not permitted to survive long. They were harried by the police, and brow-beaten by the Fascist *squadristi*, until their existence became impossible. This was not known outside Italy because Mussolini left intact the largest and best known Socialist organization, the G.C.L., the General Confederation of Labour. But, while the central body remained untouched, the many branches which it directed were either dissolved or put under a State Commissioner until the G.C.L. had no organization left to control. It then dissolved itself and was claimed as a convert to Fascism.

The Corporate State. Mussolini's economic advisers had elaborated the theory of the 'corporate state'. They argued that the nineteenth-century movement for unity had succeeded only in a political sense and it was the task of Fascism to create an economically integrated state. In its most utopian form the theory of the corporate state, which was to be still further developed by Salazar of Portugal, envisaged the replacement of political bodies by elected groups of economic experts, and the ultimate 'withering away' of the State in a political sense. This 'withering away' of the State had, of course, been a tenet of communist theory, but there is no reason to suppose that Mussolini ever gave the idea a moment's consideration. Giuseppe Bottai, Minister of Education in the 1930's and one of the purer theorists of Fascism, was continually reminding Mussolini of the original 'corporative philosophy' of the regime. The Duce listened to him with the amused tolerance usually given to small children—a tolerance which was more than Bottai with his twisted ideas deserved. The corporate state was to be based on twenty-two 'corporations'—directing and co-ordinating bodies, representative of both employers and workers, and superimposed upon the confederations. But the corporations did not come into existence until 1934, and by then Mussolini's real interest lay in the conquest of an overseas empire. A new legislative assembly, called the 'Chamber of Fasces and Corporations' did not replace the old Chamber of Deputies until 1938.

In 1927 the Labour Charter or *Carta del Lavoro* was published. It nominally established the old Socialist ideal of the right to work, but also riveted the control of the State over both capital and labour.

Dopolavoro. Nothing reveals more clearly the grim and humourless determination of Mussolini to dominate every phase of the national life, and to close every avenue of spontaneous initiative amongst the Italian people, than the working of the much trumpeted Dopolavoro, the association which controlled the recreations and pleasures of the people. Every form of sport and amusement had to be affiliated to a national organization, of which the presidents and secretaries were appointed by the Government. The national Olympic Committee, raised to a dependent organ of the State, became the guardian angel of Italian recreation. A golf club could not henceforth arrange inter-club matches, dismiss an employee, or build a new bathroom in the clubhouse, without the permission of the Commissione Federale del Golf. Tourist clubs, football and cyclist clubs, bands and dancing associations, even chess and mandoline playing, alike must submit to Fascist supervision or be dissolved. All this official interference had a political purpose which was carefully concealed. The Dopolavoro offered a fine field for propaganda, and the successes at the Olympic games, for which athletes were trained at public expense, served as a useful advertisement for the new Italy. Moreover, Fascist secretaries and organizers kept a keen and spying eye on what was called 'the moral and spiritual phenomena' of recreation. Information as to the political opinions even of Alpine climbers and mandoline players was always welcome to the Fascists.

Such in outline was the work of Fascist penetration. The degree of pressure which the Party could exert was very great. For example, the Minister of Transport ruled in March 1928 that in contracts for railway construction preference must always be given to Fascist estimates and that labour exchanges must do the same when finding work for the unemployed. Things were difficult for the independent workman who could not produce his card of membership of a Fascist union. The leaders of industry were equally at the mercy of the Head of the Government: Benni, for instance, President of the Confederation of Industrial Employers, a deputy and director or chairman of twenty other important concerns, was dismissed by Mussolini and replaced by Pirelli, who in his turn, was removed to make room for Count Volpi. Thus it becomes clear that however much the Government depended upon the industrial magnates, there was no question of permitting dictation, and that workmen and employers alike were at the mercy of the will of the Party as embodied in the Duce.

THE VATICAN TREATY

By the year 1927 the political, administrative, and economic life of Italy was in the hands of Fascism. There remained, however, one big problem in the national life as yet unsolved, the relations of Church and State. There was perhaps nothing which would stir such heart-felt gratitude to the Duce, not only in Italy but throughout the whole Catholic world, as a successful solution of this vexed question. The relationship between Church and State had been governed since 1870 by the Law of Guarantees, but this was not officially recognized by the Vatican and an armed neutrality separated pope and king. Mussolini's attitude towards the Church had from the first been respectful and even friendly. The Cross was replaced in the elementary schools, religious instruction was given, religious processions were not disturbed, and the civil authorities assisted in the transit of pilgrims during the Anno Santo. Mussolini had no wish to create clerical opposition, and his general attitude created a sympathetic atmosphere in which to open negotiations. Pius XI had already served Fascism by helping to kill Don Sturzo's Popolari. In 1926 he let it be known by an indirect message to a leading Fascist, Barone, that he was ready for an understanding between Church and State. Two conditions were laid down as essential; a treaty reconstituting a Pontifical State, however small, and a concordat conferring upon the religious sacrament of marriage the legal effect of the civil rite. In great secrecy negotiations were opened upon this basis.

The preliminaries were hardly completed, however, when they were held up by a struggle for the control of the Catholic Scouts (Esploratori Cattolici). After two years of opposition the Church yielded, and the organization was absorbed in the Fascist Balilla. The negotiations were then reopened and in

February 1929 the Lateran Agreements were signed. The death of Barone in the middle of the work led to the personal intervention of Mussolini and the final and critical stage of the negotiations was carried through by Mussolini and the pope in person.

The Lateran Agreements consist of two documents, a treaty and a concordat. The former closed the *dissidio,* which had existed between Church and State since the Law of Guarantees, by the creation of the Vatican State in the absolute possession of the Holy See, and by the papal recognition of the kingdom of Italy under the house of Savoy. Thus the 'Roman Question' was settled. The concordat defined the relations between the ecclesiastical and the civil governments. The Catholic religion was declared the religion of the State. All the sovereign rights and diplomatic privileges included in the Law of Guarantees were confirmed, and the full liberty of the Church in all spiritual matters was recognized.

The price that the Church paid for these concessions by the Fascists was heavy, for it meant the control of the Church in Italy by the State. It was 'established' in accordance with the Fascist dictum 'everything within the State, nothing outside the State', but the world-wide control of the Church beyond the confines of Italy was not interfered with. 'The Reconciliation' as it was called was received with universal joy, and for months the Vatican was flooded with testimonies of gratitude and thanksgiving.

Church and Fascism. The only criterion by which the voice of the Church can be judged is that of the pope himself, and while Pius XI lived, he spoke upon such questions as national education, racialism, and supernationalism with courageous Christian frankness. The same cannot be said of the archbishops and bishops, who too often showed servility to Fascism and a spirit of adulation towards the Duce, though there were notable exceptions. Nor were the outspoken words of the pope in his addresses and allocutions freely and widely heard, for the Catholic press in Italy was muzzled, and they frequently remained unreported save in the columns of the official Vatican organ, the *Osservatore Romano,* which when once it issued beyond the narrow confines of the Vatican City was liable to immediate confiscation by the police.

4. FOREIGN AFFAIRS, 1923–1940

The foreign policy of Italy from 1923 to 1940 was the special province of Mussolini, and can only be understood as the expression of his cynical and perverse genius. At the Lausanne Conference he obtained his first tangible gain for Italy in the acquisition of the islands of Rhodes and the Dodecanese, thus establishing a commercial base in the eastern Mediterranean, where Italy had always had an active trade. In pursuance of his policy in the course of the next few years commercial treaties were signed with nearly every country in Europe, with Poland, Czechoslovakia, and Austria (1923), with Russia and Switzerland (1924), and with Hungary, Spain, Albania, and Greece in 1925. But these good commercial relations were not established without periods of difficulty and even danger. The sensitive spots in Italy's foreign relations lay on the east coast of the Adriatic, with Yugoslavia, Albania, and Greece. These three countries occupied the Dalmatian coast from Fiume in the north to Corfu, and Italy was suspicious of all three alike, and a mutual settlement proved prolonged and difficult. The first trouble was with Greece.

THE CORFU INCIDENT

In August 1923 Greek irregulars murdered the Italian General Tellini and his staff, engaged in delimitation work on the Greek boundary under the direction of the Conference of Ambassadors sitting in Paris. An ultimatum with a time limit was at once sent to Athens, demanding a full official apology; the celebration of a Mass for the victims to be attended by the Greek Government; a salute by the Greek fleet to the Italian flag, and an indemnity of half a million sterling. As the Greek Government did not promptly comply, the Italian fleet bombarded and occupied the island of Corfu. Greece desired to refer the controversy to the League of Nations, which Italy refused, as being outside its competence, but agreed to accept the decision of the Conference of Ambassadors. The Conference supported Italy and the conditions imposed were carried out and the indemnity paid, one-fifth of which Mussolini devoted to the families of the victims killed by the Corfu bombardment. Corfu was then evacuated. This incident aroused comment and suspicion. France was sympathetic, but in England there was strong criticism of Italy's action. This irritated Mussolini and led to bitter remarks regarding England's pro-Greek policy. In the west the incident left behind an uneasy feeling that the Fascist Government was a danger to peace, but in the Balkans this display of strength greatly increased Italy's prestige. Three years later good relations with Greece were re-established, and Italy was later instrumental in healing the breach between Greece and Turkey due to the disastrous expulsion of Greece from Asia Minor.

FRANCE, ALBANIA, AND YUGOSLAVIA

The problem of Yugoslavia and Albania was a far more intricate question, complicated by the policy of France. Italy had always a special interest in Albania, and it was an axiom of her policy not to allow Albania to fall into the hands of any Balkan state. This was well recognized, and in 1921 the League of Nations after the recognition of Albanian independence entrusted the defence of her integrity to Italy. Racial difficulties and jealousies required constant watchfulness and firmness combined with tact. Another factor, which made the position worse, arose with the formation of the Yugoslav State. The component parts of the new state consisted of the Serbs, who throughout the war had fought with the Allies, and the Croats and Slovenes, who had fought for Austria; no troops had opposed Italy more staunchly than these. The Treaty of Rapallo and the Santa Margherita Conventions were still unratified when Mussolini came to power. Though he thought them unsatisfactory, Mussolini presented them to the Chamber and had them approved. In 1924 he reopened the whole question with Belgrade and finally by the

Treaty of Rome—ratified as the Nettuno Conventions in 1925—put the relations of the two countries on a sound basis.

The relations of Italy with France after the appearance of Fascism were never good. Paris became the centre of a bitter and influential group of anti-Fascist exiles. More important was the French policy of drawing the new countries, Poland, Czechoslovakia, and Yugoslavia, into her orbit, supplying them with financial help and armaments and training their armies. A French-Yugoslav alliance and an attack on Albania were always feared. Mussolini endeavoured to strengthen his hold over Albania by a commercial treaty and by the development of her resources. It was known in 1926 that France was making approaches to Yugoslavia, but it was not until a year later that a treaty was signed. Within a month a similar treaty between Italy and Albania was announced.

The effect of all this political activity threw Italy very much into the limelight. The country, and Mussolini himself, were gratified and flattered by the number of prominent personages who found their way to Rome—kings and queens, premiers, and foreign ministers. Mussolini himself was always 'news', and Fascism was apt at propaganda and advertisement.

In 1924 Mussolini had astonished Europe by formal recognition of the new Soviet Government and the conclusion of a commercial treaty. It was an unexpected reversal of policy, but a good commercial move, opening the Straits and the Black Sea to Italian shipping and industrial products.

GERMANY AND AUSTRIA

In 1925 Italy was again prominent in the management of the Treaty of Locarno. The deliberations for a security pact guaranteeing the Rhineland frontier occupied many months, and the mutual irritation between France and Italy made the attitude of Italy doubtful. However, Mussolini took his place boldly beside England and Belgium, despite an ill-timed outburst of anti-Fascist feeling in the French press, and put his signature to the treaty, undertaking thereby to go to the help of either France or Germany in the case of an unprovoked attack.

The spirit of the Locarno Treaty appeared to be strengthened when at the close of the year Italy and Germany signed yet another commercial treaty. This gave great satisfaction in Italy because it opened the largest market on the continent to Italian goods. There was in Germany at this moment much anti-Italian feeling due to Mussolini's opposition to the projected *Anschluss* between Austria and Germany. In revenge the German press and official circles backed the Austrian agitation against the treatment of the German minority in the Alto Adige, formerly the Austrian Tyrol. Nothing came of this nor of a similar agitation in 1928. Likewise the attempt to gain indirect control of Austria by a Customs Union was defeated. The obvious anger of the Pan-German party over this failure exposed the political motive that lay behind it. It was a form of pressure in the *Anschluss* campaign to obtain the union of Austria with Germany. The maintenance of Austrian independence was a vital question for Italy. Austria was no danger as she was, but to have a revengeful Austria across the border united to the vast power of Germany was to surrender the independence of Italy. Mussolini knew it, and in reference to the relation between the *Anschluss* and the Alto Adige agitation he told the Chamber of Deputies that such union could not be permitted.

TENSION WITH FORMER ALLIES

For ten years Mussolini maintained a foreign policy of peace. In 1928 he signed a treaty with Turkey and yet another of peace and friendship to last twenty years with Abyssinia. At the Naval Conference in 1930 he supported disarmament and declared that Italy was prepared to reduce her armaments to any level, provided the rest of the world did the same. And yet the man himself never ceased to be regarded as a disturbing factor. Though there was no obvious reason at that time to suspect his sincerity, the periodic outbursts of the Duce and his unexpected actions reacted violently on the frayed nerves of Europe. A perfectly legitimate visit to Italy's north African colonies, accompanied with that theatrical element of pomp and circumstance with which he loved to be surrounded, caused the mobilization of half the Turkish army and wild rumours of an Italo-Greek attack on Asia Minor.

The year 1930 revealed for the first time signs of a possible regrouping of the Powers. Since the war the Allies had remained united in opposition to Germany, with Russia standing apart, but now a tendency was discernible, first on the side of Russia and then of Italy, to approach Germany. The first open manifestation of this new alignment was observed at the preparatory commission for the Disarmament Conference held in 1930, at which Italy voted with Germany against France and England. The cause of the Italian action was the persistent refusal of France to allow her parity in naval construction, to which Italy felt entitled as a Mediterranean Power. But while Mussolini made bellicose speeches, Grandi was put forward in the Chamber of Deputies to offer olive branches. This two-faced policy was the result of Italy's fundamental need of allies. Despite all the brave talk of independence and no dictation, Mussolini knew well enough that Italy could not stand alone. The Fascists, however, were tired of France and England. Not only was there the chronic soreness left by inadequate compensation at the Peace Conference, but they were exasperated at the refusal of both Powers to accept Fascism at its own valuation. Hence Mussolini blew hot and cold, in ignorance or deliberate disregard of how deeply Fascism alienated the human and political sympathies of Italy's two allies.

The unfortunate quarrel with France had its source on Italy's side in a belief strongly held in Nationalist circles, and which can be traced back to Mazzini, that France was decadent and that both her political and cultural influence was destined to pass to a renascent Italy. Hence the jealousy with which she regarded French predominance in the Levant and eastern Europe. Already France by alliances and financial aid had become the strongest Power upon the continent, and the efforts of Italy to secure the Balkans as a sphere of influence and the eastern Mediterranean as a centre for her trade had failed to materialize. It was even worse when Italy turned to England, which blocked her advance both east and west with Gibraltar, Malta, and Suez.

But all that the Italians could do was to rant provocatively about the 'Italianity' of Malta and Corsica. Russia was too far off and Germany too weak to offer at present any counterpoise.

ECONOMIC CRISIS AND FAILURE OF INTERNATIONALISM, 1930–2

The economic blizzard which swept across the world in 1931 threatened the collapse of the entire financial and economic structure of modern industrial civilization. Italy, as every other country, felt its cruel force. The budget for that year revealed a heavy deficit with the prospect of worse to come. Foreign trade declined, unemployment increased, and for some years the unemployed exceeded a million, in spite of their absorption by extensive public works. In the autumn of 1931 the Government formed an Istituto Mobiliare Italiano for the financing of industry. The firm hold of the Government over industry, and the relatively small amount of capital invested abroad, helped to pull the country through the crisis and Italy escaped comparatively lightly.

The financial collapse of 1931 had forced mankind to realize that the world-wide economic system built up by western civilization had bound the world into a unit. The nations had been compelled to recognize that even for the bare necessities of life, food, clothes, and shelter, each was dependent on the industry and resources of other countries. The obvious solution to such a state of things lay in a policy of pooling resources. To this end two world conferences were held in 1932. The first was the Disarmament Conference. The aim of this was to establish such an equilibrium of forces that the world would be given time to recover its stability. The second was the World Economic Conference. This sought to find, amid the tangled web of finance and industry, a resultant upon which could be built a better system of international production and distribution. Both failed; and in each case it was the spirit of nationalism which proved the disintegrating factor. The Disarmament Conference met in February of 1932. Hitler was appointed Chancellor of the Reich in January 1933. In October 1933 Germany with-drew not only from the Disarmament Conference, but also from the League of Nations. In November the Conference adjourned until the following year.

The repercussion of this double failure upon the national policy of Italy was severe. The collapse of the economic confer-ence, due to America's insistence on the priority of a sound internal national policy, led to the development of a programme of 'self-sufficiency', the 'battle of wheat', the accumulation of raw materials, the provision of substitutes, and eventually a comprehensive preparation for an economic blockade.

THE REVIVAL OF GERMANY

Even more vital for Italy's future was the rise of Hitler and Nat-ional Socialism. It brought Mussolini closer to the necessity of deciding with which of the two groups, his former allies or the new Germany, he was to link the fortunes of his country. For the time being, however, he compromised by proposing, in 1932, what came to be known as the 'Four-Power Pact'. England, France, Germany, and Italy were to settle the problems of Europe, to take over, in fact, the work for which the League of Nations was designed. But the new Holy Alliance did not materialize. It was modified and watered down by France, attacked by the Little Entente, and regarded with suspicion by England. The final draft initialed in June remained a dead letter.

Two years later, in July 1934, the murder of Dollfuss and the Nazi *Putsch* in Austria were a shock to Mussolini's pro-German tendency. With a sudden realization that the independence of Italy was at stake, he acted. There were 100,000 troops on manoeuvres in the north, and he ordered 40,000 of them to move at once to the frontier. The threat was sufficient, the *Putsch* was called off, and this time the *Anschluss* remained unrealized. This action was the summit of Mussolini's peace policy. Hence-forward he passed gradually from the orbit of the Allies into that of Germany.

FRANCE AND THE ABYSSINIAN WAR

The fear of German rearmament drove France temporarily back into the old Italian friendship. Mussolini made characteristic use of this. From 1918 the rivalry between the two countries had been persistent. Their interests and aims, as well as their fundamental principles (since the emergence of Fascism), had clashed everywhere, in Tunis and Libya, in the Levant and the Balkans, and even in Abyssinia where the French possession of the Jibuti railway thwarted the influence of Italy. Each had been busy gathering satellites; round France stood Poland and the Little Entente, all, like their patron, inspired by fear of Germany, while Bulgaria, Hungary, and the nationalist element in Austria looked to Italy. But now, in the face of a resurgent Germany, these secondary alliances appeared of small import compared with the mutual help to be derived from a close union between the two principals. At the time this was felt as keenly in Rome as in Paris, and in January 1935 a bargain was struck and the feud temporarily buried. France and Italy agreed upon a common policy in central Europe, and the Italians received a number of material concessions in Africa. Italy also made concessions to France respecting the nationality of Italians in Tunisia, which, however, were not to come into practical effect for twenty years. There was also a strong suspicion that the real payment of Italy was an understanding that France would not oppose her aims in Abyssinia. After the Franco-Italian agreement was signed, General De Bono was appointed High Commissioner of Eritrea and Somaliland, whither he had been sent on a preliminary mission as early as 1932. Military preparations were hurried on. In June Eden went to Rome with further peace proposals which were promptly turned down, and on 2 October national mobilization was declared in Italy and war began.

Italy's attack on Abyssinia met with universal condemnation. That a prominent member of the League and a signatory of the Kellogg Pact should thus openly flout the principle of collective security by an unprovoked war on a weak fellow-member, for whom she herself had acted as sponsor, outraged every country that had signed the covenant. The principle involved was clear. If an aggressor named by the League, as Italy had been, was to go unpunished and to be exempt from the sanctions laid down to meet this very contingency, then the League of Nations was useless as an effective constraint on war. Fifty-two nations took this standpoint and voted that sanctions should be imposed, the only exceptions being Austria, Bulgaria, and Hungary, Italy's three satellites. The influence of the League, already weakened by failure to take action against Japan's invasion of Manchuria, would be ruined if it failed for the second time to establish a precedent for imposing sanctions upon an aggressor. But the political implications involved were dangerous. If Italy replied to sanctions by force, and, as she threatened to do, left the League, abandoned the 1935 agreement with France, and bombarded the British fleet in the Mediterranean from the air, a new world war would be let loose. Britain, as usual, was in no position to implement her ardent support of a moral principle with effective material force. With her army demobilized and her navy reduced by naval agreements with Japan and the United States, she was unprepared to go to extremes. As to France, Mussolini's threat to annul the new friendship brought the Government quickly to heel, and he found a useful and ingenious ally in the astute Laval, unburdened by moral scruples but determined not to lose Italian support.

Laval tried to find a pacific solution to the problem. Aided by Sir Samuel Hoare, the English Foreign Secretary, he proposed the Hoare-Laval pact. This, under the deceptive title of an 'exchange of territories', handed over half Abyssinia to Italy in exchange for the port of Assab as an outlet for what was left of Abyssinia. But public opinion in England, bent on the vindication of the League, was too strong. The Foreign Secretary resigned, and sanctions went forward. Laval was still to be reckoned with. He engineered delays, induced the Council to postpone the vital oil-sanctions—the only ones that Mussolini dreaded—and so hampered the general application of restrictive measures that they were scarcely in force before the fighting was over. Against an army without artillery, aeroplanes, or gas masks, poison gas and the bombing of troops and civilians proved decisive, though not as quickly as had been expected by the Italians, nor as quickly as unopposed mechanized warfare moved in 1940-41. However, on 9 May 1936 Mussolini, from the balcony of the Palazzo Venezia in Rome, proclaimed with grandiloquent phrase the fall of Abyssinia. In due course the fact was accepted by Europe, sanctions were removed, and Italy, with her glittering, but expensive and unproductive prize, was accepted back into the diplomatic comity of Europe.

THE POLITICAL CONSEQUENCES OF SANCTIONS

The imposition of sanctions produced a bitter feeling in Italy, chiefly against England. It was also a main factor in turning Mussolini towards a German alliance. Germany had been careful in no way to add to Italy's difficulties, but at the same time she had made good use of Italy's preoccupation with Abyssinia to strengthen her economic grip on the Balkans, so that Mussolini found a far more dangerous rival than France disputing his influence in that area. Another result of sanctions was the elaboration of the principle of autarky or economic self-sufficiency, which had already been put in practice in the 'battle of wheat', an endeavour to render the country independent of foreign imports of grain. A scheme of economic and industrial nationalization was now announced by Mussolini which was intended to provide Italy with coal, iron, rubber, and oil. But all that was in fact possible was the development of minor substitutes and arrangements for alternative sources of supply in case of economic blockade. The change, however, shows that Mussolini clearly anticipated the necessity of an alternative to sea-borne trade, and the possibility of a breach with England. Germany alone could open a new source of raw materials to Italy and was already aiming at self-sufficiency and the production of *ersatz* materials.

Italy and Germany next found themselves working together in the Spanish Civil War, which broke out in July 1936. Unlike the Abyssinian campaign this did not separate but drew together Church and State in Italy. Spain was the last stronghold of medieval Catholicism in Europe, and the preservation of the traditional connexion between Church and State from destruction by the Anarchist and Communist elements in Spanish republicanism constituted a first charge on papal energy. Hence the Roman Church was fully prepared to support the Fascist policy of interference and Mussolini found a useful rallying cry in resistance to Communism and the 'Bolshevik' peril. But Italy's main interest in Spain was the establishment of her own power on the open flank of France and of the British sea routes in the Atlantic and Mediterranean.

The development of submarine piracy quickly involved English interests, and England called together the International Supervisory Committee on Non-Intervention. On this there sat delegates from Germany and Italy who, with their tongues in their cheeks, arranged to patrol the Mediterranean and stop the activities of their own submarines. At Rome and Berlin the English line of action must have appeared the last word in weakness and gullibility. The collaboration initiated in Spain soon developed. In November Count Ciano, the Italian Foreign Minister, went to Berlin, and on his return there occurred the earliest mention of the word 'Axis', and the first clear indication of a new orientation of the Powers.

THE FOUNDATION OF THE AXIS

Italian policy was now definitely drawn into the orbit of Nazism. Friendship with Russia was sacrificed, and Mussolini echoed the strident tones of Hitler in his denunciation of Russian Bolshevism as the European public enemy. An elaborate scheme for army, navy, and aircraft extension was announced and the self-sufficiency programme developed. In short, Italy was brought into line with the Nazi programme.

The formation of the 'Axis' in 1936 thus entangled the policy of Mussolini with that of Hitler. This new political term meant that round the directing policy of either Rome or Berlin, the states of central and eastern Europe should rotate; while retaining their own governments, composed of men sympathetic to the Axis policy, their political and economic life was to be controlled and directed from the centre round which they revolved. As yet the aims of the two centres did not coincide. Rome wanted Austrian independence and the revision of the boundaries of Hungary and Bulgaria, while Berlin meant to have ultimate dominance everywhere, including Rome. In comparison with the forceful and continuous propaganda of Germany the efforts of Italy to establish her influence were weak, and the more closely Mussolini identified Italian aims with those of Berlin so much the less could the dependent states rely on her power to protect them against Nazism. The financial weakness of Italy likewise tended to her disadvantage. She could not fulfil her promises of financial assistance, and the enthusiasm aroused in Hungary by the visit of the king and queen of Italy to Budapest was neutralized by the refusal of export credits, and Italy's failure to take up her option on the Hungarian surplus of wheat.

The real weakness of Italy was revealed in her failure to defend the independence of Austria in spite of her 'eight million bayonets'. After Mussolini's successful intervention in 1934 Italian support steadily waned. In 1936 the Austrian Premier, von Schuschnigg, thought of a Hapsburg restoration to create a centre around which the country could rally, and went to Venice to consult Mussolini. The outcome dissipated all hopes of effective Italian support, and Austria was left without help in her struggle to keep her independence.

Throughout 1937 Italy's power to help Austria or any other of her central European friends steadily diminished. Her armed forces and supplies were being scattered to remote quarters; 3,000 miles away in Abyssinia she had to supply and maintain an army of 250,000 men. In Spain there was a 'volunteer' or expeditionary force of up to 100,000 men, a far greater intervention than anything undertaken by either Hitler on the one side or by Stalin on the other. Despite a 'Gentleman's Agreement' (January 1937) with England to maintain the *status quo* in the Mediterranean, English public opinion became steadily more hostile. Pressure was too great. In September Mussolini made a visit to Berlin and finally committed himself.

Italy signed the Germano–Japanese anti-Comintern Pact, an act described by Hitler as the creation of a 'great political triangle'. Next year, in February 1938, Hitler, after the usual preliminaries, invaded and annexed Austria. Four years before, when Austria faced a like crisis, Mussolini had moved troops to the frontier and the *Putsch* had failed. There was nothing of that kind now. For sixteen years he had declared that Germany on the Brenner meant Italy's doom. In his greed for empire and his hatred of democracy he had scattered his forces, alienated his allies, bound himself to the age-long enemy of his country, and brought the Germans to his back door. Mussolini added insult to injury by inviting the triumphant Führer to Rome. The first week in May Hitler came, while the pope left the Vatican, protesting at the presence in the Eternal City of a cross that was not Christian. A few months later, with the unerring instinct of the sycophant, the Fascist Grand Council issued the National Racial Code against the Jews, and again the pope protested.

APPEASEMENT

Meanwhile Italian diplomacy was engaged with the English Foreign Office, which had launched a curious sort of counter-attack aimed at detaching Italy from Germany. Chamberlain had embarked upon the path of 'appeasement' or 'peace at almost any price'. In the hands of Lord Halifax the issue was clarified to a demand for the effective withdrawal of Italian troops from Spain on the one side and the recognition of Italy's conquest of Abyssinia on the other. An agreement was reached in April (1938), but it was not ratified until the autumn, since Mussolini would not withdraw his troops until General Franco's victory was assured. In the end, both sides obtained what they desired. The Italian troops were finally repatriated and the king of Italy was addressed as 'Emperor of Ethiopia'.

Much less satisfactory was the attempt made by France to come to a similar arrangement with Italy. The assistance given to the Spanish Republicans by France was a barrier against any real *rapprochement*. Nor would France recognize the Ethiopian

Empire. Although she opened conversations the difficulties soon became apparent. The Italian press, always officially inspired, at once preferred a series of grievances concerning Tunisia, Jibuti, and the Suez Canal dues. In the autumn there was a startling outburst in the Chamber, allusions to France being at once greeted by loud cries of 'Tunis! Corsica! Nice!' The result was a strong spontaneous expression of loyalty in the French colonies and a noticeable stiffening of both official and unofficial opinion in France itself. France might be weak before Germany, but there would be no knuckling down to Italy. In reply the 1935 Laval agreement was formally repudiated by Mussolini. This intransigeance was of course inspired by the disastrous diplomatic defeat inflicted by Hitler upon England and France at Munich in October 1938, when Czechoslovakia was sacrificed to the appeasement policy.

ALBANIA

By the spring of 1939, after the striking success of Germany in the seizure of Austria and of the Sudetenland, it was time for a show of strength on the part of Italy, and Mussolini looked round for a victim. Albania was selected as a country whose conquest would not be likely to create immediate international complications. Albanian independence had been upheld by Italy for many years, but King Zog had recently shown a tendency to exercise it by himself, and in a small way to play off Yugoslavia against Italy. This was, of course, intolerable to the Great Power across the Adriatic, whose economic hold on Albania was firmly established and who had, moreover, invested considerable capital in the country; besides, the possession of Albania had advantages. Apart from her small but useful supply of oil and bauxite, Albania would provide a useful base for the invasion of Greece and also a check upon Yugoslavia. So in great secrecy an expedition was prepared, and, following the German technique, a quarrel was picked with King Zog, and then, without warning, troops were landed and the country quickly overrun. It was typical that Good Friday (7 April) was chosen for the departure of the expeditionary force. Six days later

Britain and France guaranteed the security of both Greece and Roumania, so that any further Italian advance meant war.

Mussolini now esteemed it wise to draw close beneath the protecting wings of the German eagle, and promptly made advances for a formal alliance which would ensure assistance in case of emergency. Germany had no objection and on 22 May a ten-year treaty of alliance was signed with pledges for mutual support, but Italy was careful to insert a clause that she would not be prepared for war for two years. From now on the policy of Mussolini consisted mainly of impotent wrigglings to assert himself in the face of the cynical indifference of Hitler, who carried out his plans without consulting his ally and regardless of their effect upon his feelings. Ciano saw Ribbentrop at Salzburg in August, and tried to convince him that war with Poland would be a mistake. The Germans, however, took no notice and events in Danzig proceeded as scheduled. A more flagrant example was afforded by the negotiations for the German pact with Russia, signed on 24 August. Of this Italy was told nothing until the day before it was completed. That it would be a rude shock to Italy to find herself suddenly an ally of Russia Hitler must have been well aware. Italy had just signed the anti-Comintern pact, and in so doing reversed her previous attitude to Russia, which she would now have to reverse again. It was perhaps in compensation for his cavalier treatment of his ally that Hitler (after the outbreak of war) decided to liquidate the problem of the German minority in the Alto Adige. This was thoroughly acceptable to Mussolini, after Hitler's claim to protect all German minorities. A plebiscite was agreed upon and about two-thirds of the German-speaking minority opted for migration to the Reich, Italy paying some seven milliards of lire for the cost of removal.

POLAND AND WAR

Germany's treaty with Russia was not only an unholy compact in the eyes of the majority of the Italian people. It pushed Italy relatively into the background. To assert himself when war between Poland and Germany became obvious (31 August),

Mussolini proposed to call an international conference to revise the Treaty of Versailles and 'save the peace'. Hitler acquiesced, but continued his invasion. France and England agreed in principle, but insisted on the withdrawal of German troops from Polish soil. Germany took no notice and carried on with her aggression, while Italy hastily declared that she would take no initiative in military operations. To this Hitler replied with contemptuous indifference that Germany had 'no need of military assistance from Italy'.

NON-BELLIGERENCY

The attack on Poland brought in England and France. To clarify her position Italy announced that she adopted an attitude of 'non-belligerency'. Whether or not the full significance of this position was realized may be doubted, but it was in fact an exceedingly astute move. A declaration of war might have led to a rapid and successful French invasion of Italy and the dislocation of Germany's plans. As it was, non-belligerency necessitated a considerable force being kept on the Italian border, created an atmosphere of uncertainty as to future moves, and enabled Italy to prepare her forces, and incidentally to keep open a wide leak on the allied blockade. With the rapid and successful liquidation of Poland, Germany began to mature her plans for the subjection of the West. In Italy the word 'Axis' was dropped and to divert the attention of the people from the horrors perpetrated in Poland, which only the papal press printed, a certain latitude was allowed to speculation and opinion in the newspapers. This proved to be decidedly anti-war, and hostile to Russia as the Finno-Russian war developed. In March 1940 Mussolini met Hitler and promised support for Germany at some unspecified time in the future. The successive conquest of Denmark and Norway, followed by that of Holland and Belgium, confirmed Italian belief in the invincibility of the German army. As the Germans pushed rapidly into France and the possibility of cheap spoils was apparent, the Fascist press began to rouse the war-like spirit in public opinion. But still it was not safe to act, and Mussolini was content 'to stand expectant by'. At last, as the German armies approached Paris, an attack on the disorganized French forces seemed to assure a splendid Italian victory, and taking courage in both hands Mussolini declared war on 10 June.

5. THE WAR, THE PEACE AND THE CONSTITUTION, 1940–1947

ITALY AT WAR, 1940–2

It could be argued that Italy was obliged to enter the war by her treaty of 22 May 1939 with Germany. By adopting the title of 'non-belligerent' Italy had made it clear that she could never be a 'neutral' in view of her pact with Germany. But the moment chosen for attacking France was so blatantly opportunist that the rest of the world could regard it only with distaste, while Germany could hardly be expected to feel grateful. Ciano believed that intervention was a mistake, and the military and naval chiefs feared that their forces were not ready for another war. Their fears were soon proved to be well grounded.

The war from Italy's point of view was inevitably fought mainly in the Mediterranean, where her underequipped armies had a disastrous record. It was clear from the defeatism of officers and men alike that the war was regarded as a 'fascist' rather than a national one. Even the Abyssinian war had been more popular. In both the Balkans and North Africa defeats had to be temporarily remedied by swift German reinforcement, only to be followed later by overwhelming defeat—defeat which culminated in the Anglo-American landing in Sicily on 10 July 1943. For two terrible years Italy was to experience what Churchill called the 'hot rake of war', as it was slowly dragged up the peninsula. Mussolini had always complained that the Germans were neglecting the Mediterranean area, and it was perhaps true that Hitler was more obsessed with his vast adventure in Russia than with the war in the North African desert. But the Italians had from the first been dependent on Germany in an economic as well as a military sense. Mussolini could not resist German demands for labour squads to work in

German industry and agriculture. The economic condition of Italy was allowed to go from bad to worse. By 1943 there was a grim shortage of food. Mussolini made the mistake of letting the Fascist Party take over distribution of rations, with the result that the Party was blamed for the confusion and growing shortage.

THE FALL OF MUSSOLINI

While the Party was losing the confidence of the country, the Duce was losing the confidence of the Party. The Fascist Grand Council had been having no formal meetings since Italy had gone to war. Several members of the Council, and especially Ciano, Bottai and Grandi, the Minister for Justice, had begun to doubt Mussolini's ability to continue as the sole government of Italy. The Duce had aged quickly during the war, and, as the national tragedy deepened, seemed increasingly incapable of taking any sort of executive action. He contented himself with privately making oracular utterances about Germany's errors, as though he no longer had any personal responsibility. He had carried out a minor purge of ministers in February 1943, but had not been thorough enough. Three days after the landings in Sicily, he met Hitler at Feltre. Italian military chiefs hoped that massive German assistance would result from the meeting, but the Duce, having listened in silence to a harangue from Hitler, returned with no assurances of help. It was then that the Fascist Grand Council decided to take matters into their own hands. They met Mussolini on 24 July. Grandi proposed that dictatorial powers should be taken away from him, and that the old organs of the constitution—king and parliament—should be given back their legitimate powers. The debate raged passionately for hours, but Grandi's motion was passed. In the early hours of 25 July Mussolini realized that the game was up, and handed in his resignation. The monarchy, which had been so illogical and pathetic an appendage of Fascism, now provided an escape from that fantastic and disastrous experiment. When the king asked Marshal Pietro Badoglio to form a new government a degree of constitutional continuity was preserved.

THE BADOGLIO PERIOD AND THE FASCIST
REPUBLIC

Badoglio's government at first seemed determined to break with its fascist past. The Fascist Party and the Chamber of Fasci and Corporations were dissolved and an amnesty was granted for political prisoners. Men of the left, socialists and Catholics, were given positions at the heads of the Syndical Confederations. Meanwhile Badoglio continued the war, in theory still allied to Germany, and forbade the formation of political parties so long as fighting should continue. He was faced with a very real strategic problem, since the Germans were still in military command of the situation to a great extent. Even so the Marshal can be charged with a faint heart or with ambiguous aims. The Germans had only about eight divisions in Italy on 25 July, and half of these were engaged in Sicily. Badoglio must have known the extent to which the underground resistance was already organized. If his policy on 25 July had been more courageous the long months of subsequent fighting on Italian soil might have been much reduced. As it was, he did not contact the Allies until the middle of August. On 8 September Eisenhower and Badoglio announced an armistice. The next day the Allies landed at Salerno, but, far from being an occupying force, suffered terrible losses at the hands of the Germans. Most of the Italian fleet sailed to Malta and surrendered, but on the Italian mainland the Germans quickly occupied Rome and the cities of north Italy. Meanwhile the king and Badoglio transferred the Government from Rome to Brindisi.

On his resignation, Mussolini had been arrested and for some weeks had been in custody. On 11 September he was rescued—or kidnapped—by German paratroops, and taken to Germany. Italy was now partitioned by a front line in a war between foreign armies. While the legal monarchical regime of Badoglio ruled the south, Mussolini established a fascist republic in the north. He gave it the name of the 'Italian Social Republic'. The word 'social' always appealed to the fascists, since it meant nothing, but brought with it a vaguely modern flavour. They were to use it again in the party name, 'Italian Social Movement', after the war. The Germans allowed Mussolini the semblance of independence in his northern republic. He formed a cabinet of Italians, including Marshal Graziani as Minister of Defence. He tried to give his new state a wide appeal by promising more working-class support in the management of industry and agriculture. But in practice the Social Republic was further to the right and closer in spirit to Nazism than the old fascist state had ever been. Those former fascists, including many journalists, who had publicly welcomed the revolution of 25 July were now obliged to go underground. More fanatical men came to the fore. Farinacci was allowed to step up anti-semitic measures. Before the signing of the Axis Pact, the Fascists had never considered the Jewish question, partly because there were so few Jews in Italy and partly because racial phobias are not often present in the Italian mentality. But in 1938 certain anti-semitic laws had been passed. Mixed marriages had been forbidden, and Jews had been deprived of professional posts. Now, in 1943, much more brutal steps were taken, culminating in November in the imprisonment of Jews in concentration camps. The anti-semitic policy was introduced under German pressure, and this may have been partly responsible for the treatment of the men of 25 July. Ciano and De Bono had not escaped to the south. In January 1944 they were found guilty of treason and shot.

THE RESISTANCE AND THE LIBERATION

Meanwhile the Allied armies advanced. An offensive in May 1944 on the Cassino front led to the occupation of Rome in June. While brilliant veteran units—like the British Sixth Armoured Division—were performing striking feats against fierce German resistance in the south, an army of another kind was forming in the north. From small beginnings the Italian resistance to Fascism had now acquired the scale of a national movement. From it, all that was best in the post-war life of Italy was to spring. The events of 25 July 1943 had constituted merely a palace revolution, a movement within the

Fascist Party. Ciano, Grandi, Bottai and even the veteran leaders of the March on Rome, De Bono and De Vecchi, had abandoned Fascism, but in doing so they had clearly not been in touch with the great underground revolution which other men had been preparing for so long. Italian authors and journalists in the free world had for many years been preaching that Fascism must be destroyed by violent revolution. After the outbreak of war, labour began to form clandestine organizations. In March 1943 factory workers bravely went on strike against the regime in Turin. When Badoglio in July banned political parties, six underground groups were already firmly in existence:— Action Party, Socialists, Communists, Liberals, Christian Democrats and Labour Democrats. In August the six groups were all demanding—in the Swiss press—an end of the war, and were supporting their demands by organized strikes. In the north the first partisan groups were formed about the same time, and by the summer of 1944 were well organized and in full liaison with the Allies. In spite of mass executions of hostages by the Fascist Republican authorities the resistance grew in strength.

Badoglio's government had declared war on Germany on 13 October 1943, but had been slow in purging fascist elements. Even on purely administrative grounds it had not been efficient. The survival of the monarchy caused a great deal of friction. Most of the army and the navy, even when strongly anti-fascist, and the big landowners of the south, who were very rarely sincerely anti-fascist, were all loyal to the Crown. Devout Catholics were more often than not monarchist in this period. The south and the Church—historically the enemies of the House of Savoy—were now, in the last days of the dynasty, its most faithful supporters. The history of the Crown in Italy had turned full circle since the *Risorgimento*. But opinion in the six political parties which had emerged in the south was on the whole opposed to the continued reign of Victor Emmanuel III, who had opened the door to Mussolini in 1922. After the Allies had entered Rome the royal functions were taken over by Victor Emmanuel's son, Umberto, and Badoglio was replaced by Ivanoe Bonomi, whose cabinet included Palmiro Togliatti, the leader of the Communists, and Alcide de Gasperi, the leader of the Christian Democrats.

The war reached its dramatic climax in the spring of 1945. As the last Allied offensive started, the partisans alone liberated Milan, Genoa and Turin. Mussolini was arrested by partisans on the shores of Lake Como, and executed on 28 April. Early in May the Germans surrendered. It had now become necessary for the Resistance groups of the north to be associated with the government in Rome. On 17 June a new administration was formed under Ferruccio Parri, a partisan leader and member of the Action Party. Parri was in office when the peace negotiations opened though he was to hand over to De Gasperi long before they were concluded. Although Italy had ended the war as a 'co-belligerent' with the Allies, she was inevitably treated to some extent as a defeated nation at the peace conferences. She was obliged to renounce all claims to an African empire, and the fate of Trieste was to hang in the balance for several years.

THE FOUNDATION OF THE ITALIAN REPUBLIC

Apart from the bitterness raised by the question of Trieste, Italians were wisely more interested in the building of a new internal regime than in the territorial questions of the peace settlement. A referendum held in June 1946 finally sealed the fate of the monarchy, 12,700,000 voting for a Republic, against 10,700,000. The house of Savoy went into exile, and Mazzini's dream of a democratic Republic of Italy became a reality, though it was soon to be dominated by his old enemy, the Catholic establishment. A constituent assembly, also elected in June 1946, spent eighteen months debating the constitution, which was finally approved on 22 December 1947. Like most democratic constitutions of the twentieth century, that of Italy places real power in a council of ministers depending upon the support of an elected assembly. The legislature consists of the assembly, or chamber of deputies, and the senate. The President of the Republic is elected by the chambers, not directly by the people. He is, in fact, only a nominal head of state; true sovereignty rests with parliament.

6. A NEW CLERICALISM, 1947–1960

THE CHRISTIAN DEMOCRATS, THE COMMUNISTS, AND THE SOCIALISTS

The first election held under the constitution on 18 April 1948 gave the Christian Democrats a clear majority. Heirs of Sturzo's Popular Party, the Christian Democrats could look back on a proud history of resistance to Fascism. Their declared policy since the end of the war had contained socialist elements—the peasants were to be given rights to the land, the workers were to be represented in factory administration, but on more specific projects of nationalization they had been ambiguous. Only in foreign affairs was their policy clear-cut. They were determined to link Italy firmly with the Western, anti-communist half of the world. Their wise and astute leader, Alcide de Gasperi, had formed governments with those moderate parties who would accept an anti-communist foreign policy—Giuseppe Saragat's Italian Workers' Socialist Party, later to be called the Social Democrats, the Liberals, Republicans and Action Party. In 1949 Italy joined NATO. Henceforth the most significant split in the Italian political scene depended upon the basic alinement in foreign policy.

The second strongest Italian party since 1948 has been the Communist Party. Emerging as a partisan group in 1945 the Italian Communist Party was well disciplined and well organized. At the end of the war peasants in north Italy with no sympathies for Communism admitted that the red-scarved or communist partisans were less inclined to loot or steal than partisans of other political complexions. Since then, Communism has given much vitality to Italian arts and literature. Like the Christian Democrats, the Communists have taken up an extreme position only with regard to foreign policy. From the beginning, in matters of internal politics, Togliatti showed surprising flexibility. He had been less determined in opposition to the monarchy than either the Socialists or Action Parties. He had joined governments under Badoglio, Bonomi, Parri and De Gasperi. He had at first refused to patronize anti-Catholic propaganda. In this he was following the doctrine of the prophet of Italian Communism, Antonio Gramsci, who had been imprisoned by the Fascists and had died in Rome in 1937. Gramsci looked to the peasantry for the communist revolution, and believed that their Catholicism had given them a sense of social integration which was an advantage rather than the reverse. The shift of Communist strength from the industrial north to the agricultural south in the 1950's seemed to bear out Gramsci's doctrine. But since 1946 the Communists have adopted an anti-clerical line, partly the cause and partly the effect of the increasing identification of interests between the Church and the Christian Democrat Party.

So long as he lived De Gasperi was determined to prevent the Christian Democrats from becoming a confessional or clerical party. He was glad that circumstances dictated alliances with purely secular parties. A lay character was given to the regime by the first president of the Republic, Luigi Einaudi, who was not a Christian Democrat. Professor of Economics and Finance at Turin, Einaudi was a sincere, quiet and highly intelligent man, whose appeal lay partly in the contrast between his personality and that of the dead Duce. De Gasperi remained in power until 1953, by which time he had lost the alliances with the other centre parties and was faced with growing divergencies within the Christian Democrat Party itself. His resignation and death the following year deprived the party of its most balanced adviser and Italy of a respected statesman.

If the world struggle between the U.S.A. and the U.S.S.R. provided the most obvious theme for hostility between the Christian Democrats and the Communists, it completely split the Italian Socialists. As early as January, 1947, Saragat formed his separate party, taking 50 out of 115 deputies with him. The left-wing socialists, who could not accept a close alliance with America, retained the name of the 'Italian Socialist Party' under the leadership of Pietro Nenni, who had been in exile in

France during the fascist period, and who had close links with left-wing socialists all over Western Europe. In 1948 Nenni had an electoral understanding with the Communists, but this was abandoned for the elections of 1953. The Hungarian revolution and its repression in 1956 drew Nenni still further away from Togliatti, and seemed to make a reunion of the Socialists possible. Nenni had already met Saragat on 26 August, but their differences proved too great. The disunity of the Socialists in the 1950's left Italy with the alternatives of increasing clericalism or government by a party eager for a close alliance with Russia.

DIVERGENCIES IN THE CHRISTIAN DEMOCRAT PARTY

The strength of the Communists, who had 143 out of the 552 deputies in 1953, and still 140 out of the 596 deputies in 1958, alone kept the Christian Democrats in a single party. De Gasperi had led the centre block of the party, most of them older survivors of the Popular Party, though with some younger men, like Mario Scelba. To left and right of the centre group were men who were not happy with De Gasperi's policy. On the right were bigoted Catholics, southern landowners and monarchists—men who had rallied to Christian Democracy solely as a force against Communism. The right wing of the party continually criticized De Gasperi for socialistic tendencies. To the left were several groups, of which those around Gronchi and Fanfani were the more important. Giovanni Gronchi was friendly with the Socialists, and not happy about Italy's membership of NATO. Always retaining an independent viewpoint, he was to be elected President of the Republic in 1955, and cause something of a stir in the party by visiting Russia in 1959. Amintore Fanfani led a group which professed to have a very advanced social policy, but talked of 'corporativism' in a manner reminiscent of the Fascists, and had far closer links with the Church than the centre had. Fanfani himself did not have the clear record of resistance to Fascism enjoyed by other leaders of Christian Democracy, but had held academic posts in Italy throughout the period 1936 to 1943. While Gronchi favoured a pact with Nenni, Fanfani was strongly opposed to the idea. In the election for the president in 1955 Fanfani opposed Gronchi, and supported instead Cesare Merzagora, the right-wing industrialist, a man—it should be added—who subsequently, as President of the Senate, proved himself to have considerable ability and integrity. But the political loyalties and aims of Fanfani are an indication of the complex situation within the Christian Democrat Party—a situation which can hardly be defined in stock terms of 'left' and 'right'. The party was almost a microcosm of Italian political life, and was united only by a common fear.

De Gasperi's last government was followed in 1953 by a government under Giuseppe Pella, who was regarded as belonging to the right-wing of the Christian Democrats. Pella's ministers were all—with one exception—members of his own party, but in the chamber he depended on the help of the Monarchists, Liberals and Republicans. For the first time it could be said that the Christian Democrats were looking to the Right for support, since the Monarchists frequently adopted fascist attitudes, while the Liberals, who represented the interests of the employers, were liberal only in name. Pella's strong action in ordering partial mobilization on the Yugoslav border when the Trieste crisis flared up in the autumn of 1953 earned him praise from groups still further to the Right.

Between 1953 and the opening of 1960, the Christian Democrats either governed with the support of the neo-fascists in the chamber, or risked splitting the party by policies which seemed socialistic to many of their own deputies. The governments of Scelba in 1954, Antonio Segni in 1955 and again in 1959, and of Fanfani in 1958, all introduced measures of social reform, of which the most impressive was the Vanoni Plan to reduce unemployment, but all faced sharp criticism from their own ranks, and usually needed the support of Saragat and the Liberals both in the chamber and in the government. On the other hand, Adone Zoli, whose government lasted from February 1957 until the general election in the spring of 1958, depended on the vote of the extreme right-wing Italian Social Movement party.

THE INFLUENCE OF THE CHURCH

Meanwhile the Government continually strengthened its links with the Catholic hierarchy. The all-pervading influence of the local cardinal in many Italian cities was greater than it had ever been since the foundation of the kingdom. The only one of Mussolini's works which had been preserved in Italy after the war was his settlement of the relationship between Church and State, between the Vatican and Italy. The Lateran Pact of 1929 had been explicitly confirmed by the Constitution of 1947. When the fascist regime collapsed, one of the few traditional landmarks which could still command loyalty in Italy was the Catholic Church. After the war nearly all political leaders had avoided identification with anti-clericalism, only a few intellectuals still supporting Cavour's theme of a 'free Church in a free State'. The political role of Catholic Action, the secular arm of the Church, was ever more thinly disguised. The relationship between the priesthood and the secular state was tested in the Bellandi case in 1958. The bishop of Prato from his pulpit publicly abused Signor Bellandi for being married according to the secular law but not the law of the Church. When Bellandi went to the courts for protection against slander the bishop was at first found guilty, but later reprieved by an appeal court. The question was inevitably raised as to whether the priesthood was recognized as being under the laws of the land. To the rest of Europe a strangely anachronistic and theocratic spirit was seen to prevail in a country in other respects so modern and enlightened.

THE NEO-FASCISTS

Still more sinister, though perhaps ultimately less likely to be a real threat to democracy was the revival of Fascism. The *Uomo Qualunque* party, founded in 1945, had been fascist in tone, and had done quite well in the elections for the Constituent Assembly in 1946, but in a few years it was largely replaced by the Italian

Social Movement (M.S.I.) or 'Missini' as they came to be called. Graziani, released from prison, was adopted by the M.S.I., but in 1953 he joined the Christian Democrats. In the general election of that year one and half million people voted for the M.S.I. The Party lost ground in the elections of 1958, but still had twenty-four deputies in the chamber. Just as Zoli's short-lived government had depended on neo-fascist votes, so were these twenty-four deputies needed to preserve the government of Fernando Tambroni, formed in February 1960. A lawyer, and a product of Catholic Action, Tambroni had formed a homogen-eously Christian Democrat government, but openly admitted that he did not mind where his support in the chamber came from. Finding that the Government needed them, the Italian Social Movement became more arrogant in their behaviour. They had adopted the fascist salute, and with it the old cult of violence. Mussolini had said 'Frontiers are not there to be discussed; they are there to be defended'. Following this policy of unreasoning nationalism, the M.S.I. demanded a strong line against the Austrians in the South Tyrol. At the beginning of July 1960 the 'Missini' were to hold their sixth national congress at Genoa. The choice of Genoa, with its left-wing traditions, was deliberately provocative. Something resembling a mass rising of the citizens prevented the congress from taking place. The police were needlessly violent in their attempts to break up the demon-stration and over a hundred people were injured. The trans-parent attempt of the Tambroni government to blame the communists for the troubles of Genoa stimulated fresh demon-strations in Reggio Emilia, Modena, Parma, Naples and Palermo. By 12 July ten people had lost their lives in clashes with the police. The 'Missini' set fire to the house of a partisan leader in Ravenna, and threw home-made bombs at the Soviet Trade Office and Communist Party headquarters in Rome. In the chamber the left-wing parties drew closer together in a common resistance to Fascism. Something of the atmosphere of 1945 was recaptured. Fearing the formation of a Popular Front, the Christian Demo-crat Party persuaded Tambroni to resign on 19 July. With the support of the Social Democrats, Republicans and Liberals in the chamber, a new government was formed at the end of the month under the little, sharp-tempered and energetic Tuscan, Amintore Fanfani.

ECONOMIC DEVELOPMENTS SINCE 1945

The news of widespread political disturbances in Italy in the summer of 1960 came as something of a shock to the outside world, since Italy had, in recent years, presented a face of prosperity and impressive material achievement. Her economic recovery since the war had in many respects been striking. In 1945 she had been faced with grave inflation and budgetary confusion. Greater disaster had been avoided only through the acceptance of American aid. But already in the first six months of 1946 foreign trade showed a remarkable recovery. The economy was greatly helped in the 1950's by the discovery of methane, or natural gas, in large quantities in the Po Valley, and of oil in Sicily and the Abruzzi. No longer was Italy so dependent on imported coal. Between 1947 and 1950 inflation was stopped —perhaps the major achievement of De Gasperi's governments. Industrial production increased quickly. The high standards of design made it easy for Italian products to find markets abroad But there was a darker side to the picture. It had been easier to cure inflation in Italy than in countries with full employment and a higher standard of living for the workers. The old problem of over-population, resulting in widespread unemployment, remained. Ezio Vanoni, Segni's Minister of Finance in 1955, introduced a ten-year plan for dealing with unemployment by big government investment in depressed areas. Vanoni died in 1956, when it was far too early to judge the success of his plan. At that date unemployment still stood around the terrible figure of two million. The people of the far south remained desperately poor and distrustful of attempts by the Government to bring them help in the form of capital, tractors and specialist advice. If the poverty of the south denied the northern industrialists a large domestic market, Italy's international policy held out great promise to them. Her membership of the European Common Market could lead to big political as well as economic developments.

CONCLUSION

Continued advances in her economy depend ultimately on a degree of political stability at home. The parliamentary system has never worked smoothly in Italy, and the crisis of July 1960 has acted as a warning that political freedom is a less hardy plant than she had seemed. One problem always faces a liberal democracy: how far can toleration be extended to political parties which would not themselves—given the power—tolerate a free party system at all? In Italy the problem is still further intensified by a clause in an appendix to the constitution forbidding the 'reorganization of the former Fascist Party, under any form whatsoever'. Whether or not the M.S.I. should be disbanded, one fact seems clear: no Italian democratic government can afford again to depend on neo-fascist votes for its survival. Twenty-four deputies in an assembly of nearly six hundred may seem very few, but the Fascist Party had only thirty-five in 1922, and then, as in July 1960, they were loyally supporting an apparently liberal government.

In Italy a bipartisan parliamentary system has never emerged. Cavour, Depretis, Crispi and Giolitti, so different in most respects, were alike in this: none of them led an integrated political party which could govern on its own; all of them formed coalitions aimed at satisfying as many groups as possible. The Christian Democrat prime ministers since the war have usually followed this tradition of coalition government, and have always had to depend on support from other parties in the assembly. In recent years the party itself has held together only as a flood-gate against Communism. Its natural tendency is to split, as the Socialist Party has split. Italian political life is thus cursed by the tendency of large parties to disintegrate, and by the need for endless combinations between individual politicians seeking office. Nevertheless it must never be forgotten that the present uncertain democracy in Italy is incomparably preferable to the totalitarian rule of the fascists.

The Republic of Italy has survived her first, difficult years. If the dangers facing her in 1960 are considerable, they are balanced by great potentialities—above all, by the prospect of integration in a wider European community.

The chief sources of this book have been Italian works—document-
ary and secondary. Some recent interpretations contained here
will not be found elsewhere in English. The following list is therefore
not a source bibliography, but simply a selection of books in English
suitable for further reading:

G. Luzzatto, *An Economic History of Italy* (London, 1961).

P. Villari, *Mediaeval Italy from Charlemagne to Henry VII* (London,
1910).

J. C. L. Sismondi, *A History of the Italian Republics* (London, 1894).

F. Gregorovius, *History of the City of Rome in the Middle Ages* (London,
1894-1902).

F. Schevill, *History of Florence* (London, repr. 1961).

D. P. Waley, *The Papal State in the Thirteenth Century* (London, 1961).

D. Hay, *The Italian Renaissance in its Historical Background* (Cambridge,
1961).

J. Burckhardt, *The Civilization of the Renaissance in Italy* (many edns.).

K. D. Vernon, *Italy 1494-1792* (Cambridge, 1909).

H. G. Koenigsberger, *The Government of Sicily under Philip II of Spain*
(London, 1951).

Harold Acton, *The Bourbons of Naples* (London, 1956). *The Last
Bourbons of Naples* (London, 1961).

G. T. Romani, *The Neapolitan Revolution of 1820-21* (Evanston, 1950).

E. E. Y. Hales, *Revolution and Papacy, 1769-1846* (London, 1960).
Mazzini and the Secret Societies (London, 1956). *Pio Nono* (London,
1954).

G. O. Griffith, *Mazzini, Prophet of Modern Europe* (London, 1932).

G. F.–H. and J. Berkeley, *Italy in the Making* (3 vols., Cambridge,
1932-40).

G. M. Trevelyan, *Manin and the Venetian Revolution of 1848* (London,
1923). *Garibaldi's Defence of the Roman Republic* (London, 1907).
Garibaldi and the Thousand (London, 1909). *Garibaldi and the
Making of Italy* (London, 1911).

A. J. Whyte, *The Political Life and Letters of Cavour, 1848-1861* (Oxford, 1930).

W. K. Hancock, *Ricasoli and the Risorgimento in Tuscany* (London, 1926).

D. Mack Smith, *Cavour and Garibaldi, 1860* (Cambridge, 1954). *Garibaldi* (London, 1957). *Italy, a Modern History* (Michigan, 1959).

B. Croce, *History of Italy, 1871-1915* (Engl. transl. 1929).

A. W. Salomone, *Italian Democracy, 1900-1914: the political scene in the Giolittian era* (Philadelphia, 1945).

R. Webster, *Christian Democracy in Italy, 1860-1960* (London, 1961).

E. Wiskemann, *The Rome-Berlin Axis* (Oxford, 1947).

M. Grindrod, *The Rebuilding of Italy, 1945-1955* (London, 1955).